CHILDREN, COMPUTERS AND THE CURRICULUM

CHILDREN, COMPUTERS AND THE CURRICULUM

An introduction to information technology and education

J. J. Wellington

Harper & Row, Publishers
London

Cambridge
Hagerstown
Philadelphia
New York

San Francisco
Mexico City
São Paulo
Sydney

First published 1985

Harper & Row Publishers
28 Tavistock Street
London WC2E 7PN

British Library Cataloguing in Publication Data

Wellington, Jerry
Children, microcomputers and the curriculum: an introduction to information technology and education.
1. Computer-assisted instruction
2. Microcomputers
I. Title
371.3'9445 LB1028.5

ISBN 0-06-318308-0

Typeset by Burns and Smith
Printed and bound by Butler & Tanner Ltd, Frome and London

Contents

To the Reader: a Preface

Every person involved in teaching should know something about the use of microcomputers in education, and *more broadly* should be aware of the possibilities and effects of new information technology in education. Information technology can be described as the 'coming together' of two related activities: communications and computing. Information technology may involve telephones, cable television, satellite communication, videodisks, large computers, microcomputers, videotex and, most important of all, the written and the spoken word in every case. Information technology therefore involves every subject across the school curriculum, since every subject depends on the written and spoken word. Subjects from English to physics, from modern languages to mathematics, are all equally involved. At the same time, all parts of the curriculum will be equally affected by it. The main focus of this collection is the effect of information technology on the *learning process*, and the *curriculum* in both primary and secondary schools. All three facets of educational computing shown in Figure 1 will be equally considered.

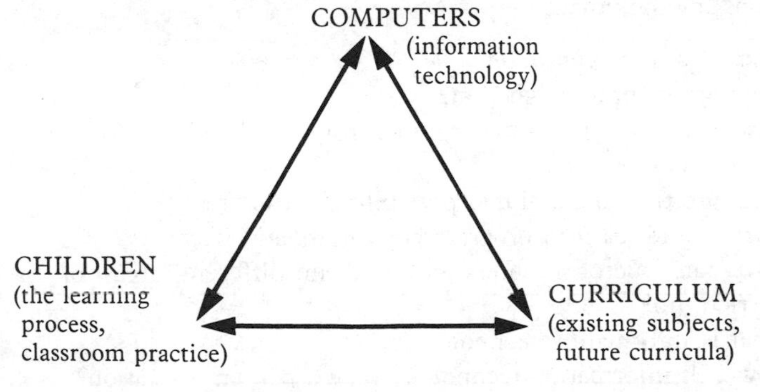

Figure 1. The three facets of educational computing

The collection begins by looking at the microcomputer itself. This is widely used as a teaching aid in schools, and is often compared to the overhead projector, the tape recorder, the blackboard and the slide/film projector as yet another versatile tool for the teacher. This is true of course. But computers are fundamentally, qualitatively different from other pieces of educational technology. Quite simply: *computers pervade society.*

Microcomputers have been compared with the programmed learning machines and language laboratories of the '60s and '70s, and described by some as 'just another passing fad'. The comparison is a poor one. Computers can certainly be used as programmed learning machines — but this is only a tiny aspect of computer technology.

Computers are now an essential element of industry, commerce, and defence. They are involved in banks, steel works, car assembly lines, supermarkets, and cruise missiles. The same can hardly be said of blackboards, overhead projectors or the teaching machines of the 1960s.

This collection is written on the assumption that only a small minority of trainee, primary and secondary school teachers wish to write their own educational programs. For that minority a plethora of books exists on 'Programming your BBC Micro', 'Making the most of your Spectrum', or 'Getting the best out of your PET'. This collection, therefore, does not teach you to program though it does discuss the educational value of programming. Nor does it include a lengthy and technical account about the insides of computers. Again, only a minority either want or need this knowledge — just as most people are content to drive cars without knowing how the engine works.

This is a book on *using* microcomputers, and other aspects of information technology, in *education.* It attempts to answer some of the following questions for the novice:

- what is a microcomputer?
- what are computers good at?
- how can you tell 'good' programs from 'bad'?
- what is CAL?
- what are the potential and possibilities of CAL?
- who should learn to program computers and why?
- how can microcomputers be used in different areas of the school curriculum?
- what is information technology?
- how will information technology play a part in education?
- how might information technology affect the school curriculum?

Above all this book *introduces* the question: how will computers affect the curriculum, and the children, in schools . . . without pretending to answer it. Points for *you* to consider, ponder and discuss will be raised throughout the text.

PART ONE

AN INTRODUCTION

UNIT 1

COMPUTERS ACROSS THE CURRICULUM

- *Computer education is now an accepted part of the school curriculum. This unit outlines the different ways in which information technology can permeate the curriculum, both as a subject in its own right and as an element of all the existing timetabled subjects.*
- *Three common ways of developing computers and computing in the school curriculum are discussed:*
  — introducing computer assisted learning as an element in all of the traditional school subjects, in both primary and secondary education;
  — creating computer awareness or appreciation courses for all pupils either as a topic or module in itself, or as an ingredient of existing subjects across the curriculum, e.g. history, mathematics, English, etc;
  — offering 'Computer Studies' as a subject in itself which can be chosen as an option leading to an examination in later years of the secondary school.

Computer assisted learning in all subjects

The first way of including computers in the school curriculum is, of course, through the use of computer assisted learning (CAL) in existing subjects. Pupils will thereby meet the computer merely as a *tool* in helping them to learn a topic, an idea or a skill.

The problems of developing CAL across the curriculum can be divided into two areas: problems of hardware and problems of software. The obvious problem with hardware, of course, is that there is simply not enough to go round in many schools. The situation should improve, but it is often made worse in secondary schools if Maths, Computer Studies or Science departments 'hog the hardware' so that History, Geography or English staff never see it, let alone use it. Teacher education has an important role to play here. Teachers can be encouraged to see the microcomputer as an important piece of educational technology (like the OHP, the projector and the duplicating machine) which they should integrate into their own planning and teaching. In this way both schools and teacher-training institutions will eventually base their microcomputers in the school or college 'General Resources Centre', so that they are not seen as number-crunchers or toys for the scientifically minded.

Software problems may be harder to overcome. Many teachers glibly complain that as well as there being an awful lot of software around, there is 'a lot of awful software'. A later unit is devoted to judging or evaluating educational software by considering various criteria.

The whole of Part II is devoted to the practice and possibilities of computer assisted learning.

Computer 'awareness' for all pupils

The second route of entry of computers into the curriculum is via computer 'awareness' or computer 'appreciation' courses. These are dealt with more broadly in some schools under the heading of 'Information Technology' courses. Such courses may be taught as timetabled subjects in themselves, i.e. by entering the curriculum 'vertically'. They may also enter the curriculum 'horizontally', i.e. by forming an ingredient, or in some cases a spice, in existing curriculum areas such as English, mathematics, science and history, e.g. the nature of communication; the history of information technology from Caxton to computers; the science of telecommunications; and the effects of computers and communications on society.

- *How could you include information technology, either as a taught ingredient in itself or as a spice added to existing topics, in your* own *area?*

A full discussion of computers and information technology awareness courses, and what might be included in them, can be found in Part V.

In practice the inclusion of computer awareness courses in many schools has led to conflicting demands on both staff and computing equipment. These conflicts are probably most obvious in schools which run 'Computer Awareness' or 'Computer Appreciation' as a timetabled subject in its own right. The conflict is made worse in secondary schools which run *Computer Studies* courses. In many cases the same teacher, often drawn from mathematics or the physical sciences, is given responsibility for organizing and teaching both Computer Studies and computer awareness courses throughout the school (see Straker 1983 and Strong 1984).

Computer Studies as a curriculum subject

Most examination courses in computer studies to CSE, 16+ and O-level involve some or all of the following elements: the history of calculators and computers; the principles of programming; an introduction to a computer language such as BASIC; the applications of computers in industry and commerce; a look at the 'inside' of a computer by considering the binary number system and computer logic; and a discussion of the social implications of computers.

The teaching of computer studies will *not* be considered in detail here, or at all in later units, as it is now a specialist subject in its own right. Teachers are trained specifically to teach computer studies in secondary schools as their main subject. The Department of Education and Science (DES) recognized the growing need for specialist teachers by creating a teacher education centre for teachers *of* new technology at Trent Polytechnic, Nottingham, in April 1984.

Its place in the curriculum as a subject in its own right has been questioned however and this will be discussed briefly here. Two common criticisms run as follows:

(a) *'How can you justify teaching computer studies to a select few when what is really needed is an introduction to the computer and its uses for* all *pupils?'*

Perhaps the easiest reply to this is that the two approaches can happily co-exist, side by side, in any school curriculum. A parallel occurs in science education; it seems highly desirable, for example, that all pupils should learn about wiring a plug and electrical safety. But this is not an argument for preventing a restricted few from learning the abstract laws and theories of electricity, and taking O- and A-level physics.

(b) The second criticism concerns the so-called relevance of parts of Computer Studies syllabi: '*Why should we make school pupils learn the details of, for example, the evolution of computers, computer hardware, logic, and binary representation? We should be teaching them how to use computers, how they are applied, and how they will affect society.*'

I couldn't agree more with the latter statement, as an aim for *all* pupils. But surely *somebody* needs to know about the inside of computers? If a similar criticism were rigidly applied to, say, the O-level physics syllabus there would be little left. After all, what is the relevance of Newtonian mechanics, Faraday's laws of induction, the wave theory of light and thermodynamics to the average citizen? Yet somebody needs to study these topics unless we want to ignore 300 years of scientific heritage. We should either apply the 'relevance' criteria to all curriculum subjects or none at all.

Perhaps the major problem for Computer Studies (as opposed to Computer Science) is its rather hybrid nature. It is neither a science, nor an art, nor a humanity. Current syllabi contain elements of mathematics, logic, programming, study of applications, appreciation of history, and speculation on social implications. Skill in all these areas is unlikely to be found in one pupil (perhaps as a direct effect of the traditional curriculum divisions). It may also be true that school administrators, parents, and employers prefer a subject which can be neatly packaged, classified, and is likely to develop and evolve at a less rapid rate.

Whatever people feel about the content, relevance and nature of Computer Studies it has almost certainly come too far to disappear as an examination subject. Total examination entries in 1982, from CSE to A-level, were in excess of 79,000. It already attracts more candidates than German and, if present trends continue, will soon reach the level of French. The statistics of one major examination board, JMB, illustrate this development and are shown in Table 1 together with a graphical representation.

- *Do you think a timetabled slot should be devoted to a study of computers? Should it be optional or compulsory? How would you justify its place on the school curriculum?*

Table 1 JMB entries for O-level and Joint 16+ examinations

Year	German	Computer Studies
1976	10 516	0
1977	11 168	1 632
1978	11 732	2 617
1979	12 038	3 637
1980	11 929	4 937
1981	11 945	7 717
1982	11 919	12 697
1983	11 542	17 755

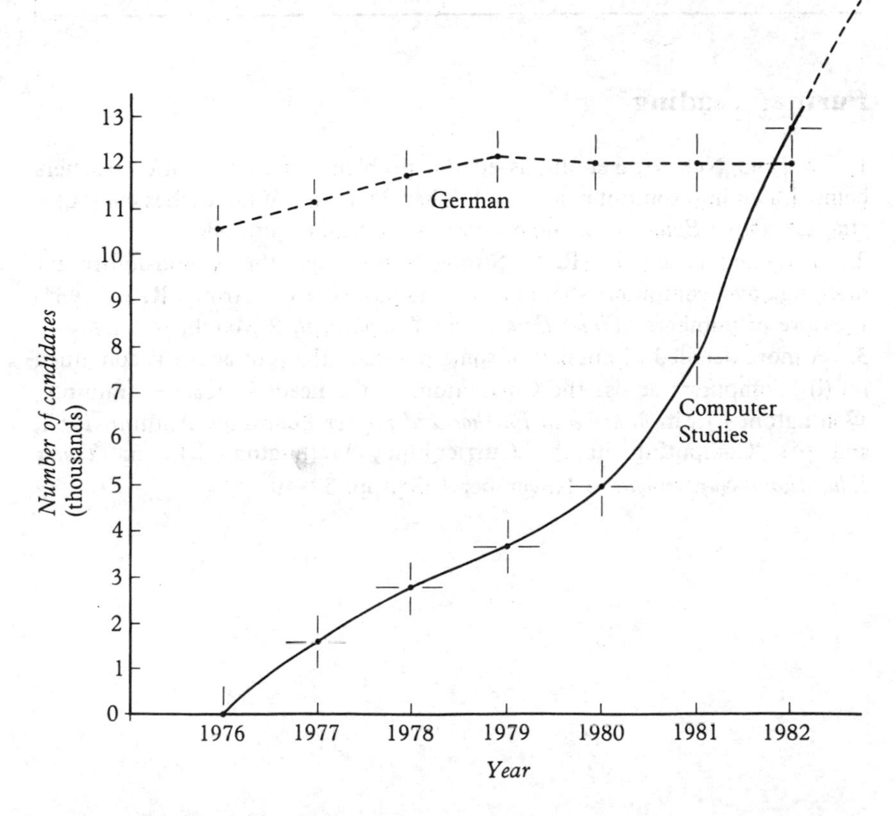

Source: *Joint Matriculation Board, Annual Report* (1983)

To Sum Up

- *The three approaches of computer assisted learning in all subjects, computer awareness for all pupils, and computer studies as an examination course, have provided the usual routes of entry of computers into the curriculum.*
- *There seems to be no insurmountable reason why the three approaches should not exist side by side at present, although in practice they may cause conflict.*
- *The future inclusion of information technology in the curriculum, and its effect upon it, may however be broader and more influential.*

Further reading

1. In 1983 Neil Straker discussed the problems of mathematics teachers being drawn into computer studies: Straker, N. (1983) Who teaches computer studies? *Times Educational Supplement*, 4 November, pp. 38–9.
2. A related article by R.W. Strong argues that the responsibility for teaching *about* computers should be spread more evenly: Strong, R.W. (1984) Pressure of numbers. *Times Educational Supplement*, 2 March, p. 43.
3. A more detailed discussion of some points in the unit above is contained in: (i) 'Computers across the Curriculum — the needs in teacher training', Wellington, J.J., in *Journal of Further and Higher Education*, Autumn 1984, and (ii) 'Computing in the Curriculum', Wellington, J.J., in *Times Educational Supplement*, 4 November 1983, pp. 39–40.

Talking points

- *Do you agree with the author's claim that microcomputers differ* fundamentally *from other teaching aids of the past and present?*
- *From your own experience of both primary and secondary schools, in what obvious ways have computers affected the curriculum? How have they actually altered the teaching and learning process, if at all, in ways which are obvious to you?*
- *Some writers consider that talk of a 'computer revolution' in society is an overstatement, an exaggeration. The extract shown below from a Penguin novel* The Soul of a New Machine *makes this claim. Have a look at the passage, written in 1982. Do you agree with its sentiments? Is the revolution more 'noticeable' now?*
- *You may have heard the glib remark: 'There's an awful lot of software around, and a lot of awful software'. Have you? Do you consider it justified?*

Extract 1:

'Wallach and I retreated from the fair, to a café some distance from the Coliseum. Sitting there, observing the more familiar chaos of a New York City street, I was struck by how unnoticeable the computer revolution was. Almost every commentator has assured the public that the computer is bringing on a revolution. By the 1970s it should have been clear that revolution was the wrong word. You leave a bazaar like the NCC* expecting to find that your perceptions of the world outside will have been altered, but there was nothing commensurate in sight — no cyborgs, half machine, half protoplasm, tripping down the street; no armies of unemployed, carrying placards denouncing the computer; no TV cameras watching us. Computers were everywhere, of course — in the café's beeping cash registers and the microwave oven and the jukebox, in the traffic lights, under the hoods of the honking cars snarled out there on the street (despite those traffic lights), in the airplanes overhead — but the visible differences somehow seemed insignificant.

* National Computer Conference

Computers had become less noticeable as they had become smaller, more reliable, more efficient, and more numerous. Surely this happened by design. Obviously, to sell the devices far and wide, manufacturers had to strive to make them easy to use and, wherever possible, invisible. Were computers a profound, unseen hand?

In *The Coming of Post-Industrial Society,* Daniel Bell asserted that new machines introduced in the nineteenth century, such as the railroad train, made larger changes in 'the lives of individuals' than computers have. Tom West liked to say: 'Let's talk about bulldozers. Bulldozers have had a hell of a lot bigger effect on people's lives.'

Obviously, computers have made differences. They have fostered the development of spaceships — as well as a great increase in junk mail. The computer boom has brought the marvellous but expensive diagnostic device known as the CAT scanner, as well as a host of other medical equipment; it has given rise to machines that play good but rather boring chess, and also, on a larger game board, to a proliferation of remote-controlled weapons in the arsenals of nations. Computers have changed ideas about waging war and about pursuing science, too. It is hard to see how contemporary geophysics or meteorology or plasma physics can advance very far without them now. Computers have changed the nature of research in mathematics, though not every mathematician would say it is for the better. And computers have become a part of the ordinary conduct of businesses of all sorts. They really help, in some cases.

Not always, though. One student of the field has estimated that about forty percent of commercial applications of computers have proved uneconomical, in the sense that the job the computer was bought to perform winds up costing more to do after the computer's arrival than it did before. Most computer companies have boasted that they aren't just selling machines, they're selling productivity. (We're not in competition with each other,' said a PR man. 'We're in competition with labor.') But that clearly isn't always true. Sometimes they're selling paper-producers that require new legions of workers to push that paper around.

Coming from the fair, it seemed to me that computers have been used in ways that are salutary, in ways that are dangerous, banal and cruel, and in ways that seem harmless if a little silly. But what fun making them can be!'

(From Chapter 13: 'Going to the Fair' in *THE SOUL OF A NEW MACHINE* by Tracy Kidder, Penguin, 1982)

UNIT 2

'WHERE DO I BEGIN?'

> *This unit:*
>
> - *suggests a way of viewing 'computer knowledge' and deciding what you need to know*
> - *outlines some possible aims and objectives*
> - *describes some of the reactions to educational computing you might encounter, and some reasons for them.*

What do you need to know?

Most people who are new to educational computing are faced with two impossible questions: 'What do I need to know?' and, as a consequence, 'Where do I begin?'. These are difficult questions simply because a person who is new to *any* area cannot possibly be aware of what they need to know or even less what they *want* to know. I will offer some suggested starting points in the next section. But first some general remarks . . .

A comprehensive knowledge about computers and computing could take a lifetime to acquire, and by then it would be hopelessly out of date. These are the two problems: the sheer volume of knowledge in this area, and the alarming rate at which existing knowledge becomes dated and new knowledge is acquired. As a student, I studied in detail the diode and triode 'valves', which formed the heart of early computers and other electronic devices like radios. Now, the only place you can find a valve is in the Science Museum.

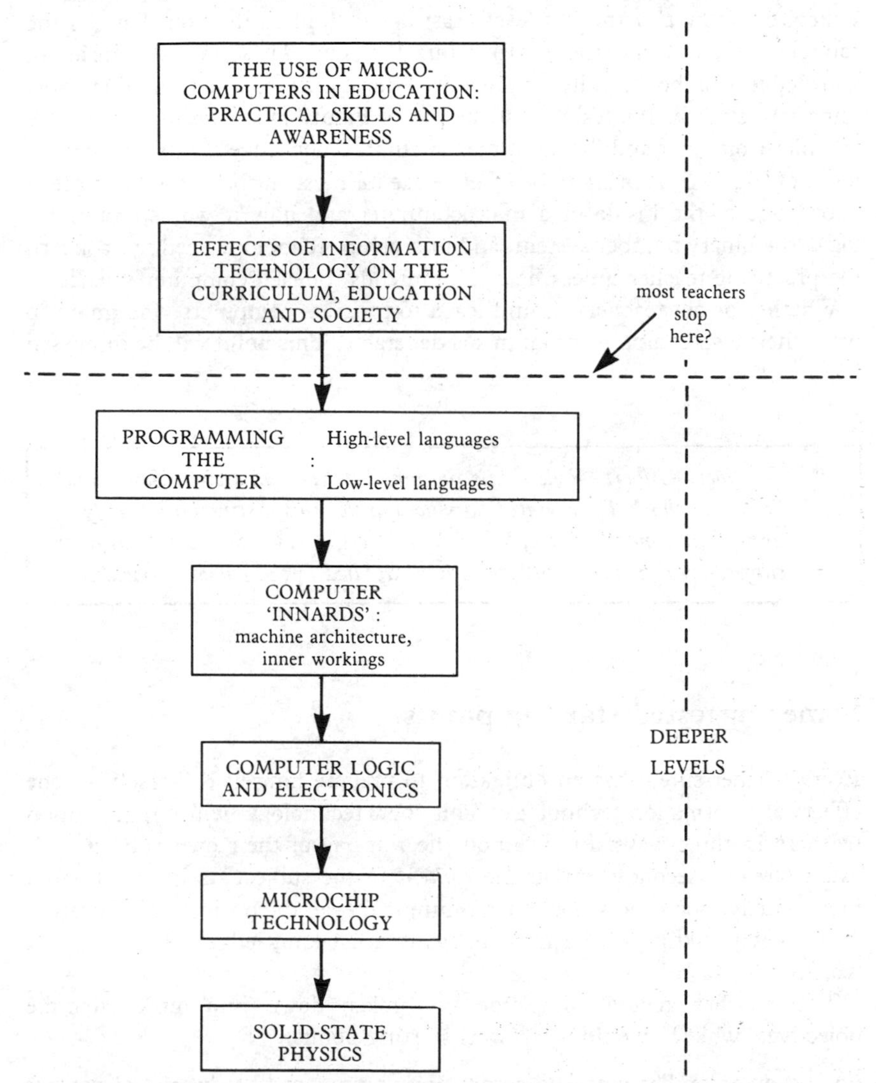

Figure 2. Levels of computer knowledge

In Figure 2 I have, somewhat crudely, divided a range of 'computer knowledge' into various levels. A simple but useful distinction was made by the Oxford philosopher, Gilbert Ryle (1949). He distinguished 'knowing how' from 'knowing that'. You can know *how* to ride a bike, swim, read or write; you know *that* the Battle of Hastings took place in 1066, Paris is the capital of France, and the Earth orbits the Sun. These two categories of knowledge can be usefully applied in educational computing. The most important skill for the teacher (at the top of Figure 2) is *knowing how* to use the microcomputer and the equipment with it. Knowledge *that,* at the deeper level, of Figure 2, is likely to be of little use for most teachers. For example, a knowledge of the inside of a microcomputer and how it works, computer logic, the binary number system, and microchip technology need not concern the practising teacher unless he or she intends to teach computer science.

Whether or not teachers should learn to program computers, and go on to write their own computer programs is debatable. This point will be discussed later.

- *Consider Gilbert Ryle's distinction between 'knowing how' and 'knowing that'. How useful do you consider this distinction? Can you apply it to concrete examples or experiences of your own, e.g. your own subject area? How usefully can it be applied to the school curriculum?*

Some suggested starting points

Every teacher surely has an obligation to prepare himself or herself for the effects of information technology. This 'new technology' will impinge upon teachers in three ways: firstly upon the *teaching* of their own subject as it exists already; secondly, upon the *content* of the subject itself; and finally, more widely, upon the school curriculum and even the business of education itself – what skills will be most relevant, what knowledge will be of most worth?

These rather general aims can be broken down into more concrete objectives, which I would suggest as starting points:

(a) become familiar with the computing equipment ('hardware') of various makes, shapes, and sizes that is used in schools;
(b) gain the ability, familiarity and confidence to use this hardware in classrooms;

(c) acquire enough basic knowledge to (i) *discuss* the uses and effects of information technology with both teachers and pupils, and (ii) keep abreast of the continual changes;
(d) make yourself aware of the *uses* of microcomputers in the teaching, and learning, of your own subject or teaching area;
(e) learn, and practise, how to select and evaluate suitable computer programs ('software') to form an integral part of your own teaching schemes and lesson plans;
(f) become aware of the possible effects of information technology on the school curriculum in general, and on your own subject or teaching area in particular.

Achieving these basic aims

As you can see, these objectives largely consist of 'knowledge how' and involve some fairly basic skills. For example, the ability to put plugs and connectors into the correct sockets is the most useful *initial* skill in using a computer in a classroom. The ability to type is also an invaluable skill for a teacher new to educational computing.

How might the aims listed above be achieved? Answer: only by using a mixture of practical, 'hands-on' experience; reading books, magazines and articles; formal and informal discussion and sharing of anecdotes; and, most importantly, by using computers with children.

The rest of this collection will hopefully provide some of the reading you need, and also point you towards further reading. But remember: reading is no substitute for practical experience.

Teachers' reactions to the microcomputer

Before launching into educational computing, and the rest of this book, it is worth remembering that any learning process involves human beings – in this case *teachers* (a special category of human). Teachers' reactions to new information technology can vary from passive or even active resistance, fear and trepidation, ostrich-like acceptance, to missionary zeal in accepting and spreading the gospel.

Can you recognize any of the following characters?

Bill Bloggs is a well-established general studies teacher: 'It's just another passing fad, like the language labs and teaching machines that we had ten (?) years ago. The novelty will soon wear off. Ignore it, it will go away. Anyway, I'm due for retirement in ten years' time.'

Gavin Plummer is an Oxbridge Arts graduate who wears corduroy trousers and a woollen shirt. He is head of Communication Studies: 'Microcomputers are dangerous. Using them in a school will debase the human side of learning, reduce social interaction and peer-group discussion, and decrease diversity and creativity. Its widespread use must be actively opposed before it dehumanizes and devalues the learning process.' (Gavin likes using education jargon.)

Jill Smith is a deputy head in charge of pastoral care: 'Microcomputers? I suppose they're just another toy for the boffins in the Maths and Science departments, who use up most of the school's grant already. Computers have got nothing to do with *my* teaching area. What's the *educational* value of some of these programs anyway? My son's got a home computer, a Sinclair-something-or-other.'

Jack Ladd is a young headmaster in an authority which prides itself on resource-based learning: 'Micros are the answer to all my prayers. I can use them to do the timetable, store pupil profiles, and write letters to parents using a word-processing program. All our pupils learn to program in BASIC, and computer assisted learning is a part of every subject.' Jack attends evening courses in microelectronics, computer logic, and assembly-level programming. He changes his micro every year.

Fred Fear has just finished his probationary year: 'I don't understand computers. I wouldn't know where to start. Most of the pupils know more about them than me. I'm worried about what'll happen if these machines catch on. What will teachers be expected to do?'

Wendy Warie is a humanities teacher, probably a Sheffield graduate. She would like to use a microcomputer more in her teaching but she is unimpressed with most of the programs available: 'The programs I do like, such as adventure games and historical simulations, are so expensive. But I have used the one or two I can afford quite successfully.' Wendy writes her own teaching materials and would like to have some of them adapted for use on, and with, a microcomputer. She can't write programs herself and has decided not to learn: 'I'm hoping the local authority will employ a full-time programmer.'

These sketches are caricatures, and I mean no disrespect to anyone or any institution in suggesting them. But I'm sure you will find hints of the above reactions amongst practising teachers *and* students in initial teacher-training.

Some of the *resistance* described can be attributed to three causes:
(i) the idea, often perpetuated, that one needs to understand computers before one can use them. How many teachers understand how an overhead projector or a video recorder works?
(ii) the often poor presentation of educational computing in computer 'newspeak' and jargonese. The topic is riddled with esoteric buzzwords, acronyms and abbreviations, which surely act as a deterrent to the unconvinced and uninitiated.
(iii) the implication that the use of microcomputers in classrooms as a teaching aid is, and will be, the main influence of information technology on education. In fact, the use of computers in classrooms will become a smaller and smaller part of the overall effect of new technology. This narrow view of the computer as a teaching machine using a restricted range of educational programs has led to the comparisons between microcomputers and programmed learning machines.

The Microelectronics Education Programme (MEP)

The initiative that has done more than any other to educate teachers in the use of new information technology is the Microelectronics Education Programme (MEP for short). This was set up in 1981 by the Department of Education and Science and will run until at least 1986. Its stated aims are: to help schools to prepare children for life in a society where devices and systems based on microelectronics are commonplace and pervasive; and to help teachers to use the technology to encourage learning in the children they teach.

The MEP has 14 regional information centres (RIC) which offer you the chance to view teaching materials, seek advice, and attend courses.

The work of the MEP and the services it offers will be mentioned at several places in later units.

Talking points

- *Which of the skills and knowledge, mentioned above, do you consider worth acquiring for your own purposes? Which skills are essential, in your view, for* all *teachers?*
- *Which of the 'reactions' described in this unit have you encountered? Do you know a Bill Smith, Fred Fear or Jack Ladd?*

Further reading

1. An outline of a possible course on information technology in teacher-training is put forward in: Wellington, J.J., 'I.T. into I.T.T. must go', *Times Educational Supplement*, 2 March 1984.
2. For a full account of the distinction between knowing how and knowing that, which can be usefully applied to any part of the school curriculum, see: Ryle, G.: *The concept of mind*, Hutchinson, London, reprinted 1969, pp. 27–29.

UNIT 3

FINDING YOUR WAY AROUND: AN INTRODUCTION TO COMPUTASPEAK

This brief unit provides an introduction to the growing volume of abbreviations, acronyms and jargon which abounds in educational computing. Some of it is useful, some of it clumsy, some just plain funny . . . more unfortunately some of the language resembles Orwell's 'Newspeak'.

Some useful terms?

In some areas the use of jargon can provide a smokescreen. By using esoteric terms, i.e. words for the initiated, the boundaries of a certain field, profession or subject can be preserved and defended. For example, trade unionists, solicitors, scientists and engineers have been accused of preserving their territory ('urinating around it') by their use of jargon.

Similar accusations have been made against the language of educational computing. This section introduces and explains some of the language. I leave the reader to decide which terms are useful and efficient, and which merely form a smokescreen for the outsider.

(1) *Hardware.* Computer equipment is called 'hardware'. This includes anything that you can fall over in a computer room, i.e. the computer itself, the keyboard, the display screen or even connecting wires and boxes. All the extra bits connected to the computer itself are called *peripherals* (peripheral =

'around the outside'). These may include *input devices*, i.e. devices for putting information into a computer, ranging from a keyboard to a microphone; and *output devices*, i.e. devices for giving information back to human beings. These may range from a display screen (or *visual display unit*) to a loudspeaker providing speech output. The whole collection of input device, output device and computer itself is called a *microcomputer system.* (A full description of microcomputers, peripherals and their use in education is given in Part II.)
(2) *Software.* Machines cannot function without people. Computers are machines. The instructions given to them by people can loosely be called 'software'. Unlike hardware, the software or set of instructions for the machine are intangible, or somehow 'in the mind'. However, computer instructions or *programs* can be stored on magnetic tape, magnetic disk or inside the computer itself. The programs that you, the *user*, put into a computer are called *applications programs.* In the case of educational computing they are — hopefully — educational programs or 'educational software'.

These programs will not run without other programs already *inside the computer*, provided by the manufacturer. The work that *you* do with the computer is controlled or masterminded by a complicated program called the *operating system.* This enables you to load programs, run them, list them on the screen, and sometimes to print things onto paper. Besides this, many microcomputers contain a 'translator' called an *interpreter.* This converts computer languages which you may have seen, like BASIC, into 'machine language' (computer languages are discussed fully in a later unit).
(3) *Backing store.* Data is information in a specially coded form that computers can manipulate. Data, and computer programs, can be stored for long periods outside a computer on *backing store.* Two common examples are magnetic *disk* and magnetic cassette *tape.* Newer ways of storing data and programs are developing all the time. Optical disks are one example. It is estimated that in the near future an optical disk will be able to store all the information in the Encyclopaedia Britannica. (There will be more about backing store or memory devices in Part II.)

Acronyms and abbreviations

Educational computing has been afflicted with more than its fair share of acronyms and abbreviations. Here is a quick Cook's tour of those you are likely to meet:

Figure 3. An example of a microcomputer system

CBL: computer based learning. This is a fairly broad term, used to mean any sort of learning related to the use of computer either as a direct teaching aid, *or* as an aid to administration or management, e.g. storing pupils' records.

CAL: computer assisted learning. This is often seen as one aspect of CBL. It usually means using a computer directly as an aid to learning.

CAI: computer assisted instruction. More narrowly, this is one aspect of CAL. It involves direct *instruction*, or even training, with the computer. CAI often involves so-called 'skill-and-drill' programs and is therefore related to the programmed learning era by many people.

CML: computer managed learning. This is often seen as one part of CBL (above). It may involve storing and processing pupils' exam results; keeping pupil profiles, marks and grades; classroom organization, registering or timetabling; or, more specifically, guiding a learner through a learning route or body of subject matter.

Definitions do vary, with all the above abbreviations. And abbreviations seem to breed. Others you may meet are: CAT (computer assisted teaching), CBT (computer based teaching), and CMI (computer managed instruction). Please let me know if you hear or see any more — I'll start a collection.

Talking points

- *Can you think of examples in other areas (e.g. professions, academic subjects) where the use of jargon is either extremely helpful and efficient* or *a totally unnecessary barrier?*
- *Have you discovered any useful acronyms not mentioned above?*
- *Some of the jargon used in the computing world can be quite amusing. You might like to discover the meaning of the following terms, which conjure up all sorts of images: bit, byte, nibble and megabyte(!) liveware, courseware and firmware (to go with hardware and software), number-crunching.*

Further reading

1. If you really want to become an expert on all the acronyms and abbreviations which abound in education, dig up: *Dictionary of Educational Acronyms, Abbreviations and Initialisms,* ed. Palmer, J. and Colby, A. (Oryx Press, 1982). It's a cure for insomniacs.
2. A comprehensive guide to all the terms you are likely to meet is provided in: *Concise Encyclopaedia of Information Technology*, compiled by Adrian Stokes (Gower, 1982).

PART TWO

COMPUTER BASED LEARNING

UNIT 4

MEET THE MICRO

This unit explains, as briefly and simply as possible:

- *what a microcomputer is*
- *what microcomputers are good at*
- *how you can load and run programs on a micro*
- *how microcomputers can be judged and compared*

What is a microcomputer?

The first electronic computers, built just after and largely as a result of World War Two, were *huge*. They occupied a large room and consumed the power of a steam engine. In the next thirty years, spurred by the invention of the transistor in 1947, computers became smaller, cheaper and more numerous. In the 1970s silicon chips were developed — a 'chip' is a tiny wafer of silicon containing an immensely complicated network of electronic circuits. Chips were the essential part of even smaller computers, called 'microcomputers'. By 1980 the computing power of 1946 could be purchased in a High Street shop and taken away in a carrier bag.

These cheap, small and plentiful microcomputers led to the sudden spread of computing in home and school education in the early 1980s, though not without problems. What would these machines be used for, apart from playing space-invaders? Who would produce the software for them? Why exactly were parents buying them? These questions will occur again and again.

The suddenly available computer power led to the microcomputer being called 'a solution in search of a problem'. Whether or not problems have been found will be a common theme in subsequent pages.

The main parts of a micro

A computer is a bit like a cow. (A dubious analogy but it will do for now.) The cow takes *in* grass, digests it, then sends milk *out* (amongst other things). A computer takes *in* information, or rather *data*. (Data is just information in a specially coded form that a computer can 'understand'.) The computer deals with or *processes* this data. It then *outputs* the processed data as information.

Following the cow analogy you can see that the cow's mouth is an 'input device'. Its stomach is a 'processor'. And its udders are an 'output device' (though not the only one). But a cow is different from a computer in two important ways:

(1) The input and output from a cow are always the same. In a computer you can feed in different input data to get a different output.

(2) With a computer you can also change the *processing*. You do this by giving it a new set of instructions, i.e. a new program.

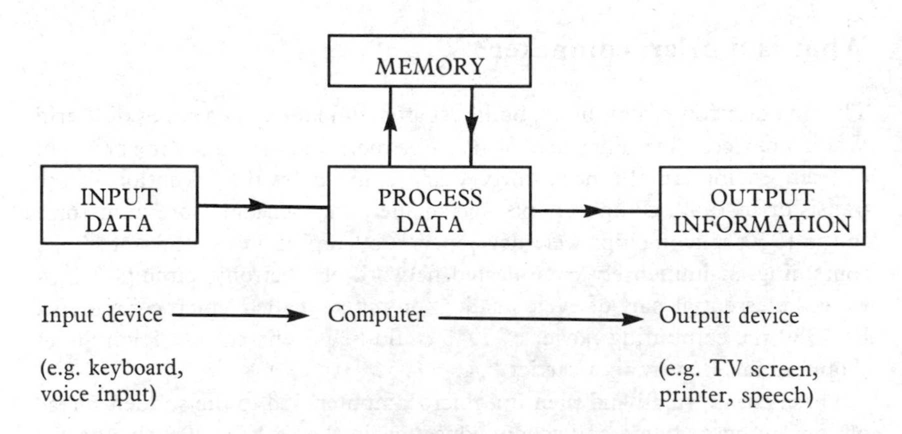

Figure 4. The main parts of a computer system

This is the job a computer does. What goes on inside the computer itself?

The heart or 'brain' of a microcomputer consists of a short-term memory *and* the part that does the processing, called the central processor. One chip may be used for the memory, and a different chip for the processor.

The memory stores the data and instructions that are given to the computer. It can be imagined as a set of pigeon-holes.

The central processor (or microprocessor) consists of two main parts:

(i) *a control unit*: this is the boss. It takes data from the memory in the right order and passes it on to the calculator. It also takes instructions one by one and makes sure they're done in the right order.

(ii) *a 'calculator'*: this unit does the donkey work. It can add and subtract, multiply and divide. It can carry out 'logical operations', e.g. putting names into alphabetical order. This unit is often called the Arithmetic and Logic Unit.

Microprocessors are used in washing machines, cameras, cars and calculators, for example, as well as in microcomputers.

This brief sketch of microcomputers is simply intended to give you a *rough* idea of what they are, and how they work. The more important question for their use in education is . . .

What are microcomputers good at?

A microcomputer, used with the right input and output devices, can be used to:

- display written words and pictures or graphics, either still or moving, on a screen;
- display information in a clear and eye-catching way using tables, colour, pie-charts etc;
- perform simple, and difficult, calculations over and over again, e.g. statistical functions, and display the results;
- store information, and be used to get at, or 'access', items of information quickly and directly;
- produce infinitely variable sound patterns and notes, e.g. music, speech of a kind;
- collect and store data by using sensors, e.g. of temperature or pressure, and then be used to display this data;

- *control devices* attached to the microcomputer, e.g. a robot arm, a set of switches, a moving vehicle (a 'buggy'), or even a lighting and heating system.

These are just some of the things that micros are good at, and all these uses can be applied in education. Whether or not a microcomputer is *fully* exploited depends on the type and quality of programs written for it. This is the subject of Units 6, 7 and 8.

Using a microcomputer

You don't need to be able to write music before you can play the piano. In the same way you can use a micro even if you know *nothing* about programming and very little about the machine itself. The two most useful skills when you first use a micro are: being able to put plugs at the end of a lead into the right sockets, and being able to use the keyboard.

For example, just to show how little skill is needed to start using a computer, here are the seven steps involved in loading and running a program:

1. Plug the micro in at the mains. Switch on.
2. Connect the micro to the VDU (visual display unit). This may be a television set, but not always.
3. Many micros still use an ordinary cassette recorder to put programs 'into them'. If so connect the tape recorder to the micro with a third lead. So three leads are involved:
   Lead 1: Mains to the micro
   Lead 2: VDU to the micro
   Lead 3: Tape recorder to the micro
When you've plugged in, and switched on, you should see a message on the screen: e.g. BBC Basic or Sinclair Spectrum.
4. Now put the cassette with your program on into the tape recorder. Rewind fully. Turn the volume up.
5. The next stage is to load the program. For example:

BBC Micro	*Spectrum*
Type CHAIN	Press the key marked LOAD

Put the name of the program
in inverted commas, e.g.

CHAIN "Welcome"	LOAD "Side a"
CHAIN "Sketch"	LOAD " "
CHAIN "......"	LOAD "......"
Press RETURN	Press ENTER

6. You have now commanded the computer to load your program. Start the tape.
7. Now watch the screen and wait for instructions, e.g. STOP THE TAPE. You may have to wait a few minutes. If things go wrong, start again from step 1.

These instructions are only included here to show you how simple it is to load a program from tape, and that no deep-level computer knowledge is required. In fact, clear loading instructions should be included with any educational program.

Software for micros is usually stored in two ways: *cassette tape*, the same tape that you record music on; or *floppy disks*. These are small flexible disks coated with a thin layer of magnetic material. Disks can be loaded far more easily than cassette tapes, and take seconds rather than minutes. *Indeed, from my experience, it is often the slowness and unreliability of cassette tapes that have put many teachers and parents off computers.* Novices who meet loading problems caused by poor quality tape, dirty heads on a tape recorder, or simply the wrong volume setting are inclined to blame the computer itself. The sooner that tapes are totally replaced by disks, the more computers are likely to be used in busy classrooms. Unfortunately, frustrating experiences with cassette tape when micros were first introduced to schools may already have deterred a huge number of unconvinced teachers.

The other disadvantage of tape is that you can only get at something towards the middle or end of a tape by going past all the bits before it. If there are several programs on the same tape you have to search for the right part of the tape to load the program you require. With floppy disks you can go directly to the part of the disk that you want by typing a simple command. This is called *direct access.*

Comparing and choosing microcomputers

In many schools, and several education authorities, teachers are not able to choose which microcomputer to buy. The choice is made for them. But for those who can make a choice, or those who simply wish to *compare* microcomputers, here is a suggested checklist.

1. What *peripherals* (outside bits) are available? Can new or unusual input devices be attached, e.g. for handicapped children? What is the keyboard like? Are the parts (the hardware) robust and durable? Can you add on and expand the system?
2. What *software* is available, and in what form? Is it on cassette, disk, a choice of both? Who produces the software — programmers who know little about education, educationists who know little about programming, or a combination of both? For parents, are there home/school connections or overlaps between the software?
3. What *maintenance* support is available if things go wrong or you need help? Is there a local sales and support service?
4. What is the microcomputer's 'memory' like? A micro has basically two types of memory and these need a brief explanation:

(i) RAM = Random Access Memory. You can put instructions and data into this memory yourself. You can also get data out again. So it should really be called 'Write into Or Read from Memory' (WORM?). This memory is like a series of pigeon-holes or *locations* which store items of data. When you switch off the micro all the data stored in RAM is lost. Some computers have more memory locations than others, e.g. 1K RAM means 1024 locations of Random Access Memory;* 16K RAM means 16 × 1024 locations of RAM are available. The amount of RAM available is important and is increasing all the time. But don't judge a micro just by the amount of RAM it has.

(ii) ROM = Read Only Memory. This is data written into the computer's memory before you buy it. You can 'read' from it but you cannot 'write' to it or change it. ROM enables most micros to operate straight away — it stays in the computer even when you switch it off. The ROM inside a computer may determine how easy it is to use (the operating system); it may determine which peripherals can be connected to it (e.g. disk drive and tape recorder, or just tape recorder); it partly determines which languages can be used with the computer, e.g. most micros contain a BASIC interpreter in ROM.

In other words, judging a computer by its two types of memory is an important, but difficult, process. It may be best to seek technical help.
5. Finally, but not least important, how much does it cost? Costs are continually changing, usually for the better. Watch out for the price cut

* In computer parlance, 1K or 1 kilo = 2^{10} or 1024.

around the corner, or the new machine ('a giant leap forward') about to emerge and make all others obsolete!

Misleading metaphors

One final comment on the language used to describe microcomputers: beware of metaphors. For example, people talk about computers in terms of:

remembering	understanding
thinking	forgetting
deciding	comparing . . . and so on.

Even the word 'memory' applied to a computer is a metaphorical use. Don't be misled by metaphors into *either* raising the status of a computer into a thinking entity *or* debasing the complexity of human thought by comparing it with the information processing performed by a computer.

Also remember: A computer is no more intelligent than a light switch; and computers do not make mistakes any more than hammers, chisels or overhead projectors do.

Talking points

- *Can you think of any other metaphors used to describe the function of a computer? Do you consider these metaphors dangerous or simply somewhat misleading?*
- *How do the microcomputers which you have seen rate on the checklist suggested above? Are there any criteria which you would add to that list?*

Further reading

1. Two readable and well-illustrated introductions to the microcomputer are: Bradbeer, R. *The Personal Computer Book* (Gower, 1982); and *The Computer Book*, produced by the BBC.
2. If you want to learn, or teach children, about the *inside* of computers (as opposed to treating them as black boxes) two introductions are: *The Computer: How it works* (Ladybird); and *Meet the Computer* by J.G. Seal (Stanley Thornes, 1982).

3. A fairly light but surprisingly detailed account of how computers work and how they evolved is contained in Gonick, Larry: *The Cartoon Guide to Computer Science* (Harper and Row, 1983).
4. Finally, you may want to read some of the imaginative speculations about 'the future of the micro'. One of the best known is *The Mighty Micro* by Chris Evans (Gollancz). A slightly more sober approach is given in *The Myth of the Micro* by Dale and Williamson.

UNIT 5

COMMUNICATING WITH A COMPUTER

Keyboards are not to be confused with computers. They are simply one of the devices for 'communicating' with computers. This unit explains and describes some of the growing number of input, output and memory devices that can be used with computers in education.

Keyboards

Most people associate microcomputers with keyboards – usually keyboards of the 'QWERTY' type, which use capital letters. These may be an ideal means of communicating with computers for many people, particularly if they can type. But it is a far from ideal input device for:

- *Young children* of pre-reading and pre-writing age who are confused by the mixture of upper-case letters (on the keyboard) and lower-case letters (appearing on a screen for example). The QWERTY layout, a remnant of the early days of mechanical typewriters, probably makes the problem worse. Alphabetical ordering, for example, may prove to be more helpful.
- *Adults and children with special educational needs:* this may vary from the slow learner, or the adult who finds reading difficult, to people who are deaf or blind or handicapped in any way. For such people the choice of device for communicating with the computer is crucial – it may also help them to communicate with other people.

Finally, putting data into a computer by typing in numbers or letters may be either too time-consuming, too clumsy, or simply inappropriate for certain uses in education.

Some of the wide range of devices that can now be connected to computers are considered below. For example:

light pens	voice input
concept keyboards	speech output
visual displays	printers
joysticks	graphics tablets

Alternative keyboards

The simplest and easiest way to adapt an upper-case keyboard is by putting a lower-case overlay on top of it. Some primary teachers welcome this simple alteration — others believe that children are *not* confused by a mixture of upper and lower case letters, and they will have to learn them eventually anyway. There is no conclusive evidence for either view.

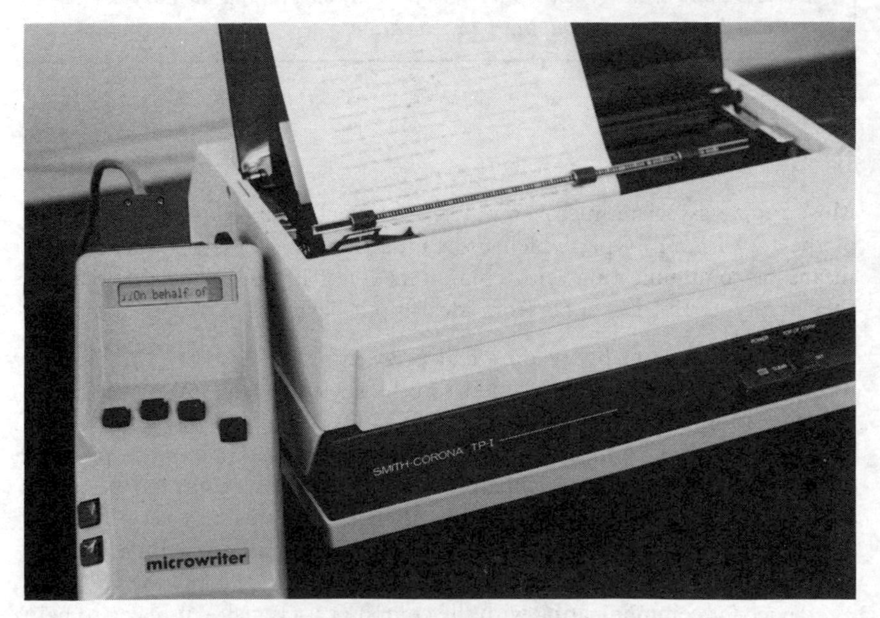

Figure 5. Alternatives to QWERTY. Quinkey microwriter (see 'Learning to Cope' *Educational Computing Special* 1983, p 12)

A second alternative is an upper-case keyboard, but with letters ordered alphabetically rather than in a QWERTY layout. Again, arguments vary as to the helpfulness of this change.

There are numerous other variations on a keyboard and a readable reference to follow up is given at the end of this unit. Two examples are handheld keyboards of various types and 'ergonomically' designed keyboards adapted for the shape and movement of human hands.

A different idea is the *overlay keyboard*. One example of this is the 'concept' keyboard. This is simply a blank A3 or A4 size tablet covered by a 16 × 8 grid of touch-sensitive pads, i.e. 128 input areas in all. The blank board is covered by an overlay of any desired layout, e.g. letters and numbers, colours, symbols, instructions, phrases, Braille, a map, road signs, symbols from a sign language for the deaf . . . anything you like. A program then has to be written to make each of the 128 pressure pads do the right thing. This is not a difficult job for a programmer. Normally *groups* of touch pads will be assigned to an *area* of the overlay: e.g. using groups of four pads will provide 128/4 or 32 different inputs on an overlay; using a larger group of 16 pads will provide 128/16 or 8 different possibilities on the overlay.

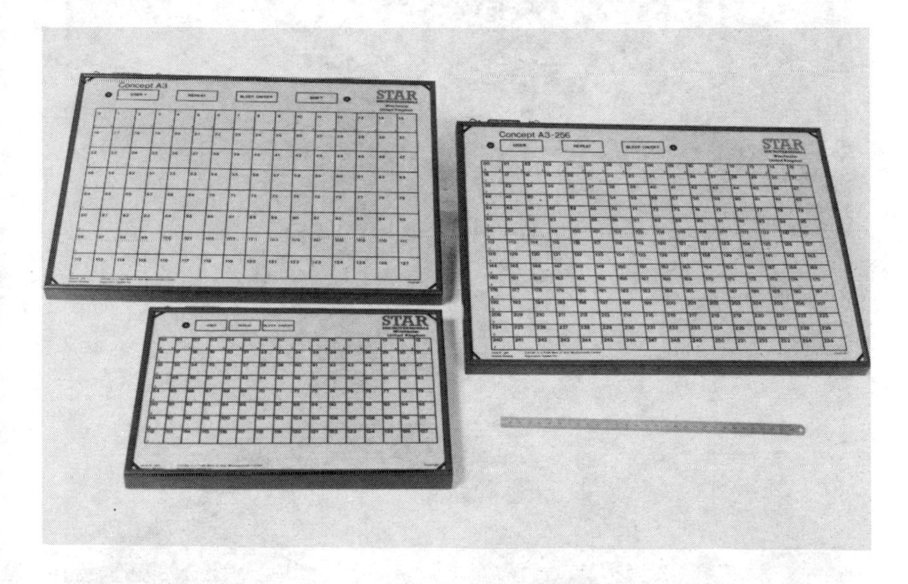

Figure 6a. Alternatives to QWERTY. A CONCEPT keyboard and overlays (photograph courtesy Star Microterminals Ltd)

Figure 6b and c Alternatives to QWERTY. Overlays in use with five and six year olds.

Given imagination from a teacher, and simple help from a programmer, the possibilities are endless for children of pre-reading age, deaf or blind children, children with other handicaps, or any educational application where a QWERTY keyboard is unsuitable. Figure 6a shows a concept keyboard, and Figures 6b and 6c show one in use.

An overlay keyboard can be connected to most microcomputers, e.g. the Apple, BBC B, RML 380-Z, by plugging a cable into the correct socket.

Other input devices

There are far too many input devices of different types to describe fully here, ranging from joysticks, paddles and switches to light pens, the 'mouse' and voice input. All will have their own uses and advantages, depending on circumstances, cost, required application and so on. Criteria for deciding which input and output devices to use are discussed at the end of this unit. But first, here is a brief explanation of *some* input devices you may come across:

Joysticks. These are simply sticks or 'handles' which can be moved in at least four directions (you may have seen them on arcade games). They can be related to a television screen and used to control the position of a letter, word or picture on it. It is a useful, robust device for picking and positioning tasks.

The 'mouse'. This is perhaps an even better device for picking out and positioning items on a screen, and even for drawing. The mouse is held against an item on the screen and a button is pressed to indicate your choice. The mouse is simply a palm-sized box connected by a wire to the computer.

Light pen. Another useful pointing device is the light pen. It looks like an ordinary pen but it has a coiled wire coming from it which plugs in to the computer. The pen detects the amount of light coming from, and exact position of, any point on the screen. This information is input to the computer. When used with a good educational program the light pen can be used for drawing, designing or simply pointing to the right answer (see Further reading).

A graphics tablet (or digitizer) can be used to transfer maps, designs, or pictures onto a screen; e.g. a map can be traced. This can be useful in design, or geography for example.

Voice input. The most convenient form of human communication is speech. As yet, speech recognition by computers is in its infancy, and is posing far more problems than speech output or speech synthesis. Eventually though, 'natural language understanding systems' will develop — this could have tremendous implications for educational computing.

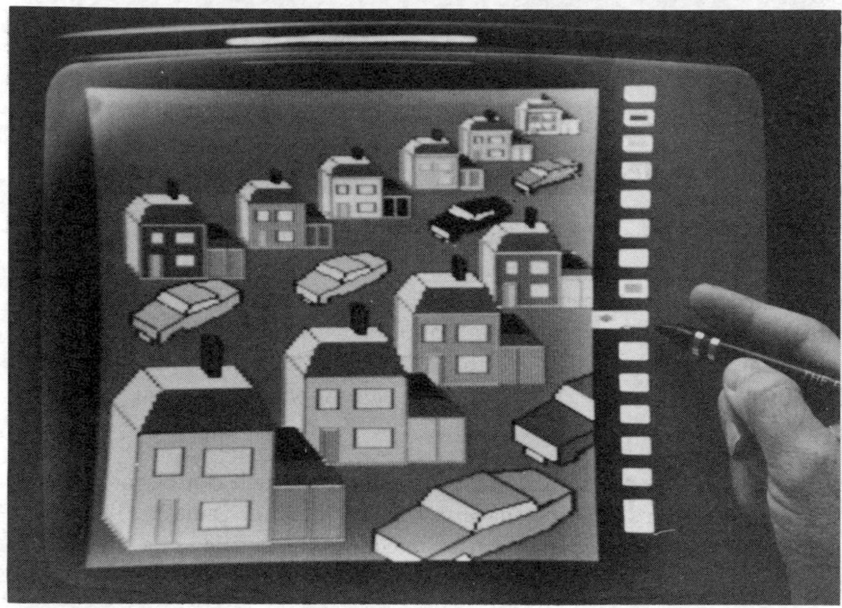

Figure 7. Alternatives to QWERTY. Light pen.

Getting information back

Presenting information to a computer-user in a suitable, interesting manner is as crucial as allowing him or her to input messages and commands in a convenient way. The way information is sent from a computer to a human depends on the ouput device. Information can be received by three senses: by seeing, by touching or by hearing (smelling has not yet been considered). For a totally blind person either *tactile* output, e.g. Braille, or voice output must be used. Otherwise a screen, or *visual display unit* is the most common way of presenting information.

A visual display unit (VDU) can be either an ordinary television screen or a computer *monitor*. A monitor usually produces clearer, more precise, text and pictures. Several guidelines have been suggested for best displaying information on a screen. For example:

- do not overfill the screen
- use short words for commands which have to be memorized, i.e. words less than six letters
- use mixed case words. People working from a screen seem to recognize words in mixed case better than words in upper case only
- design the screen layout so that the user's eyes move naturally from one item of information to the *next* item required.

These are just a few suggested guidelines or criteria. They will be referred to again in the unit on evaluating educational software.

One problem with a visual display unit is the problem of eye strain or eye fatigue. If a VDU is used for long periods, under unsuitable lighting conditions, severe eye strain can result. This is not yet a problem in primary and secondary schools with their limited numbers of computers and varied timetabling. But it has already become a 'union matter' in the use of word processors. No secretary is allowed to work with a VDU for more than two hours at a stretch, or four hours in any one day. Similar recommendations may soon be relevant to schools if the number of micros they possess continues to grow. This should already be the concern of parents whose children spend long periods with a home computer and television screen.

Other forms of output

The second common form of computer output is output on paper ('hard copy' in computer jargon). This can be produced by:

- various types of printer: dot-matrix printers, for example, form letters and graphics by a collection of tiny dots in the right places. Better quality, but more expensive, are ink-jet and daisywheel printers. Fastest of all, excellent quality but very expensive, are laser printers.

  Most schools now are likely to use printers, usually a cheaper type, to produce output that children can take away, keep, or even show their parents — output on a VDU is neither permanent nor portable.
- *plotters* of various types to produce drawings, graphs, maps or pictures (in a sense, the opposite of a graphics tablet). These may be flat-bed plotters or drum plotters.

In some ways the most exciting form of computer output is *sound*: speech, music or just noise. Microcomputers can be programmed to output notes over a wide range of pitch, loudness and duration. These notes can be put together

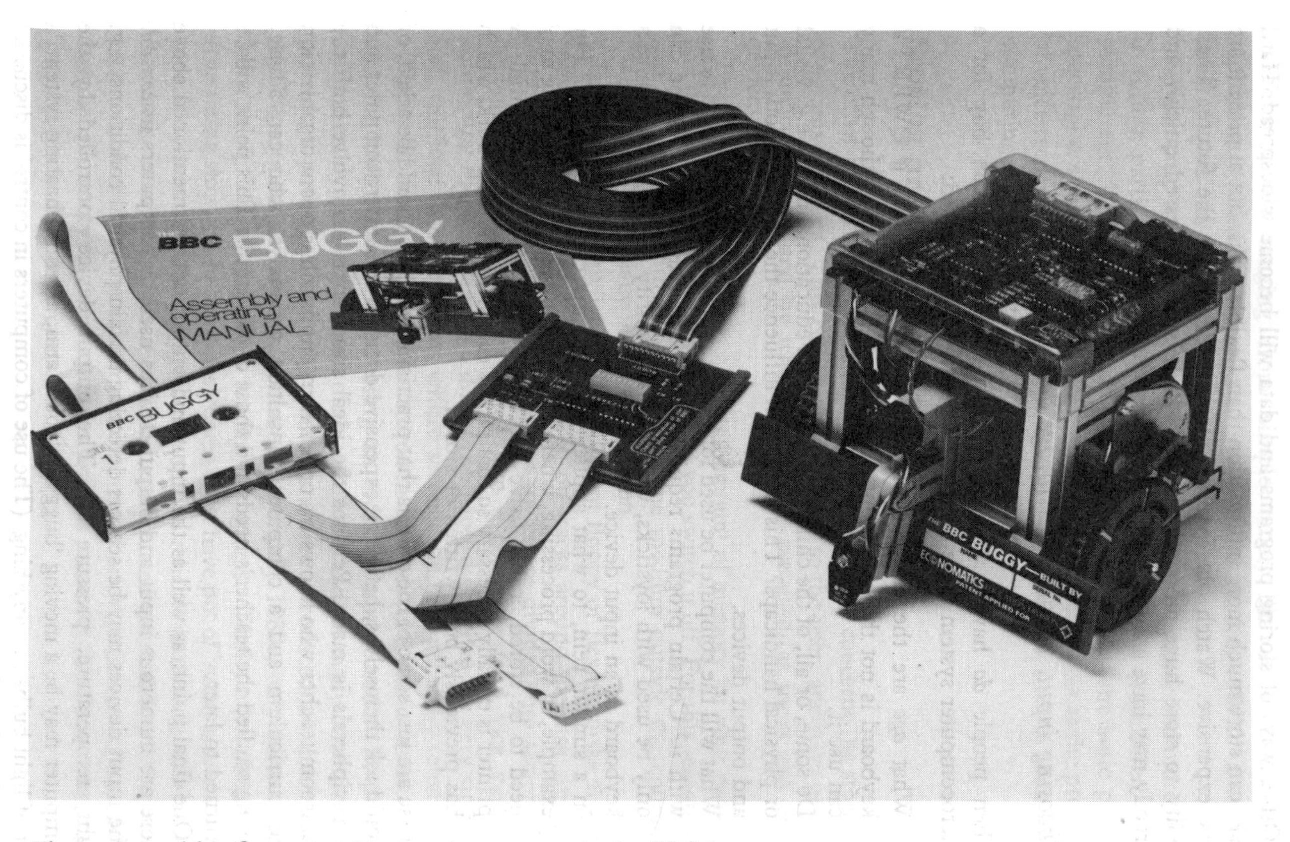

Figure 8a and b Computers in control, one example the BBC buggy

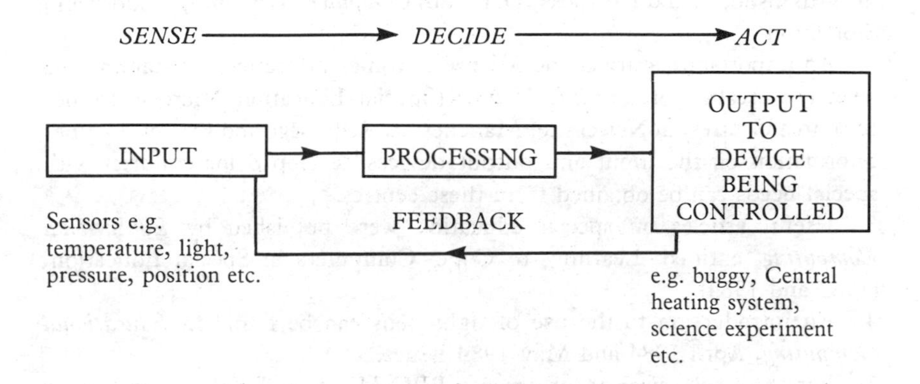

Talking points

- *From your own observations, how useful — or off-putting — do you consider a QWERTY keyboard to be?*
- *In computer parlance, input and output devices which human beings find easy and helpful to communicate with are called 'user-friendly'. Which input and output devices described above would you call user-friendly?*
- *How far do you consider that teachers' and parents' reactions to microcomputers have been influenced or even determined by the input and output devices commonly associated with them, e.g. tape recorders, keyboards? Do you think that attitudes will change and improve as these peripheral parts develop, e.g. voice output and input? Or do you consider that attitudes are determined more by people's perceptions of the computer itself and its 'processing power'?*

Further reading

1. A full and detailed account of input, output and storage devices is given in: Wilkinson, B. and Horrocks, D. (1980) *Computer Peripherals*, Hodder and Stoughton.
2. An important feature of the Microelectronics Education Programme has been the creation of four SEMERCs (Special Education Microelectronics Resource Centres) in Newcastle, Manchester, Redbridge and Bristol. Further information on the input and output devices developed for children with special needs can be obtained from these centres.
3. Useful articles on special education were published by *Educational Computing*, entitled 'Learning to Cope: Computers in Special Education' (1983 and 1984).
4. An introduction to the use of light pens can be found in *Educational Computing*, April 1984 and May 1984 issues.
5. For those who wish to program a BBC Micro, and make it sing, draw pictures and dance, consult Macgregor, J. and Watt, A. (1983) *The BBC Micro Book: BASIC, sound and graphics*. Addison-Wesley.
6. *Microcomputers and Special Educational Needs: a guide to good practice* by Bob Hogg is available cheaply from: The National Council for Special Education, 1, Wood Street, Stratford-upon-Avon CV37 6JE.
7. A short booklet describing how peripherals such as printers and graphics tablets are 'interfaced with' (connected to) computers, is: *Connecting Computers to Peripherals* by Michael Thorne (Longman, 1983).

UNIT 6:

TYPES OF EDUCATIONAL PROGRAM

This unit describes the different types *of educational program which are currently being used on microcomputers. Later, in Unit 7, some guidelines for judging or evaluating such programs are put forward. A broader and more general discussion of potential types and future possibilities of computer assisted learning follows in Unit 8.*

Educational programs, and computer assisted learning, can be classified in many different ways. The types suggested below may not form an exhaustive classification, and they will overlap in some cases, but they should form an introductory guide for you in making sense of the wide range of software available. These types can be seen as lying on a continuum with the computer program in control at one extreme, but the learner in complete control at the other (Figure 9).

Teaching programs

In a sense, only human beings can act as teachers so the word is used metaphorically here. A program can 'teach' the person using it by providing:
1. *Drill and practice* (or 'skill-and-drill').
(a) Programs can test, drive home, or provide revision in a body of knowledge, i.e. they can test or be used to improve *factual recall*, e.g. of scientific or historical facts, French vocabulary etc.

Computer programming children ←→ Children programming computer

TEACHING PROGRAMS	LEARNING PROGRAMS	TOOLS	OPEN-ENDED USE?
Skill-and-drill; Tutorial	Educational games; Simulations	Databases; Word-processing	e.g. Logo in use

Figure 9 Types of educational program

(b) Programs can be used to test a particular *skill*, e.g. addition, spelling, telling the time.
(c) At a slightly higher level, a program can be used to provide practice in using either a principle or a concept, i.e. to develop *understanding*, for example by using a scientific principle over and over again in different circumstances; or developing a concept such as area, volume or angularity.

In other words, drill and practice programs can provide almost endless practice in improving either factual recall, a skill, grasp of a concept, or understanding and application of concepts.

2. *Direct instruction/tutorial programs.*

A computer program can provide direct instruction in either factual knowledge, a concept, or a skill. This often involves breaking a learning task down into a series of sub-tasks, sequencing these, and providing immediate *feedback* to the learner at each stage (ranging from: 'Well done!' to a few bars of 'Rule Britannia', or even graphic monsters waving their arms at you).

This type of CAL is often seen simply as an unwelcome recurrence of the programmed learning of the 1960s. Yet, in my view, *good* software of this type can be defended: endless practice can be offered — microcomputers do not become impatient, tired, or irritable. Young learners are not intimidated by a machine, nor are they led into any of the undesirable teacher-pupil games and strategies often seen in classrooms. Learners can work at their own pace — they can be given many chances. A good program can also provide remedial help after each sub-task, with the help of graphics, for example in explaining fractions. With this kind of CAL the computer may be little more than a sophisticated version of the teaching machines of the 1960s — the computer *is* firmly in control. But software of this type can be defended provided it is seen as just one limited use of the micro.

3. *An electronic teaching aid.*
A third use of the computer as a 'teacher' involves using a VDU linked to it as a visual aid, sometimes called an electronic blackboard. A large enough screen can be used to demonstrate to a whole class an *idea*, a *concept* or a *process* not easily demonstrable with, say, an overhead projector or a blackboard, e.g. the idea of angles in elementary maths; a process, such as the passage of boats and ships through canal locks; graphs, tables and charts as means of displaying information; or a concept, such as the movement and interference of waves. The microcomputer and VDU provides an ideal visual teaching aid with their facilities for graphics, animation and sound.

'Learning' programs

The distinction between teaching and learning is rarely an easy one to make. Where does teaching end and learning begin? But I will assume the distinction here simply for convenience. Learning programs tend to impose slightly less control on the user in terms of, for example, route through the material. Three types, with successively more control by the learner, are suggested here:
1. *Educational games.*
In a sense many educational games are simply drill-and-practice programs which have the added spice of (for example) a competitive edge such as beating the clock or your partner, or a goal such as building a wall on the screen or climbing out of a deep cave. As with the direct teaching programs mentioned above they can be used to develop a skill, a concept, or recall of factual knowledge. However, in educational games the learning is somehow less directed, more 'oblique', than in drill-and-practice.
2. *Adventure games.*
Adventure games involve placing the learner in an imaginary situation, e.g. on an ocean with pirate and treasure ships; in the land of the Hobbit; inside a secret garden, with the user (or users) to do certain things or make certain moves. Children using the adventure game can choose their own route and decide on their own responses. Such games can be ideal for developing certain skills (e.g. the use of co-ordinates and direction-finding) *or* enhancing language development generally by encouraging 'interaction' between computer and user, and discussion amongst the children using the program.
3. *Simulations.*
Educational games are akin to simulations — both are ideal for generating

discussion and encouraging decision-making. But genuine simulations go slightly further by developing a 'What happens if . . .?' approach, i.e. learning by discovery.

Simulations are based on a model of a situation, usually real but sometimes imaginary. A model can be defined as a *simplified representation*. In a simulation the model is ready-created by the programmer. The user can then alter and experiment with the external conditions and variables affecting the model, but cannot tamper with the model itself, i.e. *internal* conditions. (In *modelling* the user creates a model of a situation and then may go on to test it, for example by seeing how well it represents and predicts reality. This type of CAL is discussed in Unit 8.)

Several examples of simulations have emerged in educational software:

(a) Copying or enhancing a *laboratory experiment*, e.g. a titration involving expensive chemicals; a radioactivity experiment. Simulations could also involve entities and situations which do not exist in real life, e.g. frictionless bodies, smooth surfaces or elastic collisions. The main advantage of a computer simulation of this type is that it can be repeated over and over again under a wide variety of conditions – not possible in the science laboratory due to constraints of time, safety and economy.

(b) Simulating a *historical situation*, perhaps an expedition, a discovery, an exploration, a siege, a campaign or an excavation. Examples include: 'Mary Rose', 'Westward Ho!', 'Round the Horn' and 'Everest Explorer'. Similarly, there is the amusing type of rule-the-kingdom simulation, e.g. 'Yellow River Kingdom'. These involve making decisions about how best to run, protect and keep alive a village, a town or a whole kingdom.

(c) Simulating a *business/marketing situation*, e.g. 'The Paraffin File', 'Litter'. These often involve competitive games to see who can make the most profit, who can stay in business the longest, or who can spend money most efficiently.

(d) *Geographical simulations*, which may involve navigating the seven seas, searching for hidden treasure or just finding your way around in an imaginary world. Simulations and games of this type can be used to teach concepts like coordinates and grid references, slope and latitude.

(e) *Pollution simulations*: these may be related to science teaching, e.g. ecology. A common example involves altering the external conditions affecting a pond. Others belong more to the humanities area, for example the effect of an oil slick on a stretch of coastline; a study of how certain industries can affect the environment.

These types of simulation are by no means exhaustive or mutually exclusive. But they have the common aims of stimulating discussion, role play and sometimes co-operation; of encouraging thinking, decision-making and conjecture ('What if . . .?'); and of developing skills, ideas and concepts in an enjoyable way.

Programs allowing the computer to be used as a tool

A computer can be used as a tool simply by using it as a calculator. At the other extreme, fairly complicated and sophisticated programs can be used for analysing data, for example by statisticians, or for displaying data in a clear and interesting way.

In education, two important uses of the computer as a tool are already widespread in primary and secondary schools: *information retrieval* and *word processing*.

1. Information retrieval.

By using a program of this type children can *store* their own information on a computer, they can *display* this information, for example on a screen or on paper, and they can get to *access* specific items of information for themselves.

An information retrieval program allows the person or persons using it to form a *database*. This can be defined as an organized collection of related data. For example, a telephone directory is a database, your address book is a database. The advantage of a database on a computer is that information can be stored in and *retrieved from it* quickly and directly.

The possibilities for creating databases in all parts of the curriculum are endless. Children could store information about the animals in the local zoo, the physical features of their classmates and possibly the teacher, the results of their science experiments, coins, postage stamps, butterflies, dinosaurs . . . anything. Storing and retrieving information from a local census, either recent or a hundred years old or both, could be particularly interesting.

Microcomputers can also be linked to *national databases*, for example by telephone. This opens up even wider possibilities and is likely to influence the curriculum as well as enriching it. A full discussion of children's 'information skills' and how they will affect the curriculum and re-open the question of 'what knowledge is of most worth' is included in Part V.

2. *Word processing.*

A word processing program simply allows text to be *manipulated*. Words can be displayed on a screen, sentences can be written, then text can be changed, moved around, and crossed out to the user's heart's content. Most word processors allow you to search for and replace words or phrases. For example, a child could write a story all about 'Daniel' then decide to change the subject to 'Rebecca'. This can usually be done with a simple command. Of course, all references to 'him' will also need to be changed to 'her' — again, this is simple to do. Once a story, report or description has been typed in, displayed on the screen and manipulated until the child is satisfied, then it can either be stored (on disk or tape) or better still printed onto paper.

The use of word processing in primary and secondary schools could encourage tremendous changes in the part played by *writing* across the curriculum. Group writing, in say twos and threes, could be encouraged. Young children could have a break from the physical effort of using pen or pencil and hammer words in at the keyboard. Children doing science experiments could type in a report together, store it and perhaps develop it later. Creative writing could become less painful and more forthcoming by allowing children to do a quick and fluent first draft, then change it, re-sequence it, add to it, or correct spellings later. In short, writing with word processors could change children's whole attitude to writing, right across the curriculum.

Word processing programs can be held on tape, disk, or in a ROM (read-only-memory) chip which can be inserted into a microcomputer. The latter is probably most suitable for a classroom. With both database and word processing programs the use of disk to store information or text is almost essential. It allows *fast* and *direct* access, which cassette tape cannot.

No programs at all — 'teaching' the computer

Many people argue that the uses of the computer mentioned so far all involve 'the computer programming the child', i.e. the program used determines what the child using it can and cannot do. Instead, it is argued, 'the child should be allowed to program the computer'. In so doing, the child can determine his or her own education, develop his own thinking, and 'explore' in his own time and pace.

The value of allowing children the freedom to program computers, rather than using educational programs, is discussed again, at various points. However, one important fact can be stated here. No child can ever have *full control* over a microcomputer, or *complete freedom* to use it as he or she wishes. He will always be constrained and limited by the software 'in' the computer *and* the hardware itself. Both are, and are likely to be in future, limiting and inhibiting in some way.

Educational programs and the curriculum

Many people argue that use of *isolated* computer programs, for example to teach a particular skill, are unlikely to affect classroom habits, let alone the school curriculum, in any obvious way. 'Packages' of computer assisted learning are far more likely to affect both *what* is taught and *how*, for example an information retrieval package, a word processing package. Similarly, a package involving a computer program, e.g. a simulation like the 'Mary Rose', *together with classroom materials* such as wallcharts, work sheets or ideas for further work, is likely to blend into, and affect, the curriculum far more than an isolated program.

The notion of CAL blending into and thereby affecting the curriculum has simply been raised here. It is an issue to look out for throughout the book.

Talking points

- *How useful do you think the classification of types of educational program offered above is? Consider the educational programs which you know and may have seen. Which category do they come under, if any? Could you add any categories to those suggested? (Answers on a postcard, please . . .)*
- *Which type of educational program do you think is likely to have the greatest effect on the school curriculum, i.e.* what *is taught and* how *it is taught?*
- *Do you consider that most educational software 'programs the child' in some way? Can the same accusation be levelled at other teaching materials and teaching situations?*
- *How far do you consider that the 1975* Bullock Report *on language is either (a) vindicated by or (b) made obsolete by, the widespread use of computer assisted learning?*

Further reading

1. A useful discussion and summary of educational adventure games can be found in *Educational Computing*, June 1983, pp. 26–7.
2. For a full discussion of classroom uses of the computer see: Taylor, R. (ed.) (1980) *The Computer in the School; Tutor, Tool, Tutee.* Teachers College Press, New York.

UNIT 7

JUDGING EDUCATIONAL SOFTWARE

Introduction

Judging educational software, like judging a textbook or an audio-visual aid, is ultimately a personal and subjective activity. It all depends on how *you* want to use it, with *your* students, in your *own* teaching situation. Even so, it is extremely useful to have some kind of checklist or aide-memoire for judging any teaching aid — particularly if you are about to make a decision which involves twenty or thirty pounds. At one extreme, various *scoring systems* have been put forward for judging educational programs. The magazine *Primary Teaching and Micros*, for example, gives programs a score out of 10 (typically ranging from 1/10 to 9/10) based on graphics, sound, documentation, packaging and so on. In a similar vein, another idea (put forward in *Educational Computing*, May 1983, page 9) uses an attitude ranking scale for children, ranging from 1 ('best liked') to 4 ('least liked'). At the other extreme, people have suggested that any *a priori*, objective judgement of computer software is an impossible dream — software can only be properly evaluated by actually using it over a period of time with real children, in school classrooms, within the constraints of the current curriculum. This is certainly true of a *full evaluation*, of a program, a textbook or any other teaching aid. But often judgements and decisions have to be made fairly quickly, in a kind of preview session. This is where a checklist comes in useful.

A possible checklist

What I hope to present here is a format for judging educational software, which can act as an aid to 'gut reaction' and intuition but does not pretend to be either a scoring system or an objective framework for evaluation. It does not form an exhaustive list but a set of criteria which can be taken one after the other. These criteria can be divided into four main groups: technical, practical, subjective and educational (see Table 2).

1. *Technical criteria.*

What form does the program take? Is it a floppy disk, cassette, or just a printed listing? Has it been written for your machine? Can you load it into your machine, e.g. is the disk the right size?

What input and output devices are required to make full use of the program.

Are there any special requirements? For example, storage requirements — is your machine's storage large enough? Do other programs need loading along with this program? Does it require high resolution graphics?

Can the teacher or child alter data statements where appropriate?

2. *Practical criteria.*

These criteria can be divided into three groups: loading and running; presentation; and organization.

(a) Loading and running. Are there clear instructions for loading the program? Are these instructions in an obvious place or hidden away in a manual?

Does the program load every time? (Nothing can be more frustrating and disrupting than seeing 'Tape loading error' and 'Please rewind tape' when working with children.)

Once loaded, are there instructions for running the program? Is the program *robust?* Does it crash if you press certain keys?

(b) Presentation. Is there a 'menu' showing, for example, the different content and levels available? Can you get back to this menu easily?

Does the program itself give clear and readable instructions? Can you easily get back to an earlier part of the program, return to the start or even escape completely?

Is the screen clear, readable and uncluttered? How much screen reading does the user have to do? Does the screen 'page' or 'scroll'? Can you read it in you own time then, for example, 'Press space bar to continue'?

Does the user have to press RETURN after each input: always? never? or just sometimes? i.e. is it consistent?

Is there any valuable use of colour, graphics, and animation, e.g. in remedial help, or reinforcement of correct answers? What use is made of sound? Can the sound be controlled, or even switched off?

Table 2 A checklist for judging software

Technical	Practical	Subjective	Educational	Printed materials
Form: disk, cassette or listing?	Does it load?	What are the reactions of teachers and pupils to it?	Is the content accurate, relevant and appropriate?	What materials come with the program: a simple users' guide; teachers' guide; documentation?
Will it run on your machine?	Is it robust?	Is it interesting and motivating?	Are the program and its instructions pitched at the right level?	Are there suitable and readable pupils' materials to use with, or alongside the program?
Any special requirements? (e.g. extra memory; high-resolution graphics; peripherals).	Can it cope with various levels and abilities?	Does it get them talking?	What educational aims does it develop: skill and drill; factual recall; understanding; analysis; evaluation?	
	Does it give clear instructions?	Do pupils find it too difficult or too easy?		
	Is the screen well presented and laid-out?			
	How much text appears?			
	Is it useful for individuals, small groups, or whole classes?			

What use is made of upper and lower case letters? For example, is there a conflict for younger children between lower-case letters on the screen and upper-case on the keyboard?

(c) Organization. Is the program for individual use? If so will pupils work one at a time, or all at once, like battery hens, hardware permitting?

Can the program be used for small groups, say two or three? Can it be used for whole-class teaching?

Is there a scoring or recording facility for either teachers or pupils?

3. *Subjective criteria.*

How do teachers and pupils react to it? Does a teacher need to be on hand all the time the program is running? Can pupils *load* and run it themselves?

Does the teacher *like* the program and enjoy using it? What are the teacher's intuitive judgements about the value of the program, its presentation, expectations, and motivation?

Do pupils like using the program? Is it interesting and motivating to them? Do you have to drag them away from it? Do they use it again and again?

Does the program stimulate talk and discussion in small groups? *Why* do they like/dislike the program? Does the program build confidence, or shatter it?

Figure 10. Judging a program — does it stimulate small group discussion?

4. *Educational criteria.*
These can be divided into content, level, aims and curriculum.
(a) Content. Is the content accurate and up to date? How much background knowledge, previous content, is assumed?

Does the program fit into your teaching scheme, or perhaps into a syllabus if you have an examination class? Does the program actually teach the areas of knowledge or skill that you want it to?

Is the program really *interactive*? Is the user involved or does he just press one key repetitively? Does the program package contain suggestions and ideas for further work, e.g. printed worksheets for you to duplicate?
(b) Level. Is the content pitched at an appropriate level? Can it cope with a mixed ability group?

Is the language level appropriate? (Some *arithmetic* programs for junior pupils require a reading age of about 16 to follow the verbal instructions.) What reading age *is* required by the program?
(c) Aims. Are the aims of the program clearly stated by its authors? Are they stated at all? Are these aims achieved or even achievable? Can the same aims be achieved *without using a microcomputer at all*?

Which of the following educational aims does the software realize?
(i) *Knowledge* and subsequent recall of a certain subject or topic, varying from knowledge of specific facts and skills to recall of laws and theories.
(ii) *Comprehension* — does the program require *understanding* of learned material, e.g. interpreting, estimating, predicting?
(iii) *Application* — does the program ask the user to apply knowledge in novel situations, e.g. to understand laws and principles, and apply them in new ways?
(iv) Is the user required to analyse material into its component parts, spot the relationship between parts, and recognize principles involved? i.e. does the user need to understand both the content and *form* of the material?
(v) *Synthesis* — this is the ability to put parts together to form a new whole, perhaps the most difficult aim to realize with an item of software. The learner is required to *create*, for example, a new story, plan, design, or proposal.
(vi) *Evaluation* — is the user asked to make *judgements*, e.g. of a report, a set of data, a statement etc?

These six aims are part of a hierarchy, based on Bloom's well-known taxonomy. The aims at the top of the hierarchy appear to be most difficult to build into educational software, but some of the better simulations now available certainly involve analysis and evaluation.

(d) Curriculum. These are perhaps the most fundamental questions of all. How will the software blend into, or affect, your current curriculum and classroom practice? Will the program support it, enhance it, extend it, change it . . . or, more dangerously, totally undermine it?

The four sets of criteria listed above can be used as a checklist for judging a CAL program. But there is one additional and crucially important question that needs to be asked: *what comes with the program?* Several points can be checked:

(i) Is there a simple, jargon-free users' guide which does not assume that you are a computer freak? Does it tell you how to load the program, run it, and what to do if things go wrong?

(ii) Is there adequate documentation with the program, including (perhaps) more technical information and a printed listing?

(iii) What materials for pupils come with the program ('courseware')? Are there any worksheets? Charts or posters? OHP transparencies or other visual aids?

(iv) Are the printed materials readable and 'understandable', both by pupils and by teachers?

Figure 11. Judging a program. Are the users asked to think and make judgements?

These questions all need to be asked in making an overall judgement of software. The material that comes with the tape, disk or whatever is surely as important as the program itself.

All the above criteria can be checked, in any order, when judging educational software. This cannot replace a proper evaluation of software in the classroom, but it may provide an aid to intuition in previewing software and making a decision which involves spending money.

Talking points

- *Do you consider that any attempt at an 'objective' system for evaluating software is worth while? What subjective elements, in your view, are involved?*
- *How useful do you consider the checklist of criteria proposed in this unit to be? Are there any items missing which you would include?*
- *How important do you feel that pupils' reactions to, and views on, a program are in judging software? How best could these views be collected, e.g. written reports, verbal comments, by overhearing their discussion ...?*
- *In what ways do you consider that judging educational software is like judging other teaching materials, e.g. textbooks, visual aids? Do the same criteria apply?*

Further reading

1. One type of ranking system for software was suggested by Jan Shaylor and Tom Stonier in *Educational Computing*, May 1983, page 9, 'Evaluating Educational Software'.

2. Some useful ideas and several suggestions for further reading are given in 'Selecting CAL Packages' by Jenny Preece and David Squires, *Computing Education*, February 1984 (Computer Education Group).

3. Chapter 7 of *Microcomputer Applications in the Classroom*, by Alan Hofmeister (Holt Rinehart & Winston, 1984) provides a useful guide to evaluating software, and further references.

4. Practical advice on selecting software, and amending programs for particular needs is given in 'Looking for quality in software' by Ian Brown in *Educational Computing*, January 1984.

UNIT 8

POTENTIAL AND POSSIBILITIES OF COMPUTER ASSISTED LEARNING

Four paradigms for CAL

In 1977 Kemmis, Atkin and Wright (see Further reading) proposed a framework for computer assisted learning which is still useful today, despite the rapid changes in technology since then. They proposed four paradigms* for applying the computer to education:

— the instructional paradigm
— the relevatory paradigm
— the conjectural paradigm
— the emancipatory paradigm

(1) *The instructional paradigm*

Early experiments with CAL largely developed from the use of programmed learning, based on the psychological theories in fashion at the time. The overall aim is often to teach a learner a given piece of subject matter, or to impart a specific skill (e.g. a new army recruit to fire a rifle). It involves breaking a learning task into a series of sub-tasks, each with its own stated prerequisites and objectives. These separate tasks are then structured and sequenced to form a coherent whole.

* Defined as a 'pattern, exemplar, model or example' by the Oxford English Dictionary.

Computer assisted learning of this type is now given names like 'skill and drill', 'drill and practice', 'instructional dialogue' and so on. Perhaps its main problem is that some teachers and others involved in education still see it as the dominant paradigm in CAL. This has probably resulted in their poor perception of educational programs and their belief that microcomputers are a passing fad in education like the programmed learning machines of the 1960s.

(2) *The revelatory paradigm*

The second type of CAL suggested by Kemmis involves guiding a student through a process of learning by discovery. The subject matter and its underlying model or theory are gradually revealed to the student as he or she uses the program.

In contrast to the instructional form, where the computer presents the subject matter and controls the student's progress 'through' it, in revelatory CAL 'the computer acts as a mediator between the student and a hidden model' of some situation (Rushby 1979, p. 28). This situation may be *real*, e.g. an industrial process, *historical*, e.g. Viking England, *theoretical*, e.g. the particle theory of matter, or even *imaginary*, e.g. a city of the future.

The revelatory paradigm in CAL in now exemplified in educational programs by numerous simulations, of various types. It seems appropriate at this point to discuss the use of simulations in education. Simulations can have various advantages, both practical and educational. In science, for example, a computer program can be used to simulate either a laboratory experiment, a natural phenomenon or an industrial process. Use of such simulations can have various advantages, for example:

- in saving money, e.g. on laboratory chemicals; the cost of transport for a museum visit or field trip.
- in saving time, e.g. in setting up an experiment; planning for and visiting an ancient castle or a factory.
- in simulating a process which could not otherwise be shown because either the time scale is too long (e.g. an ecological process, radioactive decay, evolution) or the time scale is too short (e.g. the wing patterns of a bird in flight).
- for safety reasons: certain experiments or physical processes may be too dangerous to carry out in a laboratory or a classroom.
- in simulating processes which are either invisible, e.g. sub-atomic reaction, or which are theoretical, or a mixture of both.

- finally, in a simulation variables can be easily and freely controlled. Indeed this makes an open-ended, discovery approach possible. The learner is given endless scope for runs, re-runs, trial and error.

While offering these advantages, simulations can have several dangers. They may lead to a tendency for teachers to use simulations, rather than the real thing, for practical reasons of money, danger, ease of organization, or even greater ease in classroom control. Besides this, the constant use of simulations by a learner can have unwanted educational side-effects:

- Simulations may give rise to unwanted misconceptions about the way physical processes and natural phenomena work. For example, pupils may be led to believe that variables are both easily controlled and independent of each other. In reality, not all variables can be as easily, as equally or as independently controlled as many simulations suggest.
- Every simulation involves manipulating certain factors with a model (or picture) of reality. Any model ignores certain features in order to concentrate on others, i.e. it is an idealization. Are pupils aware that they are only using a model of reality? Whose model? On what assumptions is the model based? Where do the facts come from? What sources have been used?

These factors must be borne in mind by any teacher using a simulation, and also transmitted to the learner if possible.

(3) *The conjectural paradigm*

This third suggested category involves increasing control by the student over the computer by allowing the student to manipulate and test his own ideas and hypotheses.

Modelling must be distinguished from simulation. Every simulation involves using a simplified representation, i.e. a model, of some situation, but in a simulation the model is ready-created by the programmer. The user can then alter and experiment with the external conditions and variables affecting the model, but cannot tamper with the model itself, i.e. internal conditions. In modelling, however, the user creates a model of a situation himself and then may go on to test it, for example by seeing how well it represents and predicts reality.

The potential of model building and model testing has hardly been tapped in educational computing, which is still more concerned with the two previous paradigms. Creating and testing models may slot most easily into science and technology courses. A model can be formed of some physical phenomenon, e.g. the expansion of a liquid, the motion of a projectile. The patterns predicted by the model could then be compared, say, with the results of an experiment. Clearly, this involves far more control by the learner over the computer. A similar modelling exercise could be used in history, e.g. by studying data in a local census, searching for patterns and forming hypotheses. These hypotheses could then be tested by studying further data, and searching for new evidence in their support.

Encouraging pupils to create, use and test their own models will have great educational value — unfortunately the educational software to enable this is likely to be the most time-consuming and expensive to produce.

(4) *The emancipatory paradigm*

The fourth and final paradigm suggested by Kemmis involves using a computer as a labour-saving device, a tool which relieves mental drudgery. As such, it can be used for calculating, for tabulating data, for statistical analysis, or even for drawing graphs. In this type of CAL the learner uses the computer as and when he wants to as an unintelligent, tedium-relieving slave in aiding his or her learning process. This relies on a distinction between two types of labour in any learning task: *authentic* labour and *inauthentic* labour. The authentic labour is the central, indispensable part of the learning task. The inauthentic labour is not an integral part, nor is it valued for its own sake, but is still necessary, e.g. doing endless calculations, searching through a filing cabinet, sorting information into alphabetical order, making a bibliographic search, etc. The distinction is not always an easy one to make. Doing calculations, for example, may be seen as a worthwhile exercise in itself. But where the distinction can be made the computer can be seen as a useful tool, e.g. in handling information in a history lesson. Programs are already available which teach children how to access, file and handle data, e.g. 'Factfile'. At a higher level, software packages for analysing social science data, e.g. 'SPSS', 'Minitab' have been used for several years.

This fourth type of CAL is perhaps unique in two ways: firstly, it uses the computer purely as a tool for the learner's convenience, to be used when and where he wants it; secondly, the computer is only partly involved in the learning process, i.e. to take over the 'inauthentic' part of the learning task.

The four proposed types of CAL are summarized in Table 3 — note the similarity between this diagram and Figure 9 in Unit 6.

Table 3 Types of CAL

1. *Instruction* (CAI)	2. *Revelatory* (Simulation)	3. *Conjectural* (Modelling)	4. *Emancipatory* (Labour-saving)
Drill and practice Programmed learning, e.g. Structured Q & A dialogue in a definite sequence Learner is led by computer	*Of real situations:* Trying out an existing model Varying external conditions Discovering the nature of a model, i.e. guided discovery learning *Of imaginary situations:* Games of adventure, logic and skill Educational games	Making and testing a model of reality Testing ideas and hypotheses Drawing conclusions and discovering patterns from a set of data, e.g. historical models	Computer as a labour-saving device, e.g. calculating, drawing graphs, capturing data, statistical analysis, filing data, retrieving information

COMPUTER IN CONTROL (Subect-centred) Content-laden ←→ STUDENT IN CONTROL (Learner-centred) Content-free

Developments in educational software

The four paradigms summarized above have provided a useful overall framework in considering CAL and, in particular, educational software. But they are likely to become rather dated and rigid as more and more open-minded and open-ended uses of the computer develop. For example, there is a tendency (particularly in primary education) to use 'packages' of classroom material based around a computer program, and consisting perhaps of wallcharts, worksheets and follow-up work of all kinds. Such packages could support, say, half a term's work and therefore have far more influence on the curriculum than an isolated computer program. Five other examples of 'open-ended' computer use which do not fit easily into the paradigms outlined above are:

- the use of word processing programs or packages: these can be used right across the curriculum (from English to science) and with almost any age group from five upwards. Their potential has yet to be fully realized. Clearly they do not fall easily into any one paradigm, although they can certainly be described as emancipatory.
- the use of information retrieval programs or packages in allowing pupils either to form their own database or to study a ready-made database is so open-ended that it defies any of the above classifications. It could involve the revelatory, the conjectural or the emancipatory aspects of CAL.
- the use of Logo or other programming language in education: this could allow the learner almost total control over the computer. He could therefore be involved in any of the four learning paradigms, particularly the revelatory, and conjectural, e.g. in investigating and discerning geometrical shapes.
- the use of the computer as an instrument to enhance collecting, analysing and displaying data.
- the use of the computer to control devices and systems — from light switches to robots and central heating systems.

All these uses are open-ended for the learner and with an open-minded approach by the teacher will find applications right across the curriculum. A full account of these applications in different curriculum areas can be found in Part IV. But a key topic in this unit is: who will have the imagination and expertise to develop these uses? Who will, and who should, produce and disseminate the software to make full use of the computer?

Producing and disseminating software

This is a huge issue, involving personalities, the law, politics and economics in addition to the complex educational considerations! I will simply put forward some of the possibilities here, and place questions against them.

Firstly, producing software: here are some of the possibilities which have been, and are being, tried or put forward.

1. *The practising teacher produces CAL materials in his or her own time.* This raises all kinds of questions. Does this make economic sense? Is this a sensible use of time for a highly trained professional person – is it like asking 'an architect to lay bricks'? Do teachers produce good educational programs anyway? Do they fully exploit the potential of a microcomputer for (say) its graphics, animation and sound facilities?
2. *The teacher on secondment (for one term or even one year) produces CAL materials in his or her own time.* This is probably a more satisfactory arrangement but almost all the questions raised above still apply.
3. *A professional computer programmer produces CAL materials.* This probably results in the worst software produced, judged on educational grounds.
4. *A team of teachers and programmers works together to produce and evaluate CAL material.* This is probably the most satisfactory solution. Teachers can be totally involved in the educational design and presentation of the materials, yet need not go to the trouble of learning computer language or the tedious task of writing in 'computer code'.

There still remains the problem of where this team should be located and how the production should be funded. This also involves the dissemination of software. Two possibilities are:

(a) that software should be produced commercially, through traditional publishing houses and new software publishers. Schools, colleges and parents would then pay a commercial price for the CAL materials and the whole system would live or die on a profit and loss basis. There are several problems with this approach: the seemingly high price of some of the commercial programs; the lack of innovation and experiment inherent in such a system, as with textbooks; the problem for teachers and parents of previewing software (since no inspection copies can be sent); the legal problem of copying both within and between schools, and between parents.
(b) that software should be produced and/or disseminated by Local Education Authority 'software centres'. Such centres may involve a team of

co-ordinator, programmers, and consultant teacher or teachers. The centre is likely to serve the schools in its own area in two ways: (i) by actually producing and developing its own software in line with local teachers' needs and requests; (ii) by judging, or even vetting, software from other sources, e.g. publishers or other LEAs. Once approved according to certain standards it can then be disseminated to local schools, perhaps under a special agreement if a commercial publisher is involved.

These are just two channels for producing and disseminating software. Other possibilities are:

- the use of subject organizations and their journals or newsletters, e.g. the Association for Science Education (ASE), Modern Languages Association (MLA) or National Association for Teachers of English (NATE).
- the use of teachers' organizations with common interests in microcomputers, e.g. Microcomputers Users in Secondary Education (MUSE) or MAPE (Microcomputers and Primary Education).
- through general literature on educational computing, e.g. books, journals and magazines.
- through the various centres of the MEP around the country, which will allow previewing, and even copying of certain 'public domain' software.
- finally, by the use of broadcasting on both television and radio. Software can be broadcast, and received and recorded ('downloaded') in a home or school, e.g. Telesoftware.

The problems of producing and disseminating software have only been touched upon here. But they are not to be underestimated. And they are likely to increase rather than decrease with technological progress, for example the use of videodisks.

Designing and creating educational courseware

I apologize for the use of strange jargon in this heading (courseware, by the way, not coarseware). It is part of the breeding 'ware' family of jargon, containing software, hardware, firmware and liveware (human beings). The term courseware is taken to encompass the whole range of educational materials associated with CAL, including the software itself. This section aims only to make a few brief remarks on creating courseware, and to provide pointers to further reading. Two things, at least, are worth mentioning: the use of authoring systems, and the idea of a 'top-down approach' to producing courseware.

The idea of a top-down approach to developing software is far from new, but its use could be valuably carried across into lesson-planning, producing educational materials, and even the writing of school textbooks. The approach essentially involves forming an overall view or plan of the material being prepared, with clear aims and goals in mind, then gradually breaking the task down into a structured series of sub-tasks, before embarking on the tasks themselves. For example, in writing a set of pupils' work sheets the first job would be one of deciding the overall plan, structure and aims of the sheets. The structure and plan of each individual sheet could then be decided, and the final job would be actually to write the sentences to be read. This could be called a 'bones before flesh' approach. If teachers are involved in producing courseware, including programs themselves, the top-down approach will surely result in clearer, more readable and well-structured material.

Such an approach can be encouraged by certain authoring systems. These are systems which will allow a teacher or lecturer to produce a CAL program without needing to use a so-called high-level computer language like BASIC (in a sense an authoring language is at a higher level). One system which encourages a top-down approach and does not require any knowledge of BASIC is *Microtext* (published by Acornsoft in 1984). This allows a teacher, for example, to structure a program in terms of 'modules' and 'frames'. The analogy with the structuring of a textbook is shown below:

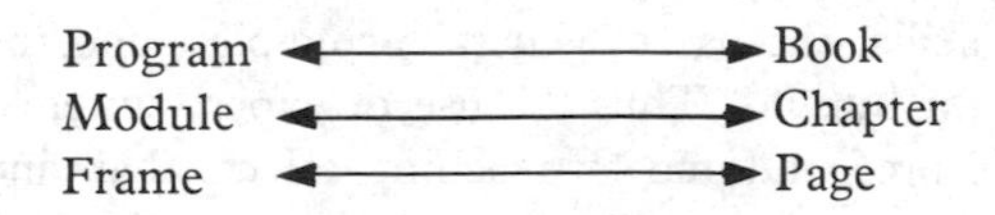

The use of authoring systems may be one way of developing good educational software in the future, although it does have opponents. The top-down approach to creating courseware of all kinds, however, should surely be widely encouraged in teaching *and* teacher-training. It may be *implicitly* used now but making its principles explicit will surely improve CAL programs and courseware in general.

Two books which discuss fully the writing and design of courseware are: *Teaching Computers to Teach* by Esther Steinberg (London: Lawrence Elbaum Associates, 1984); and *Creating Courseware* by Ruth Landa (Harper & Row, 1984).

The possibilities of artificial intelligence in CAL

One final area, surrounded by much speculation, is the use of 'artificial intelligence' in teaching and learning. As the term carries such an aura and so many connotations it might be best to confine discussion to so-called knowledge-based expert systems. The two best-known examples are in medical diagnosis and in oil prospecting. Forming an 'intelligent' knowledge-based system involves pooling as much available knowledge on a given subject as can be obtained, and structuring this knowledge into a framework or database so that it can easily be accessed, searched and questioned. The system must also be able to explain its own reasoning, for example why, in a medical program, it is asking you a certain question or following a certain pattern of 'thought'.

Such expert systems already have valuable commercial applications. Indeed their application might be wider (in conveyancing and accounting for example) were it not for the ability of the professions to protect themselves. The value and influence in education could be endless, yet they need not pose a threat to teachers. For example there is already far more knowledge in even the most highly specialized areas of the sciences than any one person could either acquire, remember, or keep up with. Teachers can no longer pretend that they 'know' physics, or chemistry or whatever. The development and use of expert systems in schools and colleges could change the whole nature of education and the learning process. Emphasis on the acquisition and storage of facts could be removed from the curriculum and laid firmly upon the development of skills, the use of general principles, and the ability of the learner to learn for himself. Thus the use of expert systems in CAL could have much more profound and far-reaching effects than any other type of computer-assisted learning. A full discussion cannot be included here but suggestions for further reading on artificial intelligence and education are given at the end of the unit.

Further reading

1. For a first-hand account of early work on CAL see Kemmis, S., Atkin, R. and Wright, E. (1977) 'How do Students Learn? — working papers on Computer Assisted Learning', Occasional Paper 5. Centre for Applied Research in Education, University of East Anglia.
2. A very readable discussion of the four paradigms can be found in Rushby, N.J. (1979) *An Introduction to Educational Computing.* Croom Helm.

3. An excellent account of educational computing and artificial intelligence is provided by O'Shea, T. and Self, J. (1982) *Learning and Teaching with Computers.* Harvester Press.
4. A collection of 22 articles on a wide range of topics connected with CAL and educational computing can be found in *World Yearbook of Education 1982/3: Computers and Education,* edited by Megarry, Walker, Nisbet and Hoyle (London: Kogan Page, 1983).
5. Elisabeth Gerver gives a readable and well-researched account of the problems and possibilities in computer-based adult and community learning in *Computers and Adult Learning* (Milton Keynes: Open University Press, 1984). The book is particularly informative on the work of the Scottish Community Education Microelectronics Program (SCEMP) set up in 1981.
6. For real enthusiasts, an ideal 'introduction' to artificial intelligence is O'Shea, T. and Eisenstadt, M. (1984) *Artificial Intelligence: tools, techniques and applications.* Harper & Row.
7. A brief and interesting comment on copying and 'piracy' of computer software, 'Computing's Blurred Vision' by Jack Schofield, was published in *The Guardian* (17 May 1984).
8. A discussion of how computer simulations provides a valuable alternative to laboratory work can be found in 'Computer Simulation of Experiments' by J.L. Moore and F.H. Thomas in *School Science Review,* Vol 64, No. 229, June 1983.

Talking points

- *Consider the four paradigms for CAL described at the start of this unit How well do programs and examples of CAL that you know fit into these categories? Are there any examples which don't fall into any? Could you suggest any other paradigms?*
- *How applicable do you consider the distinction between inauthentic and authentic labour in a learning process? How well does it apply in your own previous learning? your own subject area?*
- *What problems of obtaining or previewing software have you come across, if any? Who do you think should be responsible for producing software?*
- *It could be argued that the 'learning of facts', the storage of information or (for example) memorizing pieces of poetry, is a key part in the training of a person's* memory skill. *Do you agree with this view? Is this still a useful, or even essential, skill for many people?*

5 [illegible]

6 [illegible]

7 [illegible]

8 [illegible]

PART THREE

THE LEARNER AND THE COMPUTER

Part Three attempts to relate the use of computers to both the practical and theoretical aspects of learning.

The first unit considers some of the immediate issues and constraints, in using computers in the classroom, with groups of children. In the second unit the relationship between educational computing and psychology is examined. This unit, written by Peter Hannon and Stuart Wooler, examines psychology's impact on educational computing and goes on to consider some of the bold psychological claims made for the use of computers. Finally, connections between gender, creativity, social class of the learner, and educational computing are raised as important issues for the future.

UNIT 9

COMPUTERS IN THE CLASSROOM

The object of Part III is to relate some of the earlier ideas (e.g. on types of educational program, judging educational software, and the potential of CAL) to practical classroom *uses of the computer and the learning process itself. This first unit suggests some fairly concrete, down-to-earth considerations on classroom management and everyday use of micros and their software.*

First remarks

Using computers in a classroom is likely to bring as many of the problems (and the advantages) as using other teaching aids has done. How many people were apprehensive, nervous or even plain frightened when they first used an overhead projector, a 16 mm projector, or a video recorder in front of an audience? Blown bulbs, the wrong size film spool, or simply forgetting to switch on at the mains must be familiar nightmares to teachers. How many times does equipment fail to arrive *when* you want it and *where* you want it? In the eyes of many teachers, audio-visual equipment seems to follow Murphy's Law: 'If anything can go wrong, it will go wrong'. The same fears and experiences are likely to be encountered in using computers in a classroom. Management and 'logistics' problems will arise, as they have done with slide and film projectors, laboratory experiments, and showing videos. But this is hardly an excuse for a return to (or in some cases a maintenance of) the use of chalk-and-talk. The points discussed in this unit may help to allay some of the fears and reduce your chances of generating your own 'horror stories'. A few introductory remarks first.

Let the *pupils themselves* set up the computer system, plug it in, and switch it on. It's good experience for them, they enjoy it, and anyway several of them are probably far better at it than you are. Some will have the same microcomputer system at home. Many children of five years and upwards will be as familiar with setting up the system as they are with using a television and a video recorder.

Let children load and run their own programs, either from tape or disk. Loading from tape may take several minutes — it makes little sense for a teacher to do it in 'real' class time. Another possibility is for a teacher to load a program from tape *before* a lesson. Programs from disk will present far fewer classroom problems.

It follows that all children should be taught how to take care of both computer hardware and software. The later section in this unit on care and safety applies equally to them. Indeed, with so many children having home computers, care and safety provides a lesson in itself.

Finally (and more generally) it can be said that the difficulties and logistic problems of introducing computers into a school are directly related to how traditional the school environment is: the more traditional the school, the greater the management problems. This may also be true of the school curriculum: the more rigid the curriculum, the larger the problems of using computers. These statements are generalizations, therefore difficult to prove or refute. But in a resource-based learning environment, for example, the computer can fit in easily as just another resource. In an open-plan, low-rise school (without stairs and steps!) equipment can be more easily transferred. With fluid timetabling, say an integrated day, as opposed to the strait-jacket of many secondary school curricula the possibility of using computer assisted learning effectively is enhanced.

The idea that the difficulty of introducing new learning methods is directly proportional to the 'traditionality' of a school and its curriculum is sheer speculation. I leave it for you to consider in reading this unit.

Children to computers . . . or computers to children

Two of the possibilities for allowing pupils to 'get their hands on' a computer are: (i) having a dedicated computer room, or CAL 'laboratory', where most of the computers are housed and maintained. Pupils or students then go to this room when they wish to use computers for whatever purpose; (ii) having computers distributed throughout an institution, perhaps in classrooms, the library, and science laboratories. In a way these are two extremes, and many schools and colleges are likely to use a combination of the two. Some of the factors, the pros and cons, of the two extremes are briefly considered below.

Class to computer — 'computer rooms'

The dedicated room is seen as the place where computers can be conveniently and safely housed, supervised and maintained. A technician may perhaps be on hand to help new users or to solve any problems. The room can often be securely locked, constantly supervised and kept free of chalk dust, excessive dirt and smoke. Temperature, ventilation and comfort can be carefully monitored. These are some of the advantages of storing most of an institution's computers in a special room: ease of security, maintenance and supervision. But there are disadvantages. Here are some for you to consider:

- Special provision has to be made to 'take the class to the computer'. This may involve prior booking (perhaps a week or two in advance), along with careful timetabling and scheduling. It will involve moving classes around, and it may involve splitting classes up.
- In practice, many computer rooms become an adjunct to the Maths or Science departments of a secondary school. This reinforces again the myth that computers are useful mainly for maths and science teaching.
- Using a computer room for CAL implies to children that learning with computers is somehow special, and can be divorced from other learning and teaching activities.
- Similarly, the use of a computer room reduces *integration* of CAL into classroom lessons, and with other teaching resources. It becomes more difficult to integrate the computer into normal classroom teaching and the curriculum itself.

Computers to the classroom

Using computers within classrooms as a teaching and learning resource along with others will certainly overcome some of the problems above. But, in practice, it may create almost as many. Movement of equipment around a building may be involved which is particularly awkward where steps, stairs and split-sites are involved. Technical support will rarely be on hand if things go wrong. Classrooms may not have adequate or correctly positioned power points. Security will be a huge problem, particularly with small microcomputers, disk drives and printers which fit easily into a carrier bag.

Table 4 Computers to the classroom versus classes to the computer room

+ (FOR)	– (AGAINST)
1. *Classes to the computer room*	
Dedicated room may lead to: ⋆ tighter security ⋆ easier maintenance ⋆ appropriate facilities (e.g. power points; suitable furniture; healthier viewing distance and positions ...) ⋆ ease of supervision (e.g. technical help on hand) ⋆ careful monitoring (e.g. of temperature, dust, ventilation etc.)	⋆ room may be seen as the province, territory or annexe of certain departments ⋆ computing seen as a 'special' activity ⋆ prior planning, timetabling and scheduling needed (rules out spontaneity?) ⋆ reduces integration with other aspects of classroom practice or curriculum
2. *Computers to the classroom*	
⋆ more likely integration into classroom practice and curriculum ⋆ seen as just another 'learning tool' ⋆ not seen as the property of one department more than another ⋆ spontaneous, unplanned use made possible	Problems of: ⋆ security ⋆ maintenance and monitoring ⋆ adequate facilities ⋆ environmental conditions e.g. chalk dust Technical support not on hand

⋆ ? Can you add to these lists? ⋆

The pros and cons of taking classes to computers versus computers to classes are crudely summarized in Table 4. In many schools and colleges a combination or mixture of the two will be in operation. An ideal solution would be for a microcomputer to be securely installed in *every classroom*, available there as a resource like a blackboard or an overhead projector. This is the target for many LEAs for their primary schools. Another possibility is for computers to be distributed in different rooms around a school or college but linked together to form a 'network'. A school network of this kind would allow computers in classrooms to co-exist with a 'central' computer room linked to them. These possibilities will need to be studied and analysed carefully before expensive decisions are made. Indeed, putting the problem the other way, the decision itself will depend on the money and hardware available.

Types of classroom use

There are several possible ways of using a computer in the classroom. (See Figure 12). At the risk of stating the obvious, here are some of them:

(a) whole class use of *one* computer: the computer may be used as a visual aid; as an aid to skill-and-drill, e.g. to generate questions at random; to run a simulation in which a whole class can be involved; or to act as a database, e.g. to file information from different people in the class.

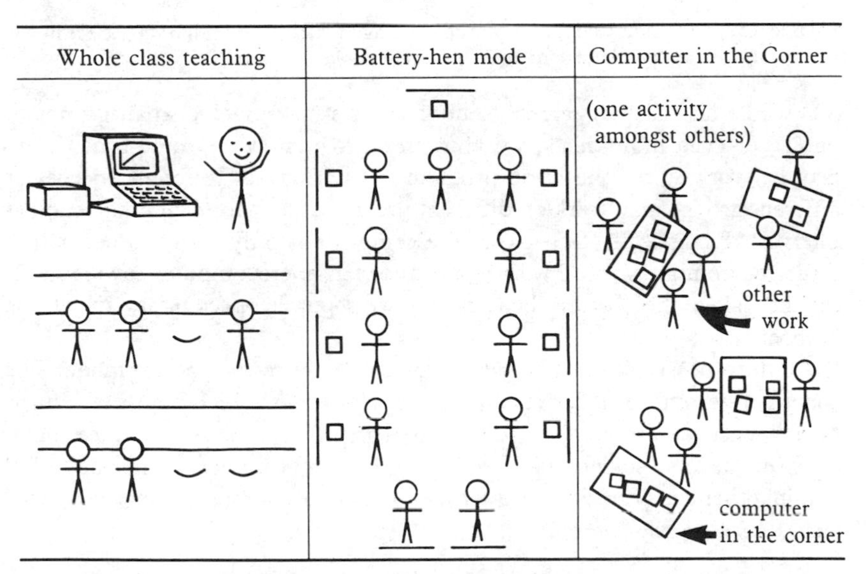

Figure 12. Using computers in the classroom, three possibilities

Figure 13. The computer in the corner. Using *Words, Words, Words* (ASK) in a primary classroom may attract onlookers!

(b) whole class use of *several* computers: this may involve small groups of pupils, or even individuals, working on a program at the same time. They may be working on the same program (most likely at different speeds) or different groups may work on different programs, perhaps changing round at intervals. Realistically this use of the computer is only likely to occur in a dedicated computer room with upwards of ten microcomputers available. It can be called the 'battery-hen' mode, with pupils 'pecking away' at the keyboard.

(c) a third possibility can be called 'the computer in the corner' mode. The computer becomes another resource in the classroom, which pupils take turns to use when necessary. Its use may be part of a circus of activities, or of experiments in a science lab. Or it may be a tool for use alongside, often within, other class activities. Either way, use of the computer is seen as simply *one activity amongst others*.

There are different ways a computer can be used in the classroom. For example it could be a | b | or c above

The *way* that a computer is used in a classroom will depend on several factors: the habits and preferences of the teacher, the nature of the room itself, the ethos and traditions of the school, and of course the facilities (hardware *and* software) available. But probably the most important factor determining classroom management is the type of *program* being used.

Table 5 Types of program and classroom use

Type of program	*Likely use . . .?*
DRILL-AND-PRACTICE REMEDIAL Certain games programs, e.g. user and computer	Individual use
VISUAL AID/ELECTRONIC BLACKBOARD/DEMON-STRATION PROGRAMS	Whole class use
SIMULATIONS	Small groups e.g. 2–5, up to a whole class
ADVENTURE GAMES	Competing groups within a class Individuals
DATABASES e.g. parish registers, census figures, readings from experiments	Occasional 'computer in the corner' use; individual use; small group use; possibly whole class use
WORD PROCESSING	Individual; small group co-operative writing; . . . even whole class use
PROGRAMS WHICH ALLOW PROGRAMMING e.g. the Logo language	Individual or small group use

A classification of different types of educational program was suggested in Unit 6, Part II. Using those labels, it would seem that drill-and-practice programs and remedial games are often best suited to *individual* use, as are certain educational games, e.g. those involving user against computer. Other educational games, particularly adventure games, are best suited to small groups (say from two to five) or even competing groups within a whole class. The same is true of simulations, which are ideally suited to use in groups of various sizes. Programs intended as a visual aid (the 'electronic blackboard') or for demonstration will obviously lend themselves to whole class use. Database or information retrieval programs are often best suited to 'computer in the corner' use by individuals or preferably small groups as a part of (say) a project, alongside or within other classroom activities. Finally, use of a word processing program is probably most suited to individual or *small group writing*, although it may even be possible to use one with a whole class.

To sum up: the actual organization will depend on the type of program being used (see Table 5). In the end it will be the job of the teacher to decide which software is appropriate for which type of classroom organization, *and vice versa*.

Taking care of software and hardware

This section is not intended as a list of handy hints on 'how to look after your micro'. It is merely a list of simple ways of reducing problems and saving time in the classroom. Many of them are habits and rules which children can follow when they handle computing equipment.

Beginning with hardware, probably the most useful skill is the ability to put leads and plugs into the right sockets. Leads and sockets can be labelled or colour-coded to make this quicker and more obvious. If equipment is being carried around, beware of *monitors*. Many are deceptively heavy and their weight is unevenly distributed. Younger pupils should not carry them. When setting up equipment beware of trailing leads and cables. With monitors or VDUs beware of eyestrain. Awkward reflections on the screen, and direct sunlight, can increase strain. Try to place the VDU in subdued light away from bright reflections. Alert pupils to the dangers of eyestrain. Don't rest the VDU directly on top of a computer cabinet; the BBC Micro, for example, is not strong enough to support it. Allow adequate ventilation around the micro and in the room itself. Beware of some of the following enemies in the room: dust, especially chalk dust; food and crumbs; dirty or greasy fingers; drinks; and cigarette smoke.

Here are some of the main points for taking care of 'software' stored on disk or tape:

- Handle disks and tapes carefully. Never touch their recording surfaces. Never bend disks.
- Keep disks and tapes away from magnetic fields, e.g. the top of a monitor.

Do not expose them to damp, extreme temperatures, or dust. Keep disks in envelopes, cassettes in cases.
- Use a felt tip pen, not a biro, to write on disk labels.
- Use good quality tapes, of a suitable length.
- Make 'back-up' copies of programs on disk or tape. These should be copied from the original so that at least one spare, unused copy exists. These copies should be stored in a suitable, secure place. (N.B. making a back-up copy is not illegal.)

These are some of the common suggestions for taking care of programs, inside and outside the classroom. It is worth re-stating here that tapes are likely to raise more organizational problems than disks. Pupils themselves will soon realize this. It often helps to pre-load a program from tape (perhaps by a pupil) so that an embarrassing and anxious waiting period will not be part of real lesson time. Organizationally it will also help to leave a program 'in the computer's memory' for as many pupils or groups as possible, before changing to another one. In other words, swapping gaily from one program to another is best left for programs on disk!

Likely effects on classroom practice

Unfortunately it has become almost a cliché to say that 'new technology will force teachers to re-think their roles'. What does this somewhat hackneyed phrase mean for classroom practice?

Firstly, teachers can no longer believe that audio-visual equipment is solely their responsibility. This may pose a threat to some teachers who see themselves as an 'authority figure'. But there will always be one or two pupils or students more competent and comfortable with computer equipment than they are. Indeed, why not? Pupils can be encouraged to set up, maintain and look after their own 'learning aids'. This leads to the second point: the boundary between *teaching* and *learning* is likely to become increasingly blurred; not that it has ever been an easy one to maintain. The activity of teaching is often said to be an over-studied and overrated activity when what really counts is the learning process. More discussion on this point follows later. Thirdly, the use of computers in the classroom is likely to encourage integration of traditional subjects. This is due partly to the open-ended nature of their use, and partly to the inter-disciplinary nature of many good educational programs. Again, this point will be discussed more fully in Part V. Finally, the imposition of a timetable and bells on the school day is likely to become an increasing intrusion in classrooms where computers are involved. With some classes the only way to get pupils out is to switch the computer off — just as many parents can only get their young children out of the bath by pulling out the plug. This drives home probably the most important observation of all: pupils from five to eighty *enjoy* learning with a computer.

Further reading

1. Excellent discussions of classroom practice and organization occur in: *Managing the Microcomputer in the Classroom*, by David Ellingham (CET on behalf of the MEP, 1982).
2. A similar collection of case-studies has been put together in *Five of the Best: Computer Programs for Primary School Children*, ed. R. Jones (CET, 1982).
3. A useful collection of guidelines for first-time users can be found in *MUSE REPORT NO. 1 — School microcomputers: uses and management* (Heinemann Computers in Education, 1982).
4. The following books all contain useful sections on classroom management and organization: *Children and Computers in the Classroom*, A.P. Mullan (Castle House, 1984); *The Microcomputer and the Primary School*, A.J. Obrist (Hodder & Stoughton, 1983); *Microcomputers in the Classroom*, Alan Maddison (Hodder & Stoughton, 1982); *Microcomputer Assisted Learning in the Primary School* (Chapter 8), Peter Gill, (Ward Lock, 1983); and *Micros in the Primary Classroom* ed. R. Jones (Edward Arnold, 1984).

Talking points

- *Have you ever witnessed, or experienced, a teaching situation where a mishap with an audio-visual aid has been a source of embarrassment? Has this influenced your view on teaching aids, such as the microcomputer?*
- *Would you feel happy about letting your own pupils or students set up computer equipment, then load and run their own programs?*
- *Do you agree with the advantages and disadvantages suggested for a computer room? Could you add any ideas or experiences of your own to the list?*
- *How do you feel that the teacher's classroom practice, organization and role will be affected by increasing use of microcomputers and other new technology?*
- *Do you agree with the sweeping assertion that 'the difficulty of introducing new technology into the daily practice of a school depends on how traditional the school ethos and buildings are'?*
- *Have a look at this passage from a recent collection of articles on microcomputers in the school curriculum:*

The first school I taught in had a raked lecture theatre into which the class would move to view a film. Thc 16 mm projector was operated by a technician, and the film ordered some while in advance from a commercial supplier. Removing the pupils from the environment of the geography room meant that the film's content was viewed in isolation from other resources and in a relatively inhibiting environment. In four years I can count the number of films I used in single digits. My second school forced me to reassess the position; not only were three 16 mm projectors available to the department, but all were on trolleys and all classrooms had blackout facilities. A regular film library service was operated by the authority with deliveries of up to six films per week. Geographical film became an integrated part of my teaching; the organizational issues no longer dominated and the environment for its use was now educational.

From: 'Microcomputers in Secondary Education' by Deryn Watson, in *Microcomputers and the Curriculum*, p.128, ed. A.V. Kelly (Harper & Row, 1984)

- *Have you experienced similar constraints yourself?*
- *Do you think that there are strong connections between this example and the introduction of micros into schools?*
- *In the light of such examples and connections, how would you assess the pros and cons rather crudely presented in Table 4 in this unit?*

Unit 10

PSYCHOLOGY AND EDUCATIONAL COMPUTING

Peter Hannon and *Stuart Wooler*

Exploring the potential of computers and information technology in education forces us to consider some underlying questions. How do children learn from computers? How might the development of children's thinking be affected? What principles should guide the design of software? What will be the personal and social consequences of the IT curriculum? Many such questions are fundamentally psychological, and it is therefore natural to turn to psychological theory for answers.

Introduction

We should be realistic about what can be expected from psychology. There is certainly no such thing as a single coherent 'Psychology of Educational Computing' or a 'Psychology of Information Technology'. To see the relevance of psychology in this area we need to understand the links between psychology and education generally. Sometimes the application of psychological knowledge results directly in an educational innovation but on the whole such cases are rare. More often psychology is linked to education because educationists turn to one psychological theory or another to justify innovations introduced primarily for other reasons. In other cases psychology enters education because, implicitly or explicitly, psychological benefits are claimed for certain educational practices. We also find psychological concepts used in describing certain curricular innovations which can, on occasions, be appropriately evaluated by means of research techniques imported from psychology. Psychology is linked with the emerging educational fields of computing and IT in all of the above ways.

In what follows we shall briefly consider the (relatively limited) ways in which psychology has already had an impact. We shall go on to consider psychological claims in this area by examining one particular example, that of Seymour Papert's notion of 'powerful ideas'. We shall then try to look further ahead by anticipating ways in which psychology might be expected to influence (and be influenced by) future developments. We also need to consider how certain psychological issues, already present in education today, might take on a new form. Our aim is to suggest a set of psychological concepts which may help us to think more clearly about how and what children learn from computers, and how some of the emerging issues might be explored.

Where psychology has had an impact

Reinforcement theory

One part of psychology which has had a fairly direct influence on educational computing is *reinforcement theory*. Developed by B.F. Skinner[1] and applied by him and many others to education, it is seen most clearly in the 'drill and practice' form of software. The theory is that learning occurs when a particular behaviour is reinforced, and the more immediate the reinforcement the better. Skinner coined the term 'programmed learning' to describe an application of this principle to education. Whatever is to be learnt is presented to the pupil a little bit at a time, various responses are required (e.g. answering a multiple choice question), and all correct responses are reinforced. In programmed learning it is often assumed that simply telling pupils when they are right is sufficient reinforcement. Early forms of programmed learning in the 1950s and 1960s, depending mainly on a paper and pencil technology, were never very popular. The advent of computers may be giving programmed learning a new lease of life. The presentation of information and pupil responses can be made more interesting. It becomes more feasible to develop 'branching programs' (as opposed to 'linear' ones) in which learners follow different routes according to the frequency and nature of their mistakes.

But from a psychological point of view there are serious limitations with reinforcement theory, and therefore with 'drill and practice' programs based on it. The theory may plausibly be applied to fairly simple kinds of learning (e.g. applying colour names, learning tables) but seems quite inadequate for precisely the more advanced kinds of learning which schools might hope to promote.

Cognitive science and expert systems

Other theories of learning have been developed in psychology, only one or two of which, however, have had much discernible influence on educational computing. An example would be Piagetian learning theory, which partly inspired Seymour Papert's ideas about the educational importance of computers (to be discussed below). In addition, distinctive theories of learning are now emerging from *cognitive science*, a new discipline in which ideas about human cognitive processes are strongly influenced by the ways in which computers solve problems.

A picture is now emerging from cognitive science in which human knowledge is seen to be of two kinds: knowledge of facts ('knowledge that') and knowledge of procedures or methods for solving problems and making inferences and judgements ('knowledge how'). The way in which a person sets about solving a problem (knowledge how) is seen to be very dependent on what the person knows about the content of the problem (knowledge that). Thus problem-solving procedures are no longer considered to be general purpose procedures applicable across all sorts of different types of problems but instead are thought of as more specific 'heuristic' rules which vary according to the factual content of the problem at hand.

It is in the current interest in 'expert systems' for educational use that the influence of this psychological theory is to be seen.[2] The expert system most often referred to is MYCIN, a computer program incorporating the knowledge of a team of doctors (both knowledge that and knowledge how) about diagnosing certain bacterial diseases.[3] By questioning doctors intensively the MYCIN developers have learnt what facts (symptoms, test results, and so on) the doctors take notice of and what rules they use for making diagnoses from these facts. All this knowledge has then been put into a program, so that the computer is capable of asking for the facts it needs to know and then using them to make diagnoses as accurate as those of a human doctor (and sometimes more so).

In addition, the user is able to question the computer about how it arrived at its conclusion, and in response the computer attempts to explain its reasoning. It is in particular this capability which is educationally interesting. Imagine a physics or geology or meteorology expert system in which the student inputs information about some states of the world — it might be a particular combination of climatic conditions — and asks the computer to infer what the resultant rainfall is likely to be. In explaining why it produced the result it did, the computer would be extending the student's factual knowledge by introducing him or her to information which it used in thinking through the problem. It would also conduct the student through its own systematic reasoning process — not only teaching students facts but teaching them how to reason with these facts.

However, while there has been a lot of talk about expert systems in education, little has been done. It is hard work (and therefore very expensive) to build an expert system as such. It is much harder to build one with the extended capacity for explaining its own reasoning in something like ordinary English[4] which is what would be needed before it could be used to much effect in schools.

Decision theory

It is too early to say for sure whether the practical problems of developing expert systems can be overcome, but even if they do prove useful for certain kinds of educational problems they are certainly not appropriate for all. They may work well for educational problems in which there are experts who know the right answers. What about those where there are no right or wrong answers? One might argue about what sort of educational topics are understood well enough to provide 'right answers'. (For example, are processes in history understood well enough for anyone to know that a set of historical conditions is bound to lead to one of a set of particular historical outcomes?) But there are some clear cases where a computer definitely cannot know a right answer; in particular those where a student must choose what to do in the light of his or her personal values and goals. No computerized system can know what they are, or dictate what they should be. Some programs deriving from the *psychology of decision making* have appeared which make a start at dealing with this problem.[5] Their aim is to encourage students to clarify their own goals and values through interaction with the computer, and to appreciate how they are interrelated and may conflict. They do not tell students how they *should* think about problems, but assume that it will be beneficial if the computer is used to present their thinking to them in a form which clarifies it and allows them to see what implications follow.

Psychological claims

Many claims have been made about the psychological benefits for children of educational computing and information technology. Amongst the most interesting and influential at the present time are those put forward by Seymour Papert in *Mindstorms*.[6] Papert is critical of much computer-aided instruction in schools in which according to his view the computer is being used to program the child rather than the child programming the computer. He shows that it is possible to design computers so that children can use them easily and as a result he argues that the way in which they learn other things changes. The children program in Logo, a sophisticated high level interactive language (or family of languages) which was developed particularly for children. One part of Logo enables children to control the movements of the now famous Turtle — a floor robot or screen equivalent which can be made to leave a trace of its travels. Through Logo quite young children can therefore learn to produce 'drawings' made up of geometrical shapes.

From an educational perspective what is interesting about Papert is the bold psychological claim he makes for what children learn from Logo environments. Not only do they learn computer programming, they are said to acquire what he calls 'powerful ideas' which influence, indeed transform, the way they think and learn even when they are far removed from physical contact with a computer. Papert leaves his readers in no doubt about what he believes the implications to be for education. 'Radical change is possible,' he says, 'and the possibility for that change is directly tied to the impact of the computer.' Few educationists could fail to be moved by the sense of intellectual excitement and humanity conveyed by Papert's writing but that should not prevent us treating what are essentially psychological claims with proper scepticism.

What are these 'powerful ideas'? There seem to be two kinds. First, there are certain ideas about computing which, by analogy, children could apply to their own learning. These include viewing what is to be learnt in terms of 'subprocedures', expecting 'bugs' in initial attempts at learning and recognizing 'debugging' as a valuable process. Papert seems to suggest that if children viewed the task of learning something as akin to devising a program to do it, they would learn to do it more quickly and possibly more successfully. Second, there are certain ideas which are powerful in a scientific sense (e.g. geometrical concepts, differential calculus, Newtonian physics, combinatorial thinking). Papert tries to demonstrate how these may be acquired through computing in 'microworlds' such as that of the Turtle.

In the first kind of powerful idea, Papert is essentially making a psychological claim about the transfer of learning — that if children learn to compute (in Logo), their learning of certain other tasks will be improved. Indeed the claim seems to be that their learning of *all* other skills will greatly benefit. This is strong stuff. It goes far beyond even those claims made in the past in education for, say, Latin or New Maths. In fact, cast in this form, the claim seems psychologically improbable, to say the least. Psychological research has not so far encountered any other form of learning with such powerful *transferability* and Papert offers no real evidence that Logo computing has had such effects.

In relation to the second kind of powerful idea the psychological claim is more modest. It may well be that certain microworlds offer an easier route to acquiring certain kinds of scientific concepts. But the psychological question here is, 'Easier than what?'. All educational methods have to be justified ultimately in relation to plausible alternatives and Papert does not compare the computing route to other, possibly humbler, methods. Indeed he does not appear to consider that there might be alternative ways of teaching, say, differential calculus, against which the computing way should be measured.

Furthermore, Papert's set of powerful ideas appear to be a rather idiosyncratic selection from all those ideas which might be considered psychologically powerful. One can see how they might appeal to a mathematician researching into artificial intelligence at the Massachusetts Institute of Technology. But if teachers and parents were asked to list general ideas about learning, thinking, and how to get on in the world which they would like children to grasp, would their lists be the same as Papert's? They might want to emphasize instead ideas of quite a different kind such as a readiness to question taken-for-granted assumptions or to look for bias, being able to understand other people's points of view, or valuing practice as a means of improving performance. Is using a computer the most direct way of acquiring such ideas?

Potential for greater psychological contribution

The issues on which psychological theory and empirical research *might* have an impact are currently perhaps more numerous than those on which it *has had* an impact. Why has psychology so far failed in this respect? Not surprisingly there seems to be more than one factor involved. Firstly the scale of the problem is large and available research methods are apparently inadequate to the task.[7] Existing methods tend to be good at discerning changes in students' capacities to cope with simple, controllable tasks, but (as we have seen in the previous section) it is sometimes profound changes in cognitive development which are claimed for computer use. The difficulties involved in measuring such psychological changes and checking their significance is daunting, and therefore progress has been painfully slow.

But even those aspects which are apparently tractable to current research methods have not yet received sufficient detailed attention. An example is group learning via the computer. There is evidence that some kinds of learning are facilitated by working in groups – but how does the introduction of a computer as the focus of attention affect the behaviour of the group? How big should the group be? How should the intra-group interaction and the group/machine interaction be managed? Limited numbers of computers in schools will dictate that a good deal of students' work with computers will take place in groups, regardless of whether or not it is a productive learning environment. How are we to get the best out of group work with computers?

Psychologists are at work on these problems, and results of interest are likely to emerge. For example, extrapolating from recent research carried out in a non-computer environment, there could be an improvement in learning for certain pupils working in pairs with a computer if it both discourages them from making very fast responses and only accepts a response when both members of the pair instruct it jointly.[8] Other, less crude, ways of trying to ensure that groups of pupils actually do work together *as a group* may emerge.

There are other issues however which are rather well understood by psychologists, but their results have been largely ignored by software developers. For example, research into the use of colour on computer screens has shown users to be very sensitive to colour and colour change. Users typically react to a colour change by looking for a reason for it[9] and confusion frequently follows if no reason can be found. A casual look at the available educational software is sufficient to show that this lesson has not been learnt by many software developers.

A further role which, though certainly not exclusive to psychologists, is one which they could usefully fulfil is that of 'whistleblower' on bad educational computing developments. For all its promise, computer power can serve to stultify more than enhance classroom practice.[10] Unfortunately to date its promises have received more attention than its pitfalls. Psychologists have a role as critics, exposing computer uses based on weak (or non-existent) assumptions about how learning is encouraged or hindered.

At a deeper level psychologists will assuredly play a part in the forthcoming fundamental debates about the appropriateness of the computer's way of thinking as a model of human thinking. The computer method of solving problems is by systematic carrying out of lists of instructions. Is this a good analogy for how people think, or is people's (mundane or creative) thinking more like taking leaps in the dark than following rules?[11] Moreover, can we even generalize with confidence about how people think, or is some people's thinking in crucial respects different from that of others? It may be that in not just wishing to acquaint our children with computers, but also in trying to teach them the reasoning processes employed by computers we are hindering the growth of their natural, intuitive 'feel' for how to develop an understanding of the world. Future generations may look back at the educational uptake of computers and see us as using computers as an educational tool rather in the fashion that an infant uses a paint brush — wildly, in an unco-ordinated manner, with no clear idea of limitations or objectives.

Other psychological questions

Social relationships and learning

One of the most striking features of children's interaction with computers in school and elsewhere is their level of concentration. What is it that makes computers so attractive? Are they actually more compelling than other objects they encounter? Part of the answer must be the way in which they provide immediate feedback about the results of action. Also they are non-judgemental. Much of children's learning is mediated by adults who tell them in one way or another whether they are right or wrong, and although this is undoubtedly a powerful source of change it can also happen that children react against it. Personal relationships can interfere with as well as promote learning.

The same aspect of computers also causes disquiet amongst some educators and parents, as yet a minority. There is a fear that there is something dehumanizing about hooking children up to computers instead of having learning take place in social settings. This view should not be lightly dismissed. It seems to some that computing will not encourage co-operative learning but something much more individual, and to that extent possibly more competitive. Does it make children better people? Anecdotal evidence and commonplace observations of children playing video games suggest that it can all go too far. This however is reminiscent of the fears expressed about television viewing twenty or so years ago and it may turn out that computers will encourage greater, not less, social interaction between learners even when they are working at their own terminals. If children are excited or challenged by what they are doing they may well be more inclined to share their experiences and knowledge with each other. The need to do so may be more urgent than when working with conventional educational materials.

Creativity

A related fear of some teachers is that computers may inhibit rather than foster the development of creativity. This fear is made more plausible by the fact that whatever children do with computers, even programming in Logo, their freedom of action is limited to what the system designer has allowed. They are inevitably forced down tramlines of one kind or another although some (e.g. drill and practice programs) are more confining than others. This criticism, however, misses the fundamental point that children are already limited by whatever adults provide for them. Also if computers were *freely* available one can imagine them encouraging exactly those forms of exploratory play which many psychologists believe underlie creativity.

Gender

There are some psychological issues in education which may be expected to take on a new, and perhaps sharper, form in the IT environment. One which has concerned many educationists and psychologists recently has been differences in the school experiences and educational attainment of boys and girls. How will this be affected in the IT environment? Educational software may well be open to criticisms which have been made of sexist materials in other parts of the curriculum. There are also suspicions that boys are making greater use of computers in schools than are girls. Some recent research suggests that both sexes expect boys to do better with computers.[12] The problem is possibly a deep-seated one bound up with complex gender-related differences in attitudes to technologies of all kinds. Further studies will be needed to determine the extent of the problem and ways in which it might be tackled.

Social class

An inescapable feature of child development is the way in which it depends on social class. So of course does educational attainment. What will be the situation in the IT environment? There is every reason to believe that the gulf between children of different classes will widen. Access to IT devices in school could be reasonably equal for all children (although our experience of the distribution of other educational resources may give grounds for doubt) but there are bound to be huge differences in home use of computers and computer-based equipment like video disks and database terminals. Entire 'curricula' are likely to be marketed by software houses or large publishing corporations. The result will be fatal to the opportunities of many working class children who will be disadvantaged in terms of the sheer amount of time they will be able to spend learning via computers. Economic differences between families are likely to be translated even more directly into educational differences.

Related to this is the whole issue of parental involvement in children's education. How will this change in the IT environment? Again the changes will be on social class lines. Parents able to afford and operate computers will be able as never before to enter the world of their children's education. Those without will be excluded.

Conclusions

The relationships between psychology, computing developments, and educational practice are complex and intriguing. For the moment computer technology is in the driving seat. Important technology-driven changes in education are under way. At the same time psychology is also being changed by the new technology and this trend can be expected to continue and accelerate. It is to be hoped that psychological theory and research will increasingly inform and shape developments in educational computing.

Reference notes and suggestions for further reading

1. See Skinner, B.F. (1968) *The technology of teaching*. New York: Appleton-Century-Crofts.
2. A related term is 'Intelligent Knowledge-Based System' (IKBS) which is sometimes used synonymously with 'expert system' and sometimes to denote a rather broader category of computer programs which have some knowledge of 'the world'.
3. See O'Shea, T. and Self, J. (1983) *Learning and teaching with computers*. Brighton: The Harvester Press. MYCIN is discussed in Chapters 2 and 4 but this book also provides valuable coverage of other issues in the field of artificial intelligence and computer-based learning.
4. The term 'intelligent tutoring system' is now becoming widely used to refer to expert systems having this extended ability to answer 'Why?' questions in a meaningful and understandable way.
5. See Wooler, S. and Wisudha, A. (1985) An educational approach to designing computer-based career guidance systems. *British Journal of Educational Technology*. **16**.
6. Papert, S. (1980) *Mindstorms*. Brighton: The Harvester Press.
7. A very useful overview of the difficulties involved in experimental testing in this area (and of several other issues raised in this chapter) is to be found in the discussion document by Sage, M. and Smith D.J. (1983) *Microcomputers in education*. London: S.S.R.C., June.
8. This possibility has been explored by T. Foot and P.H. Light at the University of Southampton following on from research reported by Glachan, M. and Light, P.H. (1982) 'Peer Interaction and Learning' in Butterworth, G. and Light P. (eds) *Social Cognition*. Brighton: Harvester Press.
9. See J. Preece, 'Graphs are not straightforward' in Green, T.R.G., Payne S.J. and van der Veer, G.C. *The psychology of computer use*. London: Academic Press.
10. A good discussion of some of the dangers of computer use is to be found in Howe, J.A.M and du Boulay B. (1979) 'Microprocessor assisted learning: turning the clock back?' in *Programmed Learning and Educational Technology* **16**, 3, 195–199.
11. Some of the most influential anti-computer arguments have been put by

J. Weizenbaum in his book *Computer Power and Human Reason: from judgment to calculation.* Harmondsworth: Penguin, 1984.
12. These findings come from M. Hughes and H. Macleod *Children on computers.* Paper presented to a B.P.S. conference, 'IT, AI and Child Development', held at the University of Sussex July 1984.

Peter Hannon is a Lecturer in Psychology in the Division of Education, Sheffield University. He is interested in developmental psychology and early childhood education.

Stuart Wooler is a Research Fellow in the Decision Analysis Unit and also teaches in the Department of Social Psychology, of the London School of Economics and Political Science. He is engaged in the development of structured decision making software for use in schools.

PART FOUR

CAL ACROSS THE CURRICULUM

Part IV examines in detail the use of computers, and other aspects of information technology, in different areas of the school curriculum. Both the primary and the secondary sectors are considered although a whole unit is devoted specifically to an overview of computers in primary education.

The units on CAL in specific *subject* areas should be of interest to those concerned with either primary or secondary education.

PART FOUR

CAL ACROSS THE CURRICULUM

Part Four [illegible] in detail the use of computers and other aspects of [illegible] in different areas of the school [illegible] primary and [illegible] secondary [illegible] and finally to an overview of [illegible]

The aims of CAL [illegible] concerned [illegible] primary [illegible] education.

UNIT 11

COMPUTERS IN PRIMARY EDUCATION

Christopher Schenk

This unit:

- *gives a brief history of computers in primary education*
- *examines the arguments for giving young children access to computers*
- *describes some of the categories of software used in primary schools*
- *looks at future developments*

Brief history

Computers did not make any significant impact on primary classrooms until the Department of Industry offer to primary schools of 1982. Before that, there were a few keen teachers experimenting with computers — and even a very few Local Education Authorities funding pilot schemes. However, in the short space of two years the DoI offer transformed the primary school scene. Before 1982 primary schools with a computer were few and far between. After 1984 nearly all primary schools had at least one computer. It is the school without the computer that has become the oddity.

The DoI offer gave pound-for-pound funding for one of three computer systems: the BBC B, the RML 480Z or the Spectrum. A substantial majority of schools opted for the BBC, though a significant minority of LEAs recommended the 480Z. No disk drives were offered, but many schools have acquired them through their own funds, and several printers, turtles and concept keyboards have also been bought.

Alongside the offer, MEP put together some in-service training materials called Microprimer. This consists of a Study Pack, containing an estimated 20 hours of self-study material, a Reader, with a number of stimulating articles in it, and about 30 programs, to introduce schools to appropriate software. The written materials are still well worth looking at. However, the software is of variable educational quality and some of it has dated very quickly. But you should be aware of the programs in Microprimer if only because every school participating in the scheme received copies of them.

The MEP Primary Project was set up in 1983 and has produced a number of packs of in-service support materials, which include some software and have been distributed to all LEAs and teacher training institutions.

At the beginning of 1982 a new national association was launched called Micros and Primary Education (MAPE). It has grown rapidly and has regional representatives all over the country. *Micro-scope*, which started out life as a Newman College publication, is now also the official journal of MAPE.

Why have computers in primary schools?

Computers have arrived in primary schools. That is an uncontestable fact. Whether they should be there is still a matter of opinion.

Various reasons have been put forward for having computers in primary schools. You might like to consider the following, some of which have a grain of truth, but none of which is sufficient in itself.

- *Why should primary schools have computers? Are these the reasons?*

  (1) To train children to be skilled computer operatives?

  (2) To introduce children to an important facet of the world outside school?

  (3) To motivate children by giving them tasks they enjoy?

  (4) To prepare children for the next stage in education?

These reasons are mainly to do with learning about computers. Far more important, in a primary classroom, is learning with the aid of computers. Perhaps the real justification for having micros in primary schools is that they can be used, as one resource among many, to support and extend what already goes on in good primary classrooms and can provide new opportunities for young children to learn through activity.

Appropriate software

What sort of software is appropriate at the primary stage of education, and how should it be used? This question can be answered by considering three broad categories of program, and examining their potential in the primary classroom.

1. Programs that support specific teaching points

Most of the software in Microprimer falls into this category. Typically these programs are fairly short, can easily be integrated with other primary school activities and can usually be used by one or more groups of children in the space of a single lesson. They can be further analysed into the following sub-categories:

(a) Drill and practice
TRAINS is a good example of this type of program. Children are presented with a series of sums, and if they get them right they are rewarded with a computer graphic of a train crossing the screen. These programs are sometimes called 'electronic work-cards'. The question needs to be asked: 'Do they do anything which could not be done equally well (and more cheaply!) with ordinary work-cards?'

For some children with special learning difficulties, who need to practice a particular skill, the motivation supplied by using a micro, and the patience of the machine, may provide a justification for using such programs. But for most children their limited value becomes apparent when they are contrasted with more imaginative uses of computers.

The programs QUIZ and MQUIZ allow children to create their own drill and practice materials. One group of children can make up a multi-choice quiz, carefully researching the answers in the class library, and present it to another group of children or even their teacher!

(b) Games of skill and strategy

These can be played against the computer, or by one group of children against another group, with the computer acting as a neutral referee. In SUBGAME, for example, children have to decide where to place digits in a subtraction sum to make the answer as large as possible. The computer also makes decisions, according to predetermined rules. The computer's decisions are always sensible, but rather cautious, so a judicious blend of logic and daring will defeat the computer at its own game.

TOYSHOP is a game for younger children in which they compete against each other. It involves money and helps them to understand coins, but also encourages them to think ahead and predict their opponent's moves.

There are a number of other games which can be used to reinforce particular skills and to extend children's powers of logical thought. Many can also be played without the computer, but less successfully, since the computer is strictly impartial!

(c) Problem solving

The computer can provide new opportunities for children to solve problems set into a meaningful context. CRASH, for example, sets the problem of devising a sequence of instructions to guide an arrow through a series of obstacles in order to reach a target. The first attempts can be corrected and refined. Children are encouraged to make mistakes — and learn from them.

Short programs, like the ones briefly described above, can be useful additions to a range of other types of work. It is no accident that the examples chosen are mathematical in content, for it is in maths, most of all, that short, specific programs come into their own. But they must be used alongside other sorts of mathematical activity, in particular the use of structured apparatus, which has a vital role to play in the building up of young children's mathematical ideas. Computer use is not seeking to replace other methods of learning, but only to enhance them.

Some schools and colleges have managed to acquire a considerable library of programs to support specific teaching points. If you are fortunate enough to have access to such a library on teaching practice, you will probably be able to find programs that are appropriate to the topics you wish to cover and to the children in your class.

On the other hand, some schools have hardly ventured beyond the 30 programs of Microprimer. If you find yourself in a situation where your choice is very restricted, resist the temptation to bring the computer in at all costs!

2. *Programs that can stimulate activities across the curriculum over a period of time*

There are a few programs that can be used as the focus for project work in the primary classroom, can hold children's attention for several weeks, and can give rise to a wide variety of classroom activities, from drama to science. They take a long time to develop, and therefore tend to be expensive. There is every indication that a growing number of good quality programs of this type will be produced in the next few years.

Two examples will show the potential these programs have in the primary classroom. The first is a simulation, based on careful research of an actual occurrence — the raising of the Mary Rose from the bed of the Solent. The second is an adventure game, an excursion into the fantasy world that exists in every child's mind, and just might be at the bottom of granny's garden!

(a) MARY ROSE, a computer simulation

The first part of the program simulates a search of the sea-bed of the Solent, using ultra-sound scanners, and exploratory dives. The discovery of the whereabouts of the Mary Rose, and the calculation of the precise latitude and longitude of the wreck, provides the password that is necessary to use the second part of the program. This entails careful preparation for 'the dive', a meticulous (and three-dimensional!) search of the wreck and the painstaking piecing together of the artefacts rescued from the sea-bed, to build up a picture of what life was like on a Tudor warship. The children play the parts, first of a deep-sea diver, and then of an archaeologist, interpreting the evidence.

An imaginative teacher, with a class of upper juniors, can use this program to inspire investigations into aspects of Tudor history, scientific speculation and experimentation about why the Mary Rose sank, creative writing, drama and a host of other activities. The work has to be carefully organized and needs to be supported with a variety of resources — from books and pictures to visits to the Mary Rose. The computer plays a powerful role, but its use has to be integrated with activities away from the keyboard for the program to have any effect.

(b) GRANNY'S GARDEN, an adventure game

This is designed for upper infants and lower juniors. In the setting of a fantasy world, the Kingdom of the Mountains, the missing children of the King and Queen must be found, and the Wicked Witch outwitted.

Mike Matson, the author of the program, describes how a class teacher might use GRANNY'S GARDEN to stimulate a wide variety of activities in a primary classroom:

> *Day 1*
> Have any of you visited your granny lately? Two grannies, Sally? I bet they spoil you, don't they? Grannies are very good at spoiling children. Mine always spoiled me, but then she didn't have to put up with me all the time. My granny died a long time ago but I can still remember her, and her house, and her garden and I used to imagine what might be on the other side of it. Have any of you got a granny with an interesting garden? Oh George! I'm sure your granny hasn't really got a garden with a jungle in it. Who else wants to tell us about an interesting garden?
>
> *Day 2*
> Yesterday you all did some lovely pictures of gardens. I liked the way Diane used real grass in her picture. Let's imagine we are in Wayne's garden. What do you think we would find if we looked behind that shed? I know, if you get into little groups and find yourselves a comfortable corner somewhere you could make up a story about how you and your friends had an adventure in one of those gardens. No, don't write it down unless you really want to.
>
> *Day 3*
> Who would like to start off with their story? All right, we'll hear yours first. Are the three of you going to take it in turns?
>
> *Day 4*
> We'll go in the hall. I've got a record of bird songs. We'll imagine that the hall is a garden and you can have your adventure there.
>
> *Day 5*
> If the ones at the front all sit on the floor you can all see the screen. We'll take it in turns to come out to the keyboard.
>
> *Week 8*
> Hooray! Now everyone has found the six missing children. Just look at all the work we've done. I've been told that if we write to the Magic Raven he will send us a certificate. What do you think we should say in our letter? Good idea, Jane. We'll write about all the things we've done. There's the play we made up, the model of the Mountain Kingdom and the plans of the woodcutter's cottage. We'll have to say that we did all these Chinese

pictures, made dragon kites, wrote some sneezing poems and made up songs about the insects. Mustn't forget all the measuring we did when we drew the map in the playground and, of course, there are all those magic spell recipes that we tried out. Did your dad really eat that cake, John? Oh yes. All your lovely stories about your adventures. Yes, thank you Timothy but I don't think we need to tell the Magic Raven about what I called the dragons. It really was a good job we wrote down what happened or else we'd still be giving them sticky buns.

3. Content-free programs that provide a flexible tool for teaching and learning

There are also some very versatile programs that have no specific content when they are first loaded, but allow children and teachers to use them for their own purposes. Three examples of these powerful tools will show that a small number of programs of this type can keep a computer in constant and productive use.

(a) Turtle graphics
The turtle is a friendly robot, with a pen in the middle, that can be controlled from a computer. The turtle can be instructed to go forward or backward by a specific number of units, and to turn right or left by a specific number of degrees. This simple beginning provides a way into the exploration of profound and intricate mathematical ideas.

Sequences of commands can be built up and given names. The computer can be taught what sequence of commands to execute when a particular name is typed in. For example, the procedure SQUARE might consist of the following commands:

```
FORWARD 40
RIGHT 90
FORWARD 40
RIGHT 90
FORWARD 40
RIGHT 90
FORWARD 40
```

Once this has been defined, the turtle will draw a square every time SQUARE is typed, and the word SQUARE can be used in the definition of other procedures.

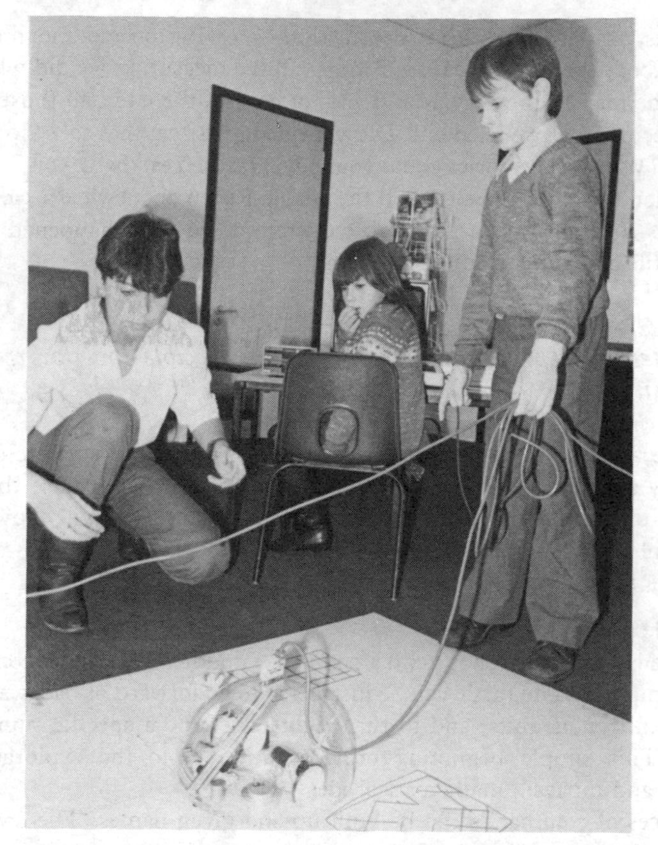

Figure 14. Turtles for the classroom. A turtle connected to the micro by cable

Most children who have the opportunity to use a turtle, naturally and spontaneously set their own goals. The problem solving which arises from trying to achieve these self-defined goals, can lead to substained logical thought, and a high level of discussion and argument between children. The turtle has the strange effect of making mathematics a passionate subject! Children really care about angles and lengths and are prepared to argue ferociously with their peers.

The finished turtle drawings are not great art. That is not the point of the exercise. The final product is unimportant compared with the process by which it came about. Along the way, many mistakes are made, but there is always an opportunity to correct them and to learn from them. One child remarked to his teacher, 'What I like about using the turtle is that there is always hope!'

Using the floor turtle, or a screen turtle that draws only on the monitor screen, children from the age of six or seven, to eleven and beyond, can set themselves challenges that significantly extend their powers of logical thought and their grasp of mathematical concepts. Surprisingly young children can make use of variables and other algebraic ideas.

Turtle graphics is a part of the computer language Logo, and the procedures that children create are the first steps towards programming in Logo. A full version of Logo can be used in order to control a turtle, but programs like ARROW and DART are widely used as substitutes.

The important teaching skill needed in order to use turtle graphics succesfully is the ability to know when to intervene with suggestions or encouragement, and when to refrain from interfering. It is essential to allow free play with the turtle; but, as in all discovery learning, the teacher's role is crucial. Sensitive questioning, occasional challenges and pertinent instruction, are all necessary at the right time. Judging when that is can be one of the most difficult tasks of the teacher.

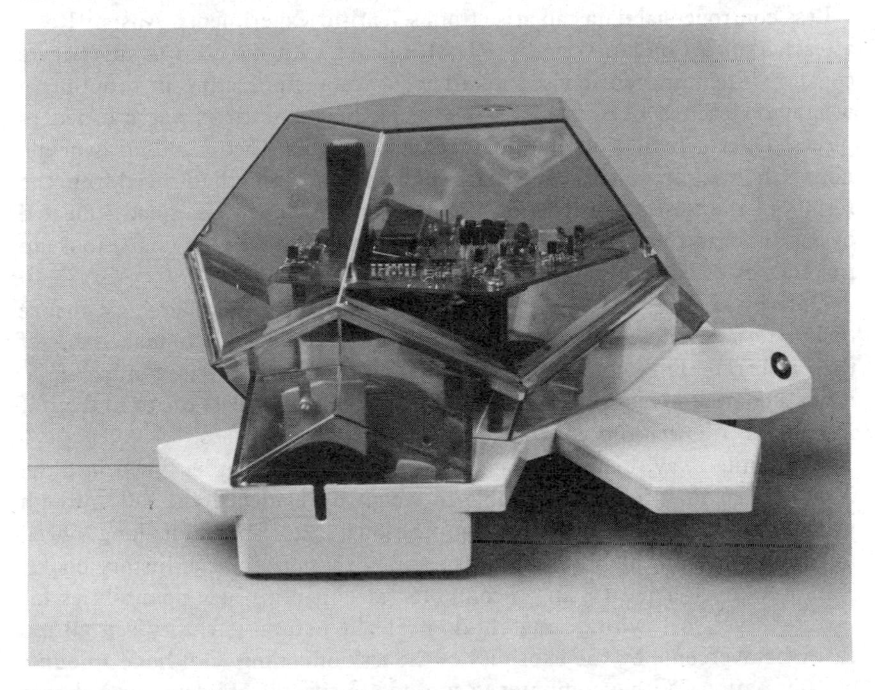

Figure 15. Turtles for the classroom. A turtle controlled by infra-red signals (Photograph Courtesy Valiant Designs Ltd)

(b) Information retrieval

Using FACTFILE, or more sophisticated information retrieval packages like QUEST or INFORM or DATAPROBE, the computer can allow children to handle large amounts of data, and make sense of a mass of information.

A simple data-file can be made with details of every child in the class. Once this has been done it can be 'interrogated' to give answers to questions like 'Which girls aged 8 or over, have black hair and are under 1 m 30 cm in height?'. Using PICFILE, block graphs and scattergrams can be constructed. Hypotheses can be put forward and tested. For example, if the right information has been put in, it might be possible to find out if there is any connection between children's favourite foods and how heavy they are. Be careful, though. There may be overweight children in the class who are particularly sensitive about their size. Issues of privacy and the uses to which information can be put often arise from this kind of work, and can provide a good opportunity to discuss some of the moral implications of information technology.

Less controversial data can arise from scientific experiments. Alistair Ross, a teacher in a London primary school, set out with his class to investigate conkers. The children devised a variety of tests culminating in dropping a weight on each conker from an increasing height until it was crushed to pieces! Over a period of time they tested more than two hundred conkers, noting the weight, volume, age, skin thickness and strength (derived from the results of the 'test to destruction') of each one of them. They had collected over a thousand pieces of information which, displayed on a chart, took up five metres of paper.

Only by entering this mass of data into a computer was there any chance that patterns would emerge and that the children could begin to make sense of their research. They could now make up and test a hypothesis. For example, it was a comparatively simple matter to interrogate their data file to find out if it really is true that old conkers are stronger than new ones.

In a similar way, historical data like census returns can be typed into the computer so that children are able to weigh up evidence and sift through primary sources, in the manner of a professional historian, and no longer need to be content with the broad and misleading generalizations of history books.

Information retrieval using a computer can open up new possibilities for investigative work with young children. Their natural curiosity can all too easily be overcome by the enormity of the task of coping with huge amounts of information. With a computer to sort and to sift, the children can be more productively employed in investigation and speculation.

(c) Word processing
Using a word processor completely changes the act of writing. The ability to alter and reorder the written word, and still produce a perfect copy that contains no trace of the many revisions and corrections it has undergone, can have a liberating effect on a reluctant writer. A word processor invites an experimental attitude to writing, and promotes a critical awareness of style and content.

Surprisingly young children can use a word processor with advantage. However, successful use does depend on regular access to a computer. In many schools this is not yet possible. It is also necessary to have a printer, and very desirable to have a disk drive, to make the best use of word processing. It is not surprising that its use in primary schools is still at an early stage, but there are strong indications that it could have a profound impact on young children's writing.

Group composition can happen naturally and productively around a word processor. Writing is too often a lonely exercise. By encouraging group discussion around the word processor children can be helped to make the difficult transition from the spoken to the written word.

Future developments

Crystal-ball gazing in this field is a dangerous occupation. Few people would have predicted two years ago that nearly every primary school in the United Kingdom would have a micro. The next few years may well see equally unexpected developments.

The pace of technological change will certainly not slow down. There are a number of technical innovations just over the horizon which could have important effects on primary education. The interactive videodisk could be used to add a new dimension to simulations and adventure games, and to the retrieval of information, by integrating video film with computer software. Speech synthesis could also have interesting repercussions on computer use in primary schools, for example in the early teaching of reading.

The possibility of gaining access to vast databases over the telephone lines or through teletext is an exciting one. It is already possible to connect a computer to systems like Prestel or Micronet through the telephone, or to down-load programs and information from CEEFAX broadcasts. However, a system like Prestel is oriented towards business customers at the moment. It may be some time before similar systems, specifically geared to educational needs, come into operation.

There will also be new forms of input devices. Already many schools have concept keyboards. These are touch-sensitive trays that connect to the computer. Different overlays can be placed on them so that, by touching particular parts, children can communicate with the computer without having to type words in laboriously. A few schools have used Microwriters which allow children to 'type' in to the computer using only five buttons. Different combinations of fingers result in the various letters of the alphabet. Light pens and touch-sensitive screens are also being further developed. Speech input, however, still seems a thing of the future.

New software is being written at an alarming rate and it is becoming increasingly difficult to keep up with it. With any luck software will begin to increase in quality as well as quantity!

Quite apart from technological developments in hardware and educational developments in software, there are also bound to be changes in teachers' attitudes. Some people predict that in a couple of years' time lots of computers will be gathering dust in the stock cupboards, piled up on top of unused OHPs and teaching machines. This will certainly happen in a few schools, but in most cases the children, the parents and the teachers (probably in that order!) will make sure that the computers remain in constant use, and that the school acquires more machines.

When computers were first introduced to primary schools, many teachers felt that they could only be used by experts. The message is now getting over to teachers that you don't need lots of technical knowledge — and in particular you don't need to know how to program — to make exciting and rewarding use of a micro with young children. Over the next few years teachers will realize that computers are here to stay and that they are for all ages, both sexes, all abilities — and all teachers. Computers in the primary school are too important to be the province of computer 'experts' — still less of computer fanatics!

Further reading

1. Further details of some of the uses to which a computer can be put in the primary classroom can be found in Obrist, A.J. (1983) *The Microcomputer and the Primary School.* Hodder and Stoughton.

2. An interesting analysis of computer use with young children, that warns of the dangers inherent in the new technology is Chandler, D. (1984) *Young Learners and the Microcomputer.* Open University Press.

3. An activity book for teachers that suggests ideas for work both at the computer and away from the keyboard is Schenk, C. (1985) *Hands on, hands off.* A & C Black.
4. A collection of articles about various aspects of the primary school curriculum is to be found in the MUSE Special Report No. 5 (April 1984) *Microcomputers in Primary Schools,* Heinemann Computers in Education. The articles are:
   Schenk, C. 'Micros and Language' (also published in the *Times Educational Supplement*, 2 March 1984).
   Straker, A. 'Micros and Primary Maths'.
   Stewart, J. 'Micros and Primary Science'.
   Hodges, M. 'Topic Work: the Role of the Micro'.
5. A stimulating account of the value of Logo, written by the guru of the Logo world, is Papert, S. (1980) *Mindstorms—Children, Computers and Powerful Ideas.* Harvester Press.
6. A practical book of classroom suggestions to do with Logo, written for children is Cunliffe, J. (1984) *Play LOGO.* André Deutsch.
7. Further ideas for making use of information retrieval can be found in Ross, A. (1984) *Making Connections.* Council for Educational Technology.

Talking points

- *Do drill and practice programs on the computer have any value?*
- *Is there any point in playing a game on a computer, that can also be played without using one?*
- *How should computer simulations be linked with direct first-hand experience?*
- *Are adventure games educational?*
- *What can children gain from using Logo?*
- *How can young children be introduced to information retrieval?*
- *Which areas of the primary curriculum could benefit from computer use?*
- *Can the computer do harm in the primary classroom?*

Program sources

TRAINS, QUIZ, MQUIZ: published by Tecmedia as part of Microprimer
SUBGAME: Longman and the Association of Teachers of Mathematics
TOYSHOP: MEP Capital Regional Information Centre
ARROW: Research Machines Limited
DART: Advisory Unit for Computer Based Education, Hatfield
GRANNY'S GARDEN: 4-MATION Educational Software, Barnstaple
MARY ROSE: Ginn & Co.

Christopher Schenk has been a lecturer in Primary Education at Liverpool University, Head Teacher of Little Milton Primary School and Deputy Director of the MEP National Primary Project. He is the author of *Hands on, Hands off*, a computer activity book for primary school teachers, to be published by A & C Black in 1985.

UNIT 12

MICROCOMPUTERS AND MATHEMATICS TEACHING

David Jesson

This unit introduces:

- *A framework for using computers in mathematics lessons*
- *Some examples of what can happen when you do this*
- *Some implications for classroom management and organization*
- *Possible ways ahead, and areas in which teachers can play a full part*
- *References to helpful sources and programs*

Introduction

'Pupils in surprisingly large numbers are finding a joy and a zest in some aspects of mathematics which they did not find before!' This is a quotation from the report *Microcomputers and Mathematics in Schools* written for the DES in 1983 by Trevor Fletcher who was until recently the Chief Inspector for Mathematics.

Any development that can encourage this kind of response must obviously be important for the curriculum as a whole, but its relevance for teachers of mathematics cannot be missed. However, that same report went on to observe that 'this reaction is not universal, and is not to be found in the majority of schools'.

As you read these two comments and look back over *your* experience of mathematics lessons, perhaps you will see that there is indeed a problem in linking this minority enthusiasm to the benefit of all pupils. And yet, in one sense, many people would not see that there is a problem at all — after all, computers are powerful number processors, so isn't it inevitable that as soon as schools get a computer it will be the mathematics department that will be the first to use it?

However, although Britain is the first country in the world to have a computer in every school, and although many maths teachers were pioneers in developing Computer Studies courses, the impact of computers on day-to-day practice in mathematics classrooms, let alone on the syllabus, is surprisingly small. In some schools computers are hardly used in mathematics classes at all. This unit has been written with the assumption that computers have a valuable role to play in making 'good practice' in mathematics teaching more accessible. Indeed a number of features which HMI found lacking in maths lessons (see for example the Mathematics section of *Aspects of Secondary Education,* HMSO 1979) can be promoted by their use.

The Cockcroft Report

In some schools, changes in methods of teaching mathematics can already be seen and these could develop rapidly given that the experience of 'joy and zest' could be made available to more pupils in more schools. One stimulus towards such change was the Cockcroft Report (HMSO 1982) which suggested that mathematics teaching at all levels should include:

exposition	discussion	practical work
problem solving	investigations	consolidation/practice

This provides a useful framework for looking at ways of using a computer in mathematics lessons. Indeed, it is interesting to note that as this unit was being written the second MEP set of materials for *Primary Maths and Micros* used just such a framework for the In-Service Notes for tutors.

Ways of using a computer

Other contributors to this book have explored different roles that the computer can play in the classroom. I want to pick out five of these:

1. Skill and drill. Here the computer simply presents the user with questions, possibly at different levels of difficulty.

2. Electronic blackboard. The computer is used as a colourful visual aid, often dynamic.
3. Simulation. Particularly useful where you want to see 'what happens in the long run' or where a simplified model of some physical process is explored.
4. Investigations. Where number sequences or other challenges which involve attempting to predict a pattern can be explored.
5. Across the curriculum. Where the computer may be used in any of the preceding modes but where the focus of the attention is on the way other subjects *use* mathematics.

It is quite instructive to link these together to form a two-dimensional grid (Table 6).

Obviously, Table 6 is not a hard and fast classification, and programs that are good for encouraging one kind of response may also be useful elswhere. However, a diagram like this does present an opportunity to see how computers can complement something (the six Cockcroft components of mathematics teaching) that has become an established part of our thinking about the curriculum.

There are of course other aspects of mathematics teaching that do not fit neatly into this framework and these will be discussed under the heading 'What more can we do?'

Classroom organization

The way that a teacher organizes the classes for mathematics teaching also has an effect on the way that computers can be used. It may well be that the availability of computers will generate pressures towards change, but at the moment there are three predominant modes of teaching in use:

A Whole class (often in relatively homogeneous groups)
B Group work
C Individualized work

Teachers are very familiar with A, and in some schools it is the method employed in the great majority of lessons. However, B and, increasingly, C are being used in response to greater awareness of different 'levels' of understanding that may be present even in supposedly homogeneous classes. (See for example *Understanding Mathematics 11–16*, Hart 1981)

Throughout primary, and increasingly in the early years of secondary schools, children meet mathematics through individualized schemes of work.

Table 6 Relationships between 'ways of using computers' and the six components of mathematics teaching identified in the Cockcroft Report

Teaching component \ Computer use	Skill and drill	Electronic blackboard	Simulation	Investigation	Across the curriculum
Exposition		✓✓	✓		
Discussion		✓✓	✓	✓	✓
Practical work		✓	✓✓		✓✓
Consolidation and practice	✓✓	✓			
Problem solving			✓✓		✓
Investigation		✓		✓✓	

Key: ✓✓ high potential for use; ✓ some potential; ☐ little potential.

The SMP 11–16 materials are one example – where up to the age of 13 a child meets many different booklets supporting different strands in the foundations of the subject. With such schemes it is rare for more than three or four children to be working on the same task at the same time. If computers are to complement and develop existing practice, then teachers must attempt to see what features need reinforcement. It must not be that teaching approaches deemed 'desirable' are neglected in order simply to incorporate new technology into the classroom. As Fletcher (1983) points out in another context, 'this can be as valueless in the new medium as in any other'. Table 7 shows one model for integrating computers into existing classrooms, which has the value of focusing attention on the role that a computer can play in each of those described earlier.

From Table 7 it appears that pupils working in groups offer most opportunities for incorporating the whole range of potential support for mathematics teaching. The classification is intentionally not complete and gaps are left for you to think about. It is however clear that the computer used with the whole class (as onlookers?) has a rather limited application.

Now we turn to consider these five roles in more detail.

1. *Skill and drill programs*

At the left hand of our classification in Tables 6 and 7 are programs that have a very specific set of aims in behavioural terms. Generally they seek to elicit a correct and sometimes a fast response to questions relating to facts that have been learned, or using techniques that have been taught and can be practised. A good example of this would be a program which tests children's knowledge of multiplication tables. At the simplest level the individual can ask for a test on, say, the 7 times table. The computer will then fire questions at the pupil in random order and, when the pupil responds, will indicate whether the answer is right or wrong.

This basic program could be added to in various ways. For example, it could keep a record of the questions the pupil got right/wrong. This could be accessed by the teacher; or they could be re-presented to the pupil. If the computer 'remembers' the answers the pupil got correct it could signal an incorrect response by presenting the 'closest' one to the present question. Suppose the pupil had correctly answered:

$1\times7=\qquad 10\times7=\qquad 5\times7=\qquad 2\times7=$

Mode of use / Class organization	*Skill and drill*	*Electronic blackboard*		*Simulation*	*Investigation*	*Across the curriculum*
		Teacher/ pupil discussion	*Pupil/ pupil discussion*			
Whole class	✗	✓		✓	✗	✓
Groups	✓ (in pairs)	✓	✓	✓	✓	✓
Individuals	✓	✓		✓	✓	

Key: ✓ This way of using the computer has clear application in this form of class organization
✗ Less appropriate way of using the computer
blank No examples of this observed to date

Table 7 A possible model for integrating computers into existing classrooms

but made a mistake with $8 \times 7 =$. The computer could respond with:

Screen 1	Screen 2
$8 \times 7 = ?$ 55	$5 \times 7 = 35$
Incorrect! You know $5 \times 7 = 35$ How many more 7's do you need to get 8×7?	$3 \times 7 = 21$ ——— So $8 \times 7 = ?$

Slightly more ambitious would be a program that chose a table at random (up to a certain limit) and then presented a number of questions about that table, including both multiplication and division facts.

More ambitious still would be a program that asked questions on any table up to 12, in any order, and finally one that did the same for any table up to a limit specified by the user (e.g. up to 25). These options could be presented in a menu:

TABLES CHALLENGE

1. Choose your table
2. Let the computer choose
3. Table Tester 1 (any up to 12)
4. Table Tester 2 (any up to *your* limit)

Enter choice

There are many varieties which may bring in some of the experiences of arcade games by giving audible prompts and both audible and visual 'rewards'. The main point to recognize however is that the programs can perform a genuinely useful role in the practice of skills and in the reinforcement of basic techniques. Carefully used — i.e. within limits defined by the teacher — they can be a valuable classroom resource, often liked by the children for the neutrality of the computer's response and the opportunity they can present for *self*-correction. It is important however that practice be related to the pupil's stage of development, for in the long run practice which is prescribed unsuitably can be expected to be as valueless in this medium as in any other!

Other areas where these ideas have been used successfully are:

Adding/subtracting (whole number, decimals, money, lengths)
Making equivalent fractions
Rounding numbers and estimating products

Plotting points
Estimating angles
Multiplying matrices

and indeed the list is limited only by the range of mathematical skills that are appropriate to school children.

The diagrams in Tables 6 and 7 are not sufficiently informative however, because once children begin to use programs in this category pupil/pupil discussion will often broaden the skill element into further investigational work which may well *deepen* the quality of children's thinking.

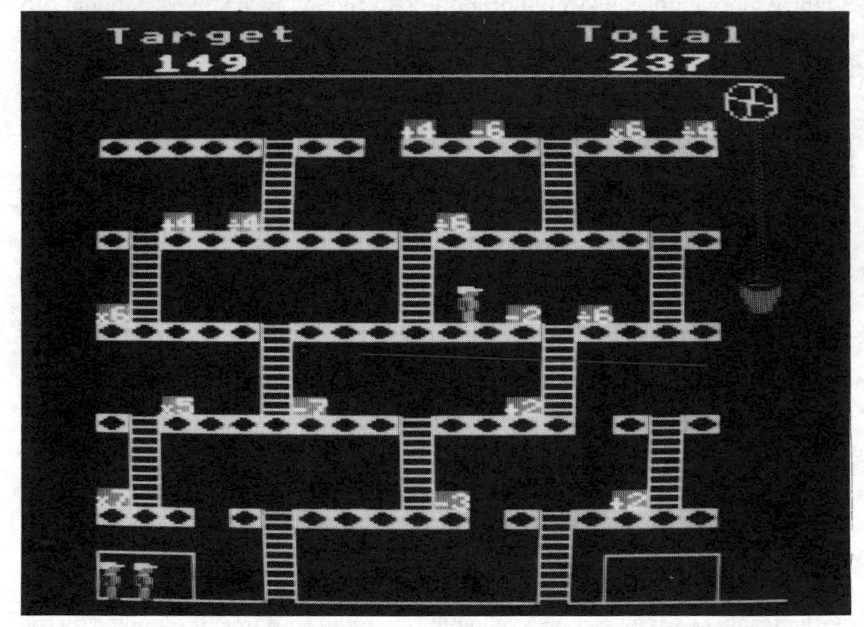

Figure 16. *NUMBER PAINTER*, the latest version of *NUMBER GULPER*

For example, NUMBER GULPER from ASK Ltd (see Figure 16) challenges children to manipulate numbers quickly and to plan how to use a set of numbers (and operations) on the screen most efficiently to get from a randomly chosen 'Made' number to the goal, the 'Make' number. The game uses simple mental arithmetic skills, but develops them so that the relationship between + and − is brought out and also between × and ÷. Repeated addition (or subtraction) is seen as a possible way of solving a multiplication (division) problem but one that is highly inefficient. The game encourages pre-planning which involves a whole range of mental arithmetic activities.

A further, and somewhat paradoxical example, is AUTOFRAC (from ITMA and published by Longman Microsoftware) which produces a continuous 'film' of fractions like:

$$\frac{21}{33} = \frac{35}{?}$$

where '?' can be in any one of the four positions. Users have to say out loud what number '?' stands for before it appears on the screen. When it has, the problem is replaced by another. I have seen pairs of children, sit, challenged, by this in ways that amazed me, having seen their behaviour in other (teacher-centred) lessons.

Currently there is a need for software which provides frameworks into which teachers can put their own examples. But even without this, opportunities exist for small single-purpose programs to be written for their pupils. There is more on this in the section 'What more can we do?'.

2. *Electronic blackboard*

Here the emphasis is on the use of the screen as a means of presenting diagrams that are accurate, colourful and dynamic — and that do better what conventional blackboard diagrams or posters attempt.

One example REFLECT (from *SMILE — the first 31 programs*) shows how lines can be reflected to form closed figures. This illustrates neatly how programs under this heading complement classroom exposition. The shapes used for reflection can be defined to be as simple or as complex as the teacher (or the pupil) desires. The position of the mirror can be anywhere on the screen and the underlying grid allows the position of the reflected image to be identified from its coordinates. How those original coordinates change under the reflection will be one focus of attention — allowing prediction and confirmation of the results.

This illustrates another point; the image can be forced off the screen by placing the mirror suitably, and then the coordinates of the image have to be found by applying the rules discovered earlier. Equally, the mirror line can intersect the shape itself, and so the idea of self-inverse points emerges. Further, if the mirror line is moved, say in a circular path around an origin, the behaviour of the image can be tracked, and the relation between reflection and rotation can be explored practically. Often it is this *dynamic* component that makes exposition so much more powerful — for, in place of the static image and pupils' imaginations, is the possibility of both demonstrating and anticipating the effects of changes. The understanding provoked by this can help enormously in liberating children's mathematics from being compartmentalized and essentially memory oriented.

In studying quadratic relations, visualization is often hindered by the graphs, which show the relationships, being time-consuming to draw. If 'enough' graphs are drawn and mulled over, then critical features like where the graph crosses the x and y axes, where the axis of the parabola lies, where the lowest (or highest) point is, can be brought into prominence. But often there is just not enough experience of actually *doing* this and so the importance of each of them is not appreciated by pupils. The result, then, is that on seeing a quadratic equation pupils are often prompted to 'factorize' or 'use the formula' to solve it without recourse to any thinking about the nature of the function itself. Obviously this is a result, but perhaps also a cause, of the kinds of question that pupils expect to be asked about such a function. But is this *all* there is to discover?

If $y=4x^2 - 7x - k$ is to be drawn on the screen (using FGP from the ATM collection, or GRAPH PLOT from Heinemann's *Mathematics with a Micro),* then clearly k has to be given a value. Suppose we choose $k=2$. The roots appear clearly at $x=-\frac{1}{4}$ and $x=2$. But if we now choose $k=0$, the graph moves upwards vertically 2 units and shows two interesting features: the roots come closer together; and part of the graph still lies below the x-axis. How far can this continue (i.e. for what value of k) until the graph just touches the x-axis? What is the x-value here?

These questions form a valuable introduction to the more general discussion of $y=ax^2+bx+c$, and of the role of (b^2-4ac) but in a context where pupils (and teachers!) are led to *specialize* using particular numbers, and to see their effect *before* launching into a generalization that for many is merely a jumble of symbols. The point here is that the vertex of the graph lies on the line $x=\frac{7}{8}$, and the distance of the vertex from the x-axis tells you whether the equation has two, one, or no real roots.

It is this compounding of movement and its cessation at a particular point that adds such a worthwhile extra dimension to the ordinary blackboard or printed page. The teacher can prepare the materials so that the sequence of critical points remain the same while the particular examples used can be easily changed.

The electronic blackboard is a resource that will be increasingly exploited in the classroom. The last two years have seen an explosion in the availability of this type of program in all kinds of subject areas. There are as yet relatively few for mathematics, which means that the ambitious teacher-programmer may be able to contribute here. The cost in man-hours is likely to be high, but almost all those that I have seen to date have been written by practising teachers.

The encouragement of discussion is difficult for many teachers, and this is particularly true for mathematics teachers. This is another area where the 'electronic blackboard' is likely to make considerable impact. Two particular examples are briefly described below: EUREKA (from the ITMA collection, Longmans) and TAKEHALF (originally from SMILE also available from ATM).

In EUREKA a man takes a bath and the level of water in it is plotted on the screen. The actions taken, such as turning the water on/off, getting in/out of the bath, putting the plug in/out can be controlled by the user to gain familiarity with the relation between action and the graph. Even quite low ability children have made realistic interpretations of graphs which they themselves have drawn in this way. The graphs can be drawn without the pictures, but equally the pictures can be drawn and the effect on the graph left open for discussion. The whole can be a source of much fruitful interaction between pupils as well as with the teacher. Teachers are usually quite good at getting children to draw graphs, much less good at interpreting what has been drawn.

TAKEHALF is quite a different program. It simply presents a film of different ways of halving a square; the different ways move into each other in smooth sequence and the effect is beautiful, satisfying and, hopefully, provocative in that the sequences really do require to be followed by discussion and drawing.

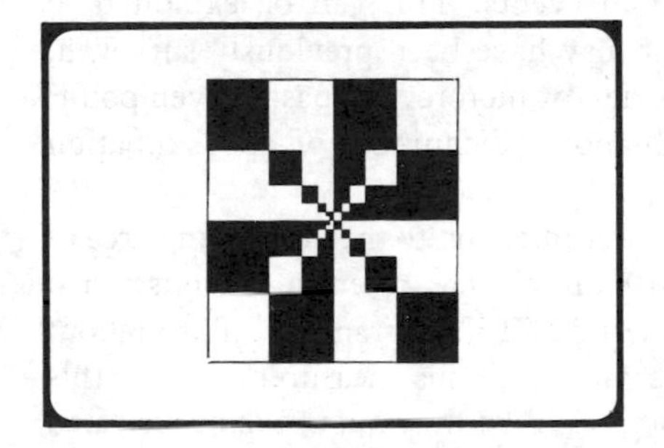
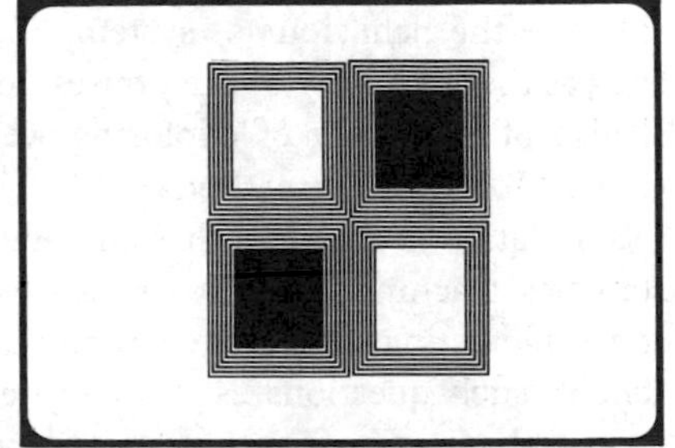

Figure 17. Takehalf *Source*: SMILE Centre.

The importance of pupil/pupil discussion in mathematics cannot be overemphasized. Being able to put your ideas into words often sharpens what it is that you think you know — but it also makes it available to others for interchange and possible challenge. These interchanges between peers can be literally re-creative in their impact. Perhaps we shouldn't be too surprised that this should be so, for we probably find the same when those challenges to our thinking are presented to us in our own language and thought style.

Thus the electronic blackboard approach has an important role to play here. Many of the programs that offer good presentations to the class can equally well provoke incisive pupil discussions. The role of the teacher here needs to be one of discreet awareness in the background, but not intervening too easily. How important it is therefore for the teacher to be familiar with the structure of the program and some at least of the possibilities it offers. It appears to be true here, as elsewhere, that undue technical sophistication either of instructions or concepts needs to be avoided if children are to be left on their own to use the resource. Self-confidence in using the program may be a prerequisite of talking about what the program shows.

3. Simulation

There is plenty of opportunity in mathematics to exploit the random number generator that most computers include. This is rather like an electronic dice throwing machine, but with the advantage that random sequences between *any* two limits can be obtained, rather than just the 1 to 6 available on an ordinary die. What happens is that unpredictable sequences of numbers are generated, but which nonetheless have many of the well-known properties of 'fairness' that we associate with random events. This can be exploited to simulate the behaviour of systems that may have been previously surveyed, such as the frequency of cars, buses, lorries, or motorcycles past a given point. It also offers a way of exploring well-known techniques of approximation called Monte Carlo methods.

Simulation in this sense has an obvious application to the developing area of statistics teaching. The Statistics 16-19 Project has recently commissioned some interesting software to support a series of TV programmes. Throughout school, such questions as 'how representative is this measurement' or 'this mean value' really require repeated samples to be drawn and then illustrated to show the relation of any reading to a mean value. Also, showing how the mean itself is affected by extreme readings is conceptually important and practically vital.

Much of the development of skill and drill programs relies on the random number generator, but it can also be a focus for discussion itself. What *are* the properties you would expect a set of random numbers to have?

Other 'models' are more physical in their make-up; for example in simulating the path of a projectile across the screen. With horizontal velocity vcos (a) where angle (a) is the direction of projection relative to the horizontal, and vertical velocity vsin (a)$-$gt; a point can be made to move across the screen by plotting successive points sequentially at (vcos (a).t, vsin (a).t $-\frac{1}{2}gt^2$) for regularly increasing values of t. Such simulations have recently been published, for example by Nelcal to accompany a course in mechanics and also include examples of vectors, relative motion, impulse and simple harmonic motion.

There are clear links between this area and 'Mathematics across the Curriculum'. Indeed many of the models used in other subject areas depend on the two basic ideas presented here.

4. *Investigation*

The microcomputer is an excellent way to launch small scale investigative work, particularly in shape and number. In one such program the screen displays a set of white tiles partially surrounded by red tiles in a pattern. The object of the investigation is first to discover a rule linking the number of red tiles to the number of white, then to make and test predictions using this rule. Another example is ERGO, produced orginally by SMILE and available also through ATM. This presents children with a 5 × 5 grid and two numbers on it, somewhere. The 25 numbers on the grid are connected by some rule which the user is invited to try to discover by making 'guesses' about the number hidden in a particular square. (The guide produced by ATM *Some lessons in mathematics with a microcomputer* gives some examples of lessons built around this program.)

Investigational work is intended to provoke open-ended questions like 'What happens if . . .?' so there may be a need for children to intervene and perhaps even change programs to answer these. For example CHAINS (which appears in *Problem Solving Workcards for use with Microcomputers* by Jim Seth, published by ATM) is an investigation based on the rules:

1. Start with a whole number
2. If even divide by two
3. If odd, multiply by 3 and add 1
4. Stop when you get a number repeated

Investigating how long the chains are with given starting points is an interesting activity in itself, as is classifying the numbers which have chains of equal length or sequences of chains with lengths increasing by 1. However it is possible to propose other 'rules'. What happens if rule 3 is changed to 'multiply by 5 and add 1' or 'multiply by 3 and subtract 1'? Here the computer is doing the arithmetic, for its own sake, but the user's attention is on the results. These results are the raw material from which guesses can be made, predictions tested and mathematical enquiry be encouraged in general.

It is likely that many of the programs in this category will be developed initially by teachers who have just one or two ideas they want to try out. Exchange of these through the growing network of LEA software and teachers' centres would seem a fruitful way of increasing the availability of this type of program.

One further aid to investigational work is the use of a subset of the Logo language called 'Turtle Graphics'. The references at the end of the unit give some examples of the use of this. Perhaps the best of these is by Richard Noss in *Maths Teaching 104* (1983) called 'Doing maths while learning Logo'. My own experience with Logo so far has shown it to be a powerful way to illuminate the relationship between the process of drawing and the properties of the shapes drawn. There is much more to it than this; suffice it to say that Papert considers that Logo offers a totally new paradigm for what we and children do in classroom.

5. *Mathematics across the curriculum*

The Cockcroft Report and recent HMI reports on individual schools have pointed to the lack of much effective work which explores the way that mathematics is used in other subjects in the curriculum. The existence of simulations in Geography, History, Biology, Economics and Home Economics, to name but a few, should make this criticism less valid in future.

Recently in my own teaching I have used a program called TRAY (made available through MEP) which in effect re-recreates a piece of text or poetry by using information about letter frequencies and combinations of letters that allows whole words or even phrases to be reconstructed. It is probably quite well known that some problems of authorship have been illuminated by simple word and phrase counts. Here the use of simple models link mathematics interestingly to language studies. Is it possible, even where a substitution code has been employed, to detect whether the underlying language is English, German, Russian or French? In the Reader supporting the first MicroPrimer Pack for primary schools there is a fascinating description of a Middle School project called 'Computers in Crime'. The authors describe their planning and its results, showing how many parts of the curriculum could be integrated into a computer-based study of this kind. (*MicroPrimer Reader*, pp. 49–61.)

These five aspects of the computer's role in the mathematics classroom have referred in the main to the use of programs that can be obtained commercially, and many teachers will rightly be happy to stop at this point. However, there are other issues which are worth discussing, even if only briefly. I will turn to these now.

What more can we do?

This section is intended to help you look at some issues which may affect the way you use computers in your classes.

What about programming as part of maths lessons?

In the early days (i.e. five years ago) it was common to find both flow charts and elementary programming activities in many CSE syllabuses. Many voices have been raised questioning whether this is either desirable or necessary. However, one project based at Trent Polytechnic has taken a rather different line and has attempted to *use* programming ideas to help children learn algebra. A report about this has been produced, and follow up work undertaken and reported on by MEP. The basic idea is to treat the 'variables' that are used in writing programs as an introduction to the notion of 'variable' in algebra. For, if we have a statement: Let $A = L \times 8$, which represents the calculation necessary to work out the area of a rectangle with one side equal to 8 cm, say, it is possible to treat A as a pigeon-hole into which different numbers are placed before the calculation can take place. In this sense A is *genuinely* a 'variable' and it is this very idea that many children find abstract and therefore difficult. It seems that some progress can be made along these lines provided the work is at an individualized level and can be tried out practically at a computer by each pupil.

Another possibility, often expressed but rarely tried out, is that one way to encourage a greater grasp of a topic is to ask children to write a program to incorporate its basic ideas. Many teachers, however, have found that it is only when *they* attempt to program that they realize their own understanding of it is put to the test. As an example, you might like to think of writing a series of instructions to solve any pair of simultaneous equations in two variables. The importance of the determinant becomes explicit in a way that may formerly only have been rather vague. Perhaps, after all, the prospect of children being expected to program as part of their maths lessons is rather too daunting to take on board for most children.

However, there are opportunities for teachers to write, and pupils to modify, brief, say 5–10 line programs in class with very specific objectives in view. Here the emphasis is not on the programming as such, but on the facility of having the computer come to our aid to do repeatedly what might be too time-consuming to do otherwise. One book already referred to, *Problem Solving Workcards for use with Microcomputers* (Seth, 1983, ATM) does just that. It provides about 30 programs (the longest is 13 lines) which encourage both teachers and pupils to type them in and explore their use. Familiarity with the computer language (BASIC in this case) can be expected to grow as these are used. Another book published recently offers more along these lines: *Explore Maths with your Micro* (Johnson, 1983, Heinemann).

Homespun programs written 'on the spot'

Whereas the focus of the last section was really on children and programming, the value of teacher-written materials should not be underrated. There are literally dozens of opportunities for using the computer as a powerful exploratory tool in lessons. For example, in a recent lesson using Pythagoras, we were looking at the different ways that information about right-angled triangles could be presented. That is, given a triangle with sides a, b and c (with c the hypotenuse), then given any two of a, b or c the other one could be found. However, there were basically two distinct types of calculation depending on whether the hypotenuse (c) was given or not. We wondered could the computer generate examples of each type? (I think the pupils really meant using *whole* numbers for each side, but that is another story!) We suggested:

Type 1: Hypotenuse given. Generate two random numbers. Square them, subtract the smaller from the larger. Find the square root of this difference.

Type 2: Generate two random numbers. Square them.

Add the squares.
Find the square root of this sum.

Now this wasn't the biggest step that mankind has taken in mathematics, but I'm convinced that the discussion it generated was very helpful in moving attention away from the numbers themselves to the appropriate strategy. Given that we had explored this situation could this be extended to calculate each angle of the triangle? And, even, could you explore what happens if $c^2 > a^2+b^2$? Or $c^2 < a^2+b^2$? Teachers' familiarity with the computer will allow such questions to be explored as part of normal classroom practice.

A resource for ALL pupils?

Some of the most interesting work being produced at the present time is in imaginatively exploiting the facilities of computers in the interests of children with special educational needs. Familiarity with BBC TV's 'Tomorrow's World' has shown some dramatic examples. Less dramatic but not less important are the needs of less able pupils generally. For these children the additional skill of having to learn how to use a typewriter keyboard (Qwerty-technology in Papert's phrase) may mean they are excluded from some of the advantages outlined in previous sections. For these children particularly the use of the overlay sheet on a 'concept keyboard' may be a distinct advance (see Figure 18). The use of this piece of technology allows the teacher to define pictures, which she draws, on a worksheet which is used in association with the program. The pictures represent possible answers to questions or choices presented to the pupil as part of the program. The worksheet is placed on top of a concept keyboard (which consists of a bank of very small pressure switches) and, when a particular picture is pressed, a signal is sent to the computer which is equivalent to 'typing it in' on the ordinary keyboard.

Designing materials to accompany software

No program that comes ready made is suitable for all the occasions that the teacher might feel it to be appropriate. So, the teacher will want to design worksheets which promote constructive use of the software with the particular objectives she has in mind for the current use. One advantage of this is that *developments* in the use of software can be shared. This is probably one of the most fruitful areas for every teacher to feel that there is a real part to play.

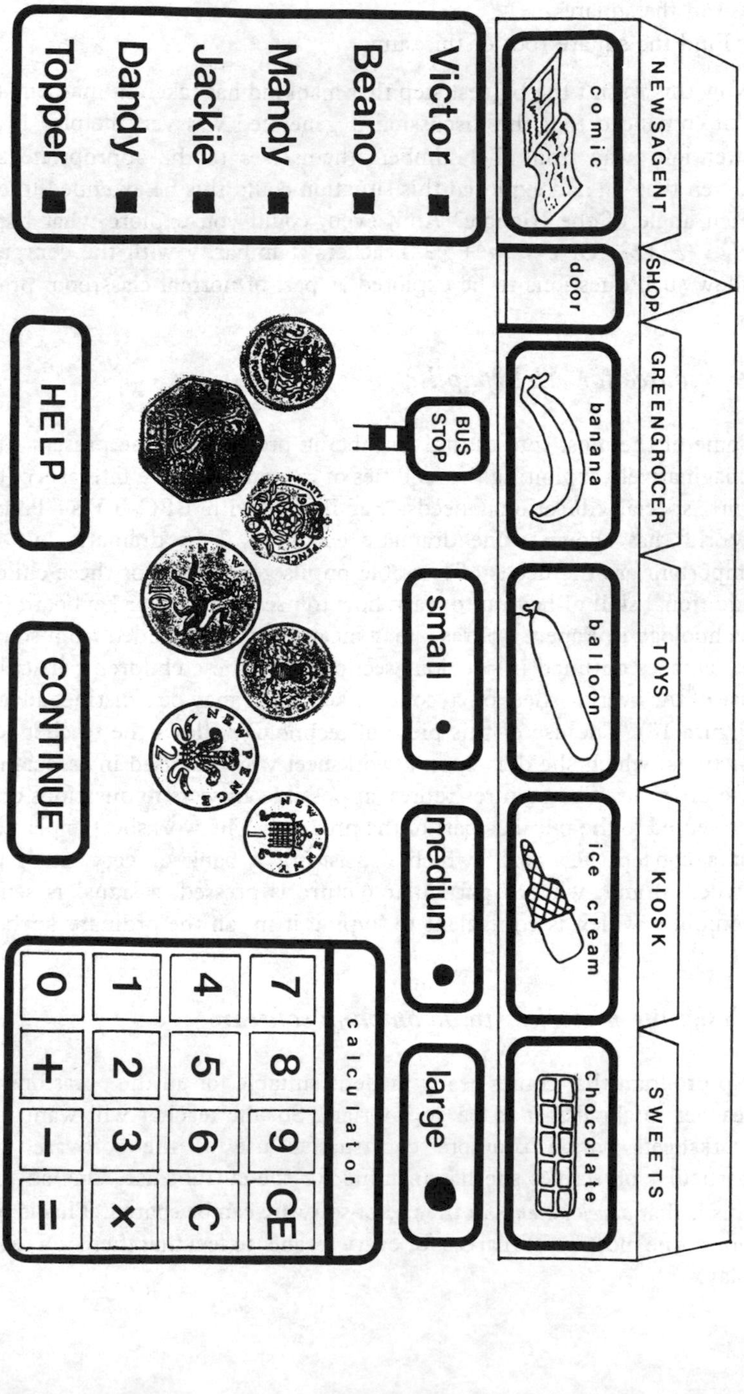

Figure 18. A CONCEPT keyboard overlay

Summary and conclusions

1. Mathematics teaching has as yet been little affected by the impact of computers.
2. A framework for using computers in the classroom is linked with current thinking about the curriculum, notably with the Cockcroft Report.
3. Different styles of computer use have been presented in this unit and some of the kinds of mathematical activity that they promote are outlined. These include problem solving and investigational work, modelling, consolidation of skills, and discussion.
4. There is a considerable role for teacher involvement in developing simple software for classroom use, and in developing teaching material to support what already exists.

Talking points

- *Do you think it is something of a paradox that computers are used so little at present in direct mathematics teaching? What examples have you seen? What would you perhaps like to see?*
- *Is computing essentially a 'mathematical' subject?*
- *Is it important for children to learn a programming language for their mathematics? If it is, what set of basic features would be sufficient for most purposes?*
- *At present about 95 per cent of all educational programs are written in BASIC. What arguments are put forward to change this? Do you think these arguments will affect the way* you *work with children and computers in the near future?*
- *Much has been written by imaginative teachers (like Seymour Papert) about the role of Logo in classrooms. What advantages can you see for using the Turtle Graphics subset of Logo that is now widely available? (See 'Doing Maths while learning Logo' by Richard Noss in* Mathematics Teaching No. 104, September, 1983.)
- *Many mathematics teachers also teach computer studies courses. What are the disadvantages of this? Can you see any advantages?*

Further reading

1. Oldknow, A. and Smith, D. (1983) *Learning Mathematics with a Micro.* Ellis Horwood. This is a first class book, the best of its kind to date. It points the way to the development of mathematical ideas through numerical experience. The section on computer geometry is particularly good. It contains a large number of programs for modification and development and looks like an invaluable resource for every mathematics teacher wishing to exploit the computer in class.
2. Association of Teachers of Mathematics (1984) *Some Lessons in Mathematics with a Microcomputer.* This is a record of lessons using the programs supplied on disk. There are 12 of these, with valuable suggestions for follow up.
3. Childs, G.T. (1983) *Maths + Computers = Fun.* Sigma Technical Press. This contains a large number of example programs in many of the common areas of mathematics syllabuses. It is written in a racy style. Readers may find the programming a little technical. There is a chapter on the conversion of programs from one machine to another, but this omits any reference to the difficult area of graphics — which are an important part of many successful programs.
4. Seth, J. (1983) *Problem Solving Workcards for use with Microcomputers*, an ATM Activity Book. As its name implies this offers a number of short programs with suggestions as to how they can be used in class to encourage exploration and investigation.
5. Johnson, D. (1984) *Explore Maths with your Micro.* Heinemann. Does just that. An interesting and challenging book, short enough not to daunt the beginner but with plenty to explore.
6. ATM (1982) *Working notes on Microcomputers in Mathematics Education.* A preliminary study to the more recent ATM publication.
7. MEP (1984) *Primary Maths and Micros.* This has been distributed free to LEAs. It is a teacher-training pack that contains not merely a collection of useful software, but is itself a statement about the best use of microcomputer software in primary schools.
8. Papert, S. (1980) *Mindstorms.* Harvester Press. The original, radical, appeal for computers to be used to open up possibilities for children rather than for 'computers to program children'. Uses Logo as a vehicle for demonstrating his ideas of the new worlds that children can explore. But is it mathematics? One indication of the seminal influence of this book is the large number of versions of Logo at the moment, not to mention 'buggies', 'turtles' and robots.

9. Hart, K. (Ed) (1981) *Children's Understanding of Mathematics 11–16.* Murray. A very useful book about what is and what is not appropriate mathematics for children of differing abilities. Its findings were made use of in the Cockcroft Report.
10. Fletcher, T.J. (1983) *Microcomputers and Mathematics.* DES. A thought-provoking little booklet that does exactly what it was intended to do — to stimulate thought about and experiment in the use of computers in mathematics teaching. It gives a perceptive overview of the current situation in schools, based on HMI observations.

Program sources

NUMBER GULPER: ASK Ltd.
Some Lessons in Mathematics with a Microcomputer: FGP: ATM
Maths Topics: Cambridge University Press
GRAPH PLOT: *Mathematics with a Micro*, Vol. 1: Heinemann
EUREKA: Longman
NELCAL Advanced Mechanics: Nelcal
REFLECT, ERGO, from *SMILE: the first 31 programs*: Smile
Mathematics with a Micro 1: Resources for Learning Development

David Jesson, lecturer in Mathematics Education at Sheffield University and formerly Head of Mathematics at Cordeaux High School in Lincolnshire, has a growing interest in the use of computers in schools but is puzzled by their slow advance into Mathematics teaching.

UNIT 13

COMPUTERS IN MODERN LANGUAGE LEARNING AND TEACHING

Graham Davies

This unit:

- *discusses the usefulness of microcomputers in modern language learning and teaching*
- *examines different types of computer programs which are suitable for language learning*
- *suggests what the teacher of modern languages should look for when selecting hardware*
- *examines some of the problems encountered in selecting, designing and producing software*
- *suggests ways in which the microcomputer can be introduced into the classroom*
- *discusses possible future developments in hardware and software.*

Introduction

When computers first appeared in substantial numbers on the educational scene in the late 1970s, teachers of modern languages did not display much enthusiasm for the new technology. It is still difficult to persuade the diehards that they may be missing something, but attitudes are rapidly changing. The negative reaction of older teachers may stem from bad experiences with technology: for example, the language laboratory, which appeared in the 1960s, failed to live up to its expectations. Another possible reason for scepticism is that the current trend in modern language teaching is towards the development of communicative skills, which, it is claimed, the 'inhuman' computer is incapable of assisting.

The main reason for the lack of interest amongst language teachers is probably ignorance or even fear of computers. For many years, courses for students of mathematics and the natural sciences have included an introduction to computers. Most students of the humanities, on the other hand, could go right through school and further or higher education — at least until the early 1980s — without touching a computer keyboard. Times are changing: some degree courses in modern languages include an 'awareness' element on computer applications to language and offer classes on programming in BASIC. In spite of this, even elementary keyboard skills are frowned upon by the more traditional-minded teacher of modern languages. This is curious when one considers how useful such skills are. No one who has to deal with large amounts of text — and this certainly includes language teachers — should remain ignorant of the most obvious example of the application of computers to language: the word processor. The word processor is, after all, only a computer dedicated to a specific task. This unit was written on a microcomputer equipped with word processing facilities — probably in less time than half the time it would have taken on a typewriter.

In what ways is the computer useful in language learning?

The two questions I am most often asked by language teachers are: Why should I use a computer at all? What can the computer do that cannot be done by other teaching aids?

I can understand what lies behind the first question. Teachers are already faced with a bewildering array of technical aids, most of which they have no time to exploit and many of which go wrong at the worst possible time — no wonder we all continually revert to chalk and talk! So why introduce yet another technical aid to add to the confusion?

One argument in favour of using the computer is that it is perceived by the younger generation as 'modern'. It is probably true that interest can quickly disappear if the teacher appears to be old-fashioned. This is not to say that the computer should be regarded solely as a gimmick to enable the teacher to appear 'with it'. Nevertheless, the introduction of a new piece of hardware into the classroom is useful for the sake of variety.

A crucial point which should be made in addressing the first question is that no teacher should be obliged to make use of a technical aid which he or she cannot get on with. We all have our particular preferences and priorities, and they should be respected. A computer comes low on my own list of priorities. A well-trained teacher with native-speaker or near-native-speaker competence still comes first, and probably always will. A good coursebook comes second, followed by an overhead projector and a language laboratory. I cannot yet see the computer playing a key role in the fostering of oral communicative skills — apart from acting as a stimulus or focus of attention — and it appears to be only of limited use in the development of written compositional skills, although both these areas are currently being investigated. The computer is, however, an extremely flexible piece of equipment which has a lot to offer in the development of specific reading and writing skills, and increasingly an important role to play in the development of listening skills. It is the computer's flexibility in these areas which makes it a particularly useful instrument, but the main reasons for giving it serious consideration are probably brought out more clearly in attempting to answer the second question: 'What can it do that other teaching aids cannot?'

The prerequisite of a teaching aid is that it should make the teacher's job at least more efficient if not easier. One aid which would make the teacher's job easier is a machine which would mark student's written work, diagnose their weaknesses, supply appropriate remedial material, mark it . . . and so on. Ploughing through piles of routine written reinforcement exercises and tests, which form part of virtually all language courses, is one essential but tedious job most teachers would happily renounce. This would give them more time to concentrate on oral communicative skills and written compositional skills.

One drawback in correcting written exercises in the traditional manner is the delay between the student completing the work and the teacher handing it back. When the work is handed back, the student usually looks at the grade at the bottom and files it away. It is then quickly forgotten. The teacher thus becomes an efficient proof-reader and the student does not learn by his or her mistakes. Another drawback is that the student may misunderstand the point of an exercise and repeat an error consistently, thus reinforcing the error. This is one area where the computer is undoubtedly useful. It is relatively easy to program a computer to present a stimulus to the learner, accept a response typed at the keyboard and supply immediate feedback. The student's work is thus 'marked' as it is produced, and the student's attention is concentrated on the problem in hand. Moreover, the computer can be programmed to review weak areas and branch to remedial exercises. These are all things which cannot be done by other teaching aids.

Whenever a new point of grammar or vocabulary is introduced it should, ideally, be reinforced until the student can produce more or less automatically a meaningful utterance containing the point. The main difficulty in reinforcement work is that some students master the point after one exercise, while others still have not grasped it after a hundred and one exercises. What usually happens is that the teacher sets as many exercises as time allows and hopes that the weaker students will catch up sooner or later. Inevitably, most of them don't.

Most of the traditional written exercises language teachers use in reinforcement work can be transferred to the computer. The computer never tires of marking, has infinite patience and will go on reinforcing a point of grammar or vocabulary until the cows come home. Typical traditional exercises suitable for the computer include:

1. *Completion exercises or gap-filling exercises:* e.g. filling in the occurrence forms of verbs, endings of adjectives, appropriate prepositions.
2. *Substitution exercises:* e.g. substituting a pronoun for a noun, or one item of vocabulary for another.
3. *Transformation exercises:* e.g. transformation of active into passive, change of tense, merging two sentences using co-ordinating or subordinating conjunctions, transformation of statements into questions, translation of short phrases and sentences.
4. *Recognition exercises:* e.g. multiple-choice exercises; matching synonyms, antonyms or collocations in two tables of words; matching lists of words with appropriate definitions.
5. *Production exercises:* e.g. providing a suitable ending for a sentence, anticipating the next word or series of words in a text. Computer assisted language learning (CALL) is probably only of limited applicability here owing to the open-ended nature of most production exercises.

It should be emphasized, however, that CALL does not simply imply the implementation of traditional material on new hardware. Many language teachers have indeed been criticized for their lack of imagination in the way they use computers. The computer screen can be used as an automatic exercise book, if that is what you want, but there are other more exciting possibilities, some of which will be examined in this unit.

Different types of CALL programs

The different categories of CALL programs, into which the activities described above can be incorporated, may be broadly summarized as follows:

1. *Exercise program:* consists essentially of:
(i) stimulus,
(ii) learner's response,
(iii) feedback to learner.
This is usually linked to material already presented to the learner. The best exercise programs include error diagnosis, branching and remediation.
2. *Test program:* similar to the exercise program, but error diagnosis, branching and remediation are usually absent. It may include the facility for storing and analysing an individual's or a group's test results.
3. *Tutorial program:* begins with presentation of information to the learner, followed by exercises. Error diagnosis, branching and remediation are usually more elaborate than in the exercise program. The Canadian CLEF programs are excellent examples of this type of program.
4. *Inquiry program:* consists essentially of a database which the learner uses to seek information by asking questions or making selections from a 'menu' of options. It may include additional features: e.g. relevant exercises may be called up to consolidate the information the learner has discovered, and records may be kept indicating what information the learner failed to find. Carsondale's programs on irregular verbs and Hodder & Stoughton's *Telem-Nantes* fall into this category.

The more imaginative types of programs, hinted at above, fall broadly into two further categories:

5. *Simulation program:* in which the learner instructs the computer to take a certain course of action. The usual pattern is:
(i) a scenario is presented to the learner,
(ii) the learner changes the parameters,
(iii) a new scenario is presented.
'Adventures' and 'text mazes' fall into this category. The learning process tends to be inductive in these programs. CALL simulations are difficult to write because they require an enormous amount of data, but they can be fun.

A simulation may include 'synthetic' language, whereby model sentences are generated according to fixed rules with the student controlling the data.

There are many examples of simulations which are not intended primarily as programs for language teachers. Nevertheless, there is no reason why the language content should not be exploited. Typical examples in English include *Yellow River Kingdom* (part of the BBC Micro's 'Welcome' package); Melbourne House Software's *The Hobbit; Hammurabi* (see Ahl 1978); and, in French, Geoffrey Smith's *Paris Trip* and *Château de Grand-père*. A team at Chelsea College, University of London, is developing other programs of this type.

More sophisticated examples of simulations include programs in which the computer acts as an interviewer, asking questions, analysing the user's responses and perhaps offering advice. It's an old idea, dating back to Weizenbaum's famous 'Eliza' program. Krutch (1981) lists a version of 'Eliza' which runs on a microcomputer.

6. *Language games:* e.g. 'Hangman', anagrams, crossword puzzles, jumbled sentences, jumbled texts. ESM's *Word Hunt, Word Sequencing* and *Sentence Sequencing* are good examples of language games. Wida Software's *Wordpack, Vocab* and *Crossword Challenge* are also worth mentioning.

There are also guessing games, in which the computer attempts to guess what the player is thinking of by asking a series of questions. *Animal* is an example of this sort of game (see Ahl 1978). An interesting feature of the program is that if the computer fails to make a correct guess the player is invited to type in a question it might have asked in order to arrive at the correct answer. The machine stores the question for future reference, thus appearing to 'learn' from the user. The first of Camsoft's German packages includes a variation of the program, in which questions are asked in German about towns in German-speaking countries.

Selecting hardware

The prerequisites of a microcomputer suitable for CALL are:

1 a good keyboard,
2 a good, fast version of a common programming language (BASIC is the best known),
3 sufficient memory (memory is sometimes referred to as RAM and measured in kilobytes or K; 32K is adequate),
4 a clear display screen with lines at least 40 characters wide,

5 a facility for producing foreign character sets under software control (sometimes referred to as user-definable or programmable characters),
6 a facility for storing programs on floppy disks, the most efficient widely available storage medium.

In addition, the computer should be capable of displaying both text and graphics in different colours, which makes for more attractive presentation on screen. It may also be useful if the computer can produce a range of sounds to enable different noises and music to be produced. If it is intended to use the computer for developing listening skills, it is essential to be able to link it with an audio cassette recorder.

Producing and designing CALL software

The main problem in CALL is the shortage of good quality software. Much commercial CALL software shows evidence of having been hastily put together by programmers whose programming expertise is indisputable, but whose knowledge of foreign languages and language teaching methodology is virtually non-existent. This raises the question: If programmers are not making a satisfactory job of it, *who* should produce CALL programs? A partial answer to this question is that the subject specialist should unquestionably be involved in determining the language content; but then *who* does the actual programming? There is a growing band of polymaths who are able to bridge the disciplines of natural and programming languages, but programming, like learning a foreign language, is no easy task. Even now, after many years of experience, I envisage spending about 20–25 hours writing a short CALL program from scratch. Such a program will keep students busy on average for 15–20 minutes. They can, of course, use it over and over again.

It would be convenient if all language teachers had at their disposal sympathetic programmers who would create software for them according to their instructions. This team approach is undoubtedly the best, but it is of course very expensive. The Canadian CLEF package was produced by a team consisting of both programmers and teachers of French; the high quality of the package bears testimony to the effectiveness of this approach.

Authoring packages

The luxury of a team of suitably qualified programmers and teachers is something most educational institutions cannot afford. No wonder many teachers decide that the only answer is do-it-yourself software. This need not be such a formidable task. The easiest way to create software of a reasonable quality is to make use of an *authoring package.* This usually includes at the very least a teacher's program and a student's program. The teacher's program enables the teacher with no knowledge of programming to insert his or her own material within a framwork provided by the program. The framework may take several different forms: multiple-choice, open-format question-answer exercises, gap-filling or Cloze exercises or even adventures and text mazes. The student's program simply enables the student to make use of the material created by the authoring package.

Even if one is fluent in a programming language, the authoring package is still the most convenient way of generating a solid body of material. This is the way I create most of the material I use with my own students. Using an authoring package, and material I have already drafted by hand, it takes me about three hours to create a set of exercises to occupy students for one hour — much more realistic than the 100 or so hours it would take if each program were written from scratch! The authoring packages I use are described below, and all are available commercially.

The easiest type of exercise to set up on the computer by means of an authoring package is the multiple choice exercise. One should not underestimate the value of a good multiple choice exercise; the idea and presentation are simple but the content can be varied. Above all, it should not be forgotten that the success of a CALL program depends ultimately on the quality of the language content and not on gimmicks.

Most multiple choice programs present on screen a series of questions to the student, who keys in the answer A, B, C, D or E. The student receives immediate feedback and at the end of the exercise the program reviews the student's errors. All the teacher has to do in order to create such an exercise is to type the questions, the correct answers and suitable distractors. Such programs are in no way examples of imaginative programming, but providing the quality of the exercise material is good they should sustain the interest of students, particularly those who require additional practice for examinations that include multiple choice sections. Wida Software's *Choicemaster* and Camsoft's *Multichoice* are examples of multiple choice authoring packages.

Other authoring packages allow the creation of open format exercises in which alternative answers are accepted (e.g. Hutchinson Software's *Questionmaster*). Then there are packages for creating gap-filling exercises (e.g. Camsoft's *Gapkit* and Pitmansoft's *Gapfill*) and Cloze exercises (e.g. Wida Software's *Clozemaster*, Camsoft's *Clozewrite* and Longman's *Readamatics*).

Open format authoring packages are particularly useful for writing transformation, substitution, recognition and, to a limited extent, production exercises. Gap-filling and Cloze packages are more limited in what they can do, but providing the teacher is imaginative in selecting material they are no less useful.

An interesting authoring package, which aims to assist the development of reading and production skills, is ESM's *Copywrite.* This takes the Cloze idea to the extreme by deleting the whole of the text from the screen and leaving just the punctuation and sets of dashes representing the missing words. The learner then tries to reconstruct the text, entering any word he or she can recall. The words are positioned by the computer in their appropriate positions. If a word occurs several times then it pops up all over the screen. The most useful aspect of this program is that it becomes an exercise in spotting collocations as the skeleton of the text builds up. It begins as a memory exercise, which is no bad thing in language learning, but also calls on a wide range of linguistic skills.

The only time I write a program completely from scratch is when I require a complex presentation strategy incorporating moving text or graphics. Moving text on screen I find useful, for example in presenting the eccentricities of word order in German or the positioning of 'ne . . . pas' and pronouns in French. Graphics I occasionally find useful but they have their limitations, which are discussed below. One can also incorporate music and a variety of other sounds into a program, but the resultant cacophony in a room full of microcomputers is distracting, if not unbearable!

Because the computer is capable of presenting graphics and sound it has led some programmers to produce programs in which the language content is trivial, or even inaccurate, but the accompanying graphics and sound are deceptively attractive. The newcomer to CALL can be fooled by the presentation: flashing colours, racing cars tearing around the screen, pictures of the Eiffel Tower building up girder by girder, congratulatory musical fanfares, rockets taking off . . . and so on. The language content in such programs may consist of nothing but a series of out-of-context questions on the conjugations of verbs or isolated items of vocabulary. In other programs the graphics are admirably executed, but one questions their relevance. Producing a picture of a pencil on screen labelled 'Das ist ein Bleistift' may be a clever piece of programming but it is an inefficient way of using the computer. A far more accurate picture of a pencil can be produced in a book, or, better still, the teacher can hold one up in class.

On the other hand, pictures in a book do not move. Here computer graphics can help, for example by making a matchstick figure move to reinforce the idea of verbs of movement and prepositions plus the accusative case in German. Sensible use is made of graphics in a recently produced series of programs by Cambridge Micro Software. In their *French Connections* a plan of a town appears on screen and the learner has to guide a figure around the streets by giving appropriate directions in French. In *Quelle Tête* the learner describes a human face by using expressions such as the French equivalents of 'a pointed chin', 'bushy eyebrows' or 'wide-set eyes'. A drawing of the face builds up on the screen according to the instructions given. A third program, *Jeu de Ménages*, displays a vertical cross-section of a house on screen, and the learner is invited to position items of furniture in the appropriate rooms. German versions of the programs are also available. These programs not only give the learner useful practice in specific areas of vocabulary but also the correct use of prepositions, gender and case.

Using a programming language

Having exploited the possibilities of various authoring packages, more ambitious teachers may wonder about creating interesting new programs themselves. Without a programmer at one's elbow, this is an undertaking which should not be considered lightly. It is an extremely time-consuming process which is guaranteed to burn up gallons of midnight oil. There are several reasons why it takes so much time to produce CALL programs without an authoring package:

First, one has to master a programming language. There are programming languages devoted to the creation of computer assisted learning programs. PILOT and TUTOR are two examples, but they are not available for every microcomputer. Acornsoft's MICROTEXT is another example and relatively easy to learn. But such languages are still restrictive, and there is no question that if one really wishes to get to grips with programming it is essential to master BASIC, the most common programming language found on microcomputers. Unfortunately, there are few textbooks or courses in BASIC which are suitable for those of us who do not have a scientific or mathematical background. My own *Talking BASIC*, however, is aimed directly at would-be programmers whose background is in the text-orientated rather than the numeric disciplines.

Learning BASIC is a slow process. It is not unlike learning a natural language; a lot of attention to detail and plenty of practice – a little every day

— are essential. Linguists make quite respectable programmers and should not be put off by people who try to persuade them that they will get nowhere unless they have a good qualification in mathematics. On the other hand, BASIC cannot be mastered in a day, despite the claims made by some textbooks and course designers. Good progress can be made with about 20 hours' tuition, but reasonable fluency cannot be achieved without many more hours of keyboard practice.

Second, having mastered BASIC, one has to consider very carefully the design of the CALL programs one wishes to write. Presentation strategies are important: Is a tutorial element necessary? Is movement of text essential? Are graphics and sound relevant? Input, matching and response analysis routines are vital considerations. This is an area full of pitfalls for the unwary. When matching the learner's response with the anticipated response, a good program should allow for alternative acceptable responses; e.g. both *der Wagen* and *das Auto* are acceptable renderings of *the car*. One must also consider how 'tolerant' the computer should be: Should allowances be made for the presence of too many or missing spaces in a response? How should responses in which only one letter is wrong or two letters transposed be evaluated? Should responses which should be in lower rather than upper case be allowed? How should the computer react to responses in which, say, the stem of a verb is correct but the ending wrong? What about diacritics? What happens if the learner presses the BREAK or CONTROL key by mistake? The considerations become quite frightening when one steps outside the safe confines of an authoring package! *Callboard* No. 4 contains a list of desirable features in input and matching routines. Pusack (1984) describes further possibilities.

It is generally considered inadequate for a computer simply to tell the learner he or she is right or wrong. Ideally, it should attempt to locate errors and offer clues and helpful notes, e.g. the statement of a rule or the presentation of a paradigm. In this way the machine becomes less of a quizmaster and more of a tutor. Sorting out the complexities of the branching this involves is no mean feat and can only be done by careful planning.

Third, having written a new program you must ensure that it works every time, whatever the user does. This process is known as 'crash-proofing' a program or making it 'robust'. There is nothing more infuriating when a program goes wrong — or 'crashes'. Finding out what made it go wrong is not always easy. Programmers usually refer to this as 'debugging', a task which may take hours or days. The programmer may do this by playing the role of a determined user setting out to sabotage the program and by retracing his steps whenever an error emerges.

Despite the difficulties of writing one's own programs, learning a programming language is a salutary experience and certainly good for the mind. Even if you decide in the end that it is easier to buy off-the-shelf programs or stick to authoring packages, you will find that you have gained a better appreciation of the problems of developing software and probably become more sympathetic towards programmers.

Classroom management and CALL — the logistics of using the micro in the classroom

It is of course all very well talking glibly about the usefulness of computers, but what about the logistics of introducing a computer into the classroom? Let us examine three possible approaches:

1. *Whole-class work:* a computer with a large display screen is used in front of the whole class.
2. *Individual resource:* a corner of the classroom, or even a special room, is reserved for an individual, a pair or a small group working on one computer.
3. *Microcomputer laboratory:* this consists of several computers, possibly linked together, and is used in much the same way as the language laboratory, with pupils working alone or in pairs at individual machines.

Whole-class work

It is easy enough to use a computer in front of the whole class as a sort of 'electronic blackboard'. Either the teacher or pupil can carry out the necessary keyboard operations, while the class watches the screen. The computer is especially useful as the focus of attention in oral work. Teachers of foreign languages habitually use a variety of stimuli to encourage pupils to talk: pictures, realia, overhead projector slides, film strips, audio and visual recordings, and so on. The computer may be added to this line-up of aids, but not all programs are suitable for use with groups, particularly large ones. In any case the computer has one significant practical disadvantage: text on a display screen cannot be read very easily by pupils at the back of the class and pictures are often difficult to discern. My own experience in displaying material on a computer screen to groups of more than about a dozen participants suggests that the overhead projector is a much more effective medium.

Some programs are ideally suited to use with the whole class. Programs like *Quelle Tête*, in which imaginative graphics play a key role, can be used by the teacher to get the class to make suggestions about the sort of face they would like the computer to draw. Programs like *Copywrite* or *Clozewrite*, in which part or the whole of a text is reconstructed, have also been used very successfully with groups. The class is encouraged to suggest what words might fit, or even to debate points of syntax or lexis. One interesting effect in such activities is that in the eyes of the class the teacher ceases to play an authoritarian role; it is the computer which has the final say. Simulations, especially adventure and text mazes, work well with whole classes, the pupils being encouraged to talk about the outcome of their decisions before and after their responses are entered at the keyboard.

The computer may be used to present something to the class in a more dynamic way than is possible with other visual aids. Dynamic presentations are both more memorable and more amusing. My own program on subordinate clause word order in German always raises a laugh when the verb scuttles off like a scared rabbit to the end of the clause. So far I have never managed to achieve the same effect with a piece of chalk or a felt-tipped pen!

Individual resource

The idea of the computer as an individual resource may not appeal to all teachers. The 'resource in the corner' may well cause some disturbance, and there is also the problem of supervision if the resource is located in another room. Nevertheless the practice is well established in some schools. Interactive programs on the computer are valuable here, particularly in remedial work. The computer may be able to help in cases where the pupil is gaining little from participation in normal classroom activities because of his or her failure to cope with a particular point. Remedial classes often carry a stigma, but the computer is just a neutral piece of high technology with the patience of Job. The computer need not be reserved just for the slower learners. All pupils can be given an opportunity to take their turn, with the teacher, or maybe even the computer, keeping a record of the programs they use.

The microcomputer laboratory

The ideal environment for CALL is the microcomputer laboratory. A few years ago this would have been inconceivable on the grounds of cost alone, but the falling prices of microcomputers and the development of systems like ECONET, which enables several microcomputers to share one disk drive, make the microcomputer laboratory a practical possibility.

In the microcomputer laboratory a group of pupils can work at the machines on a one-to-one basis or in pairs, each machine running a different program. In this way the advantage of immediate feedback to the learner is retained while the teacher supervises the work of the group as a whole, ensuring that the weaker pupils tackle material with which they can cope and the more able pupils move on to material which stretches their intellect. Unlike the language laboratory, the microcomputer laboratory is a truly universal resource and can be used by all subject areas. Another advantage is that it can be used on an *ad hoc* basis by pupils in private study periods.

Future developments

There are several possible directions in which CALL can go in the future, depending on what happens in the development of software and hardware. Some trends are already visible. Much of the current software has been criticized for being too preoccupied with grammar and having little to offer the teacher who favours the communicative approach. Teachers of English are particularly vociferous in their criticism of drills. Chandler (1982a) talks of 'such an unimaginative, even dangerous, abuse of the creative potential of the micro', while Sanders and Kenner (1984) make a plea for 'communicative courseware'. The latter advocate a move away from structural drills towards activities which focus on the content of language rather than its form. They suggest the need for programs which aim to promote activities and to stimulate the learner to *use* language rather than simply memorize it. The types of programs they suggest have already been mentioned above under the categories 'simulations' and 'games'.

Here is not the place to debate an ancient internecine feud over language teaching methodologies. Suffice it to say that while it is undoubtedly useful to exploit the computer's potential in helping to establish morphological and syntactic patterns, it would be short-sighted to regard it as solely as a drill-and-practice machine.

Higgins and Johns (1984) stress the need for 'exploratory' programs such as *Loan*, in which the learner explores what could or could not be said in an attempt to borrow different sums of money from sources ranging from a close relative to a bank manager. Their programs *Textbag* and *Close-up* offer alternative approaches. *Textbag* invites the learner to restore a masked text by 'buying' hidden words, while *Close-up* gradually reveals a text, inviting the learner to hazard a guess at a fitting title from a given list. Under the heading 'artificial intelligence' they refer to programs in which the machine simulates human intelligence by attempting to make sense of responses entered by the learner at the keyboard. The experimental program *John and Mary* falls into this category. Here the computer answers questions, confirms statements and carries out commands relating to a graphic representation of two people and a room. Such programs are extremely crude at present, but they may serve to demonstrate to the learner the machine's limitations in handling natural language.

The computer can also be used to help students develop compositional skills. Brian Farrington, University of Aberdeen, is working on an impressive series of programs on the Apple II, which guide the advanced learner through the stages of translating a passage of English prose into French (see Farrington 1981). Each program is well conceived and able to route the student through different paths representing alternative approaches to the translation. Advice is offered when the student gets stuck. At the other end of the spectrum is Daniel Chandler's *Storymaker* (see Chandler 1982b), which suggests to the learner possible themes on which to base a story in English. ESM's *Adventure Storywriter* is a more sophisticated program which is designed to facilitate creative story writing.

All the computer programs mentioned so far have ignored the most important aspect of language — the human voice. This is because the hardware is still relatively primitive. Yet it is not difficult to link a microcomputer with an audio cassette recorder. The Atari CALL courses and Tandberg's AECAL system prove that the audio-link is a reality, though by no means foolproof. The Atari programs offer a linear approach while the Tandberg system uses a random access cassette recorder. The Tandberg system incorporates an authoring package which enables listening exercises to be set up relatively easily (see Last 1984a). The compact disk player is another device which may also yield fruitful results.

Research into computers linked with a video cassette recorder or videodisk player is also going on, but it may be some time before the software becomes robust and the hardware becomes cheap enough. Nevertheless it is something to look forward to. The June 1982 issue of *BYTE* magazine was almost euphoric about the possibilities of microcomputers linked to videodisk players. Certainly, the videodisk player is a natural partner for the microcomputer in that it too offers the possibility of random access. Imagine the following scenario: The learner is sitting at a videodisk player which is displaying a menu of situational dialogues in French. The learner chooses a dialogue showing a guest registering at an hotel. The dialogue is presented on screen, using native French speakers in a real French hotel. The learner may choose to see the dialogue with or without subtitles and with or without translations. Sections of the dialogue may be reviewed at the press of a key. After the dialogue has been presented and the learner has reviewed it to his own satisfaction a set of exercises is offered, covering vocabulary, structures and general comprehension. The exercises may be presented as visual and/or audio stimuli. Depending on the learner's responses, which are typed at the keyboard, sections of the dialogue may be presented again and again until it is clear that the learner has fully understood the material.

Schneider and Bennion (1984) describe two approaches to videodisk CALL. In the first, the videodisk recording simulates a visit by an American tourist to a Mexican town. The computer screen offers choices to the tourist, who is confronted by the natives speaking Spanish. Depending on the tourist's answers to a series of multiple-choice questions, with the option of hearing and seeing a native speaker produce the chosen utterance, different parts of the town may be explored. In the second, a videodisk recording centres on a Mexican worker in a city in the northern USA. What type of day he has when he ventures into the culturally unfamiliar outside world depends on choices made by the user.

After linking computers with recordings of natural human voices, the next logical step would seem to be to go the whole hog and get the computer to produce a synthetic voice. It is already possible to produce a synthetic voice on a computer which is completely indistinguishable from a natural human voice. The snag, however, is that it is costly. Most affordable synthetic voice devices sound like the popular Texas Instruments 'Speak 'n' Spell' machine — hardly precise enough for language teaching. Nevertheless progress is being made, although it may be many years before the language teacher is offered anything which threatens to replace the audio cassette recorder.

Even further behind is research into voice analysis. So far it has not proved possible to get computers to analyse human speech with anything like the accuracy a language teacher needs. There are devices which can match a word or phrase spoken by a student against the 'perfect' rendering of a native speaker, but they are somewhat indiscriminate. They can measure 'how right' the attempted utterance is on a crude percentage basis and can even display the waveform on the computer screen. They cannot, however, pinpoint the errors which would cause a native speaker to misunderstand what was being said or allow for 'acceptable' errors such as the mispronunciation of English 'this' as 'zis'.

Whatever route CALL takes, there is no doubt that it offers many exciting possibilities. Primitive though the present hardware may be, language teachers will find more than enough potential in the microcomputer to occupy them for many years to come.

Talking points

- *What advantages do you think a microcomputer has over traditional aids for whole-class teaching?*
- *20th century technology and 19th century methodology: Is this a fair assessment of current approaches to CALL?*
- *What roles can the microcomputer play in a communicative language course?*
- *How valuable are computer graphics in CALL?*
- *Under what circumstances might voice synthesis and voice analysis be useful in CALL?*

Further reading

Ahl, D. (1978) *Basic Computer Games*, Morristown, New Jersey, USA: Creative Computing Press.

Ahmad, K., Corbett, G. and Rogers, M. (1984) *Computers, Language Learning and Language Teaching*. Cambridge: Cambridge University Press.

Callboard: a regular newsletter on CALL. Subscription enquiries to 19 High Street, Eccleshall, Stafford ST21 6BW.

Chandler, D. (1982a) Great Expectations. *Educational Computing,* **3**, 9, pp. 39–40.

Chandler, D. (1982b) I don't know what to write. *Educational Computing,* **39**, pp. 39–40.

Chandler, D. (ed.) (1983) *Exploring English with Microcomputers.* London: Council for Educational Technology.

Davies, G.D. (1982a) Authoring Techniques and Computer Assisted Language Learning. *INTUS NEWS* **6**, 2, pp. 46–57.

Davies, G.D. (1982b) Doing It Yourself. *The EFL Gazette* **37**, pp. 6–7.

Davies, G.D. (1984) *Talking BASIC.* Eastbourne, Cassell/Holt-Saunders.

Davies, G.D. and Steel, D.H. (1982) Micros in Modern Languages. *Educational Computing* **3**, 8, pp. 30–31.
Davies, G.D. and Higgins, J. (1982) *Computers, Language and Language Learning*. London: CILT.
Farrington, B. (1981) Computer Based Exercises for Language Learning at University Level. In Smith, P.R. (ed.) (1981) *Computer Assisted Learning*. Oxford: Pergamon, pp. 113–116.
Godfrey, D. and Sterling, S. (1982) *The Elements of CAL*. Virginia, USA: Reston Publishing Company Inc.
Higgins, J. and Johns, T. (1984) *Computers in Language Learning*. London: Collins.
Kenning, M. and Kenning, M-M. (1983) *An Introduction to the Use of Computers in Language Teaching*. Oxford: Oxford University Press.
Krutch, J. (1981) *Experiments in Artificial Intelligence for Small Computers*. Indianapolis, USA: Howard W. Sams.
Last, R.W. (1984a) A New Lease of Life for the Language Laboratory? *Language Monthly* **7**, pp. 10–11.
Last, R.W. (1984b) *Language Teaching and the Micro*. Oxford: Blackwell.
Pusack, J.P. (1984) Answer Processing and Error Correction in Foreign Language CAI. In Wyatt, D.H. (ed.) (1984), pp. 53–64.
Sanders, D. and Kenner, R. (1984) Whither CAI? The Need for Communicative Courseware. In Wyatt, D.H. (ed.) (1984).
Schneider, E.W. and Bennion, J.L. (1984) Veni, Vidi, Vici via Videodisc: a Simulator for Instructional Conversations. In Wyatt, D.H. (ed.) (1984), pp. 41–46.
Wyatt, D.H. (ed.) (1984) *Computer Assisted Language Instruction*. Oxford: Pergamon.

Useful addresses

CILT, Centre for Information on Language Teaching and Research, Regent's College, Inner Circle, Regent's Park, London NW1 4NS. CILT issues a comprehensive bibliography on CALL (No. B 32).

CLEF Project (French CALL project), The Program Coordinator, University of Western Ontario, London, Ontario, Canada N6A 3K7. CLEF is published by Gessler, New York.

Graham Davies is a Senior Lecturer in German at Ealing College. He writes computer software and has lectured on CALL in Norway, France, Canada and Africa.

UNIT 14

CAL AND ENGLISH TEACHING

Malcolm Salt

This unit:

- *discusses the potential of the microcomputer in English lessons*
- *outlines various ways of using computers in current English courses*
- *describes the type of CAL programs that can be used by English teachers*
- *suggests some ways in which the current kind of English syllabus can be modified and expanded to cope with pupil needs*

Introduction

A few years ago, many English departments did not even contain microcomputers. In this unit, an attempt is made to review current classroom practice, the types of computer programs that are available, and the associated literature that has been produced to help teachers master this new technology. Some of the innovations pioneered at the Abbot Beyne school are detailed and, where possible, the work of other specialists is described. Since this aspect of English teaching is so new, many current computer programs are bound to have their teething troubles and drawbacks. I only wish to suggest *some* of the ways in which they can be used effectively in the classroom. As with most other resources, the crucial factor is still the enthusiasm of the English teacher, and his/her ability to present the material in a stimulating and meaningful manner.

The potential of the microcomputer in the English classroom

Barry Midgley (1983) succinctly outlines his ideas on the teaching potential of the microcomputer for English. He stresses collaborative opportunities for writing stories, plays and poems, and the accompanying possibilities for discussion and constructive argument. Midgley stresses the importance of group decision-making, clear and logical thinking, and the development of concentration skills. He sees the computer as a means of helping pupils to frame 'significant' questions, and values the acquisition of keyboard skills. Midgley finds much of interest in such activities as word processing and the selection, storage and retrieval of information. Above all, he clearly recognizes the computer's power to act as a creative and 'liberating' resource for both teachers and pupils alike.

This summary of Midgley's views effectively focuses on many of the concepts and activities that are at the heart of English teaching. As a senior English adviser, Midgley does not advocate that English teachers be replaced by machines. He is much more positive, and suggests ways in which the computer might enliven and enrich our teaching of English.

Types of program that can be used in the English classroom

In a recent book, Bitter and Camuse (1984) describe some of the main types of computer assisted learning programs. They identify 'drill and practice, tutorial, simulation . . . and problem solving' materials, and then deal with each type of software in some detail. The drill and practice programs commonly introduce vocabulary items or particular language structures, and they often ask the pupil to memorize facts, or refine a particular skill. Tutorial software 'utilizes written explanations, descriptions, questions, problems and graphic illustrations for concept development', and seeks to prepare the ground for further applied study. Simulations 'allow the students to experience situations which would be difficult or impossible to duplicate in a classroom setting', and they provide a means for personal and group involvement with a topic or theme or social situation. In practice, such simulations can be centred on activities like exploration and business enterprise, but they can just as easily cope with school experiences or purely imaginary circumstances. They are linked to programs of the problem-solving kind, for here 'the student applies what is already known, learns from mistakes, and refines skill as (s)he gains mastery of certain problem solving techniques'. Taken together, these types of programs provide some of the English learning opportunities and experiences mentioned in the previous section. This will become clear as we go on to examine some specific classroom applications.

Classroom applications

(a) Drill and practice programs Drill and practice programs are still popular because they duplicate many of the exercises found in the traditional language books. The best of them go further and establish a context for the vocabulary items or language skills that are being drilled, thus returning a student to areas of the living language.

According to the publishers, *Wordpower* (by Sulis Software) 'increases and enriches your vocabulary, teaches you to use words more accurately' and 'helps you to spell correctly'. The program does this by presenting a large range of opposites, synonyms, nouns/adjectives, collectives and similes. In other words, the value to the classroom English teacher resides in simple recognition of words, the excitement that is generated by the 'game' element, and the possible conversations that might take place between the various players. I have used this program with special groups, and for special, limited purposes. It has certainly helped children with a very low level of motivation, and done something to return their interests to mainstream English lessons. My teaching stipulation is that such pupils must be given further opportunities actually to use and manipulate the words, that they have seen or learned — in actual stories or poems.

Longman Software's *Wild Words* is treated in a similar manner. It concentrates on 'language spelling rules' and because the student has to move a chimpanzee actually to catch the necessary letters for a word, this program illustrates the graphical ingenuity that can be applied to increase involvement and (hopefully) learning. Longman also produces *Famous Blast Words* where the player literally shoots down letters, and *Margana* where the emphasis is on forming anagrams.

Another type of drill and practice program features language skills — sentence structures, or such specific things as question patterns. A typical example might be *Sentence Sequencing* (by Educational Software for Microcomputers). Here, the user is asked to manipulate and 'rearrange' sentences into a correct order; but the important thing to stress is that the programmers arranged for the teacher to input material as well, thus ensuring a greater flexibility. Drill and practice programs need to be carefully introduced into the classroom. If they are integrated into a well thought out English course they can be of value, but detailed follow-up work is essential.

(b) Tutorial programs In a tutorial program, notes, helpful hints and practice passages are usually provided together with a means of automatically assessing the pupil's success in dealing with the material at hand. In the best of these programs, graded passages are used to cater for individual needs, and progress is carefully monitored. *Copywrite* (by Educational Software for Microcomputers) is a less developed piece of 'tutorial' software. It encourages 'reading and comprehension practice at all levels of ability' by using Cloze procedures. Graded passages are selected by the teacher, and there is a scoring system to record attainment and offer help.

Summary and Comprehension Guidelines (Sussex Software) is a fully fledged tutorial program. The author provides notes and hints for teachers and pupils, and uses the power of the computer to generate 'help' options where they might be needed. This format is of immediate interest to English teachers because language is examined in appropriate contexts, and there is ample scope for individual or group work. Some of my pupils seem to enjoy this opportunity to work alone. The consensus is that this program is a useful revision aid. Small groups use it in their spare time. By its very nature, tutorial software will soon find a place in many subject libraries.

(c) Simulation programs Simulation software is exciting to use. It engages the imagination, and can be integrated into a range of valuable classroom activities — note taking, fact selection, the presentation of arguments, oral work and discussion, analysis, the development of sequencing skills, and the planning and writing of essays and reports. The range of simulation programs is enormous.

Commodore's *Rail Boss* is both an adventure and a business simulation game. Players must plot to extend their railway from the east coast of America to the west coast, but they are also required to obtain the necessary revenue, interpret surveys, and overcome unexpected events. Whenever I have used this program, it has generated a good deal of pupil interaction. The children seem willing to review the consequences of their decisions, and plan alternative strategies. In this context, the piece of software becomes 'but one part of a larger pack' of activities, to use Richard Knott's words from his article in Chandler (1983).

The Longman Micro Software catalogue contains a useful variety of other simulation programs. *Pirates* is an adventure that requires a good deal of verbal and mental reasoning to solve the problems that are posed. *Transpots* is a program that ably illustrates the flexibility of the computer: it centres on the need to locate a factory in the south-west of England, and requires a range of activities and skills. Some mathematics is involved, but the overall effect is to produce a suitable context for all kinds of language and drama work. Almost all these simulation programs can lead to role play and improvisation.

Teachers can actually generate their own simulations using what are called Business Spreadsheets — computer programs that allow the operator to input large amounts of factual and numerical data. Lists of results, general accounts and profit and loss balances can all be represented. *Business Games* (Acornsoft Education) refines this idea and caters for up to eight participants. It deals with the world of high finance, but generates dramatic tension whenever the various items are purchased, sold or exchanged. Anyone who has used similar programs will vouch for the enthusiasm that soon grips the players.

(d) Problem solving programs Seymour Papert (1980) has eloquently defined how 'very powerful kinds of learning are taking place' when young pupils are learning a computer language like Logo. They 'are learning a language for talking about shapes and fluxes of shapes, about velocities and rates of change, about processes and procedures'. It is impossible to overestimate how important it is for all our students to grasp these concepts and communicate them to others; and learning these languages depends on the ability to communicate successfully — solving problems, reading instructions, interpreting notes, comparing observations and formulating theories. My own attitude is that if an English teacher feels confident enough, there is a good deal to be gained from teaching a computer language to interested pupils. Such activities will probably have to take place after school. (The subject is discussed again in the section on innovations at Abbot Beyne.)

Smaller programs have been evolved to cater for specific needs, *Tree of Knowledge* (ESM) is a classification program that helps to develop reasoning skills, and *Sheepdog* (Longman Software) is a piece of software for younger pupils that has similar aims, but a different format. The range of these resource materials is enormous. *Magic Garden* (Acornsoft) is based on horticulture, and *Watchperson* (MEP) is aimed at the young and concentrates on route planning. In nearly every case, the programmers seek to bolster motivation, provide graded sequences of activities, and encourage concentration and reflection. Indeed, this kind of software has a great deal to offer the modern English teacher.

Other kinds of English programs

We are all familiar with the sequencing exercises that are used to help students plan their stories and plays coherently. By its very nature, a computer is ideally suited to help with these lessons. *Paint Brush* (HesWare–Thorn EMI) is a program that enables a pupil to rapidly draw a sequence of pictures. I use it to liberate the imagination, and to encourage the depth of descriptive detail that is sometimes needed; but the illustrations can also help certain pupils actually to establish the core events in a story, and hence to plan it more powerfully. In extreme cases, one picture can serve as the basis for one paragraph. Here, an important point is that the computer illustrations can be talked about and discussed before any writing actually begins. *Author* (ESM) goes much further in that it allows text to be displayed on the screen, and helps the writer to design, create and edit the material. A computer program can do this by offering different format options, asking pertinent questions, and referring the user to 'help' or information screens. It can also be programmed to display sequences of events and even conclusions, and these facilities allow the writer to reflect on the planning choices that are essential for any piece of writing. The power and flexibility are impressive. *Adventure Story Writer* (ESM) has some of the facilities described above, and *Author* (ESM) can serve as a bulletin board, class diary, or magazine. It even helps with word puzzles, and can be formatted to function as a kind of resource bank for individual classes – storing materials, dates, sources of information, and even workcards.

Crucially, a computer speeds up the illustrative processes and helps the English teacher to plan for the classroom needs of individuals or small groups. The latest software attempts to utilize these capabilities fully. We have already mentioned Cloze passages, but *Readamatics* (Longman Micro Software) goes much further. It is designed to enable the average English teacher to write and edit suitable passages, and also includes a provision for testing the readability and measuring the reading age of any piece of text. There is a wide range of existing material for each pupil to review, and *Readamatics* offers help with spelling, vocabulary and word selection. For good measure, a pupil's progress is recorded and assessed.

Language work is also featured in a recent book by Higgins and Johns (1984). The authors describe a series of fascinating 'text games' that have been devised 'to develop the student's ability to form appropriate hypotheses and to guess intelligently' when they are confronted by texts. These games emphasize 'language as information and the way that information hangs together', and the student is always assigned an 'active' role in the learning process. Undoubtedly, the work of those two authors is a guide to future developments.

The word processor

In his article 'Why English teachers should use computers', Anthony Adams (Chandler 1983) makes at least two very important observations. English departments are seen as central to 'a comprehensive programme of computer education in schools, a kind of computers-across-the curriculum approach', and the 'remarkable capacity' of the word processor is both recognized and demonstrated. With such a program, a pupil can type in text, edit it, store it, correct it, and shape it. First drafts can be discussed, spellings checked, descriptive words added, phrases and whole sentences moved, and paragraph sequences amended. There is already a good deal of evidence to suggest that pupils are generally highly motivated by this chance to polish, and experiment with, their own writing. My own students enjoy the chance to reflect on their work before having a finished copy printed. If necessary, they can store materials indefinitely. They also like combining individual lines into experimental poems, and putting playscripts together. The word processor has an inherent flexibility, and English teachers are in a good position to harness its services.

Indeed, since many of these programs have the ability to search a text for single letters or combinations of letters, they are important tools for textual analysis — able to identify words, symbols or images for further study. To make matters even easier, some of this software has been specifically designed for school use. *View* (Acornsoft) is available for the BBC B; *Word* (the Chiltern Advisory Unit) is a simulation program for the RML 380Z that 'illustrates some of the main features of a word processor'; and *Edword* (Clwyd Technics) is a program that is directly marketed for teachers and schools. It has easy to remember mnemonic commands, clear error messages, and a simplified operating system; but its value also comes from the total resource package that accompanies *Edword* — a user book, keyboard inserts, wallcharts, and a collection of information sheets. Interestingly, it is often through using such a word processor that our pupils begin to acquire keyboard skills. This explains why writers like Anthony Adams are excited at the thought of these programs being widely used in English classrooms.

Programs associated with literature texts

Many teachers are disappointed when they first encounter this type of software. It tends to appear limited in relation to the texts themselves. *Pride and Prejudice* (Sussex Software) is a program divided into sections on characters, story, themes, social background, and style; and *Critical Analysis*, by the same company, deals with such topics as rhyme and metre before advancing to a discussion of more subtle, critical concepts. My students value such programs as revision aids; but, where it is used, they find the multi-choice question a limiting format. They want to *handle* language. In future, literature programs will probably be more interactive. No doubt resource banks will be created full of incidental information about authors, readers and historical contexts. At present, the best software deals with other topics. *Text Grader* (Hutchinson) is an invaluable program for establishing the reading age of any text, according to eight different measures. A boring task is transformed, and all our pupils stand to benefit from this kind of efficiency.

Information technology

Communications and viewdata systems There is no doubt that students students are often tremendously excited by lessons on information technology, but there are skills to be acquired before they can successfully manipulate the software and hardware involved. We emphasize the crucial need for correct typing, and have evolved exercises to encourage a high level of screen comprehension. The aim is to identify important commands, and ensure fast reaction times. Prestel and other viewdata systems usually have introductory menus. Pupils move from these to the requisite pages of information. To proceed rapidly, they must scan and review each screenful of information, and make decisions about it. The context is the important thing: pupils retrieve information, create letters or reports, make decisions, interpret documents, and communicate with other users. Clearly, information technology is a growing force in our lives, and it generates strong motivation for pupils to refine their English skills. In my experience, they are more than willing to do so.

Database A small group of pupils kindled my interest in databases. They simply wanted to know how information is stored in a computer. Our investigations led to a writing project and display, but they also led me to think more deeply about the role of the database in our society. My pupils were more practical: they collected information on rates of pocket money, hobbies, holiday locations and the weather. When we started on the pocket money project, our initial classroom discussions focused on the specific kinds of information to be collected, and the design of questionnaires. We broke into small groups and worked out ideas before coming to a class consensus. Thus, every pupil started with some notes and plans in their exercise books, and a brief summary of aims and expectations. From the beginning, oral work was emphasized with these second years. We concentrated on the differing amounts of money paid to boys and girls, the relationship between remuneration and pupil age, and the nature of the tasks performed for this reward. The questionnaire led to discussions at home, each student typed in the collected data, and we all had a wonderful time experimenting with the database and discovering just what could be collated by the computer, and what could not. Naturally, we ended up with tables of names and numbers, but we also documented our successes and failure.

In this way, the English project included computer information as well. It generated enough enthusiasm for various pupils to opt for further research; and, at the end, I was left with a genuine feeling of satisfaction at the range of activities covered and the depth and intensity of pupil participation. Stewart (Chandler 1983) confirms the computer's ability to stimulate group and class discussions but, as always, the onus is on the subject teacher to choose a suitable topic and use the software correctly.

The Abbot Beyne experience

At Abbot Beyne, a complementary English course has been evolved to help all the pupils to make sense of the new technology, and learn how to handle it. This course runs in spare time, and the emphasis is upon the development of communication skills. Students are encouraged to master difficult spatial, numerical and social concepts, and every attempt is made to foster a rich language learning environment. In order to cater for children of all abilities and ages, we base some of the course on ordinary home computers, and offer to teach interested parents. The supporting literature is rewritten to feature a step-by-step approach. A special strategy has also been evolved to help the girls with their computing: they enjoy the advantages of program examples that are based on social and personal situations, and can select from a wide range of 'arts' software.

At first sight, some of the topics on the syllabus might seem a little odd. We teach Logo, BASIC and machine code. What have these to do with English? The answer is that in pursuing these studies the pupils find themselves using all the resources of English to establish an understanding of the concepts involved. Papert (1980) has demonstrated the exciting intellectual processes involved in learning a computer language. We don't aim for a full, professional computing standard, but our pupils do gain an awareness of how large programs work by developing small routines of their own. Admittedly, this is a small fraction of the entire English course, but it is crucial for an insight into what computers are, and what they do. The skills acquired will help the children to face, shape and influence the new technological age.

For similar reasons, we study speech synthesis, graphics, robotics, business spreadsheets, musical synthesizers and financial programs. A description of the robotics component might help to illustrate just what is going on. The Memocon Crawler (from *Prism*) has first to be assembled. This means interpreting technical English and following instructions precisely. The robot then has to be programmed, and this entails learning its language by carefully studying the documents provided. The pupils then work out routines, and keep a strict diary of events.

I am invariably asked to introduce 'robots' into the normal English and Drama lessons. Beryl Maxwell (Kelly 1984) describes a similar project, and she talks about her primary pupils experiencing the 'joy of discovery' and becoming 'totally absorbed'. This is exactly the learning environment that I am after. The crucial point to remember is that the software is only as exciting as the teacher makes it. I incorporate my speech synthesizers into plays, use dedicated graphics programs to generate poetry, and adapt the business spreadsheets to simulate work experiences.

It is difficult to quantify the effects of such a course, but certainly an immediate impetus is given to a school's 'language across the curriculum' policy. Social skills are refined in the mixed teaching groups, technical reading is encouraged, and the sociology of the computer studied. Perhaps the parents should have the last word. They report that their children have gained the kind of confidence that enables them to pursue personal research projects, and argue forcibly and logically. We are back to the sense of Barry Midgley's remarks in the opening section.

The problems of a classroom teacher

All heads of English will be faced with the problems of providing enough in-service computer training for staff, and finding the spare time to review the available software. Every teacher will worry about transporting equipment to the classroom, and gaining access to library resources at the appropriate time. In a computer lesson, numerous groups might be concentrating on a variety of activities. This means allocating space for each group, and preventing the computer from attracting the attention of those not directly working at the keyboard. More seriously, teachers often have to create the materials for group activity. Only the sharing of resources and ideas will prevent an overload of work. In addition *all* pupil programs need to be reviewed before they are presented in class. This procedure eliminates the errors that cause complaints and frustration.

One main question remains. How well will the English computer programs fit into the scheme of a term's work? A pragmatic approach is needed here. But it would be unfortunate if valuable opportunities for innovation were missed merely on grounds of ignorance or, worse, of prejudice. Proceed cautiously, and build up your confidence gradually.

Talking points

- *How do you and your colleagues intend to acquire a basic confidence with handling computers?*
- *What kinds of English computer programs do you want to start with? How are you going to review the available software?*
- *Are you willing to share your computing materials and experiences with colleagues, and perhaps with English teachers from local schools and computer groups?*
- *How are the computers stored and used in your school? Do you understand how a computer laboratory works? Would it be possible for you to experiment with small teaching groups?*
- *Just how crucial is the role of the teacher in an English computer lesson?*

Further reading

These books and articles encapsulate different areas of English teaching.

1. For a step-by-step approach to English computing see Salt, M.J. (1984) *An English Computer Book*. Abbot Beyne School, Burton on Trent.
2. English computer software for home micros is listed in Salt, M.J. (1984) *English, the Electric Language Catalogue.* Abbot Beyne School.

3. See M.J. Salt on 'How to interest girls in English computing' in *Personal Computing Today*. October 1984.
4. The social implications of the micro revolution are handled in Shallis, M. (1984) *The Silicon Idol*. Oxford: OUP.
5. If you want to investigate learning activities that you might be able to program for yourself, see Orwig, G.W. and Hodges, W.S. (1982) *The Computer Tutor*. Boston: Little, Brown and Company.
6. For language teaching, read Higgins, J. and Johns, T. (1984) *Computers in Language Learning*. London: Collins ELT and Addison-Wesley Publishing.
7. NATE has contributed to computer research in Chandler, D. (1983) *Exploring English with Microcomputers*. London: Council for Educational Technology.
8. More general essays are available in Kelly, A.V. (ed) (1984) *Microcomputers and the Curriculum*. London: Harper & Row.

Authors cited in text

1. Adams, A. Why English teachers should use computers. In Chandler, D. (1983) *Exploring English with Microcomputers*, London: CET, pp.19–24.
2. Bitter, G.G. and Camuse, R.A. (1984) *Using a Microcomputer in the Classroom*. Reston (USA): Reston Publishing Company, pp. 39–64
3. Higgins, J. and Johns, T. (1984) *Computers in Language Learning*, London: Collins ELT and Addison-Wesley, p.59.
4. Knott, R. Computer awareness and creative English — Mission Impossible? In Chandler, D. (1983) *Exploring English with Microcomputers*. London: CET, pp. 25–29
5. Maxwell, B. 'Why Logo?' in Kelly, A.V. (1984) *Microcomputers and the Curriculum*. London: Harper and Row pp. 84–106.
6. Midgley, B. (1983) *English Occasional Paper 17: Microcomputers and the Teaching of English*. Staffordshire LEA.
7. Papert, S. (1980) *Mindstorms*. New York: Basic Books, p.13
8. Stewart, J. Does the use of microcomputers inhibit the development of language in children? In Chandler, D. (1983) *Exploring English with Microcomputers*. London: CET, pp. 59–74

Program sources

Wild words, Famous Blast Words, Margana, Pirates, Transpots, Sheepdog, Readamatics: Longman.

Sentence Sequencing, Copywrite: Educational Software for Microcomputers.
Wordpower: Sulis Software.
Summary and Comprehension Guidelines (RML 380Z), Pride and Prejudice, Critical Analysis 1: Sussex Software.
Rail Boss: Commodore.

Business Games, Tree of Knowledge, Magic Garden, View: Acornsoft.
Watchperson: MEP Micro Primer Software, Pack 3.
Paint Brush: HesWare.
Author: ESM.
Word: Chiltern Advisory Unit for Computer Based Learning.
Edword: Clywd Technics.
Text Grader: Hutchinson.
Memocon Crawler: Prism.

Malcolm Salt is Head of English at the Abbot Beyne School, Burton on Trent, and Director of 'National English resources Sharing Scheme'. He was formerly Lecturer in English, University of Sierra Leone.

UNIT 15

THE HUMANITIES

Ashley Kent

Introduction

Definitions of the 'humanities' are difficult, despite the deceptively simple but all-embracing Oxford English Dictionary version which suggests they are 'learning or literature concerned with human culture'. The term is interpreted here equally widely, but examples are drawn only from economics, geography and history. However, many of the general observations in this unit can be applied to the other humanities, and to the social sciences.

Economics, geography and history lagged well behind science and mathematics education in seizing the opportunities of CAL in the late 1970s and early 1980s. However, increased interest was shown first by geography and now economics and history, as evidenced by the great increase in CAL programs, articles and books published on these subject areas in 1983 and 1984.

Geography has remained ahead of economics and history for a variety of reasons. Firstly, GAPE[1] was established by David Walker in 1974 and raised the consciousness of geographers to the potential of CAL. Secondly, the Computers in the Curriculum Project early on (1979) published a suite of geography programs; and thirdly, an influential book by Shepherd et al.

(1980) was read by many geographers (and, interestingly, by many non-geographers). Finally, the nature of modern geography and its related pedagogy suited the medium of CAL well.

Categories of CAL in the humanities

Various attempts have been made to classify types of learning (Kemmis 1976), pupil/teacher/micro interactions (Shepherd et al. 1980), and software. Figure 19 is an attempt to relate types of learning with programs having particular subject intent.

Information handling (Category 1) is of growing significance for each of the three subject areas and a number of programs now published are used across subject boundaries. Information about any sort of data an be held on a disk. One disk can hold up to 1000 items under each of 20 headings — around 20,000 separate pieces of information. Information-retrieval or information-handling programs allow pupil and teacher to select the data. The most important task for the user is to ask the right questions of the programs in order to extract the required information and to present it in the form in which it is needed, whether as a table, list, map, graph or diagram. Freeman (1984) explains how the QUERY 'family' of information handling programs including QUEST can act as a tool to aid teaching and learning by making possible fast and accurate interrogations of a vast amount of data. As Ross (1984) explains, such work often involves three stages. First, the number of columns (fields) of data has to be decided upon; second, the information has to be entered into the resultant table and usually stored on disk (in Micro SCAN for instance); and third, the user can ask any number of enquiries of the data set. To subjects in danger of drowning in a surfeit of historical and contemporary economic, social and geographical data, such programs offer major classroom advantages. The skills of data handling and retrieval are vital in today's computer age, and such work can be a key contribution that subjects can make to pupils' computer literacy.

Statistical analysis (Category 2) represents a further set of skills demanded by the social sciences and is helpful in many other areas. By doing the computations, the micro allows the student to concentrate on the interpretation of the statistics and not the calculations themselves. Displaying the statistics as well as calculating them helps with understanding and interpretation. For instance, PROFILE needs slope angle data to be collected in the field, then displays hill slope profiles or beach profiles as a section.

1. Information handling
2. Statistical analysis
3. Simulations: (a) Models and systems (b) Decision-making exercises and games
4. Reinforcement of knowledge, skills, ideas
5. Other uses of CAL
   (a) Teaching materials produced
   (b) Electronic blackboard
   (c) Managing resources
   (d) Management of learning
   (e) Video/micro link

Some programs as examples of these categories

Category	*Program name and source*	*Subject area*	*Topic*
1	QUERY (AUCBE)	H, G, E	Interrogates data sets
1	CENSUS ANALYSIS (L)	H	1851 Census data
1	BARCHART (ILEA)	H, G, E	Prints data in variety of forms of barcharts
1	SCAN (ILEA)	H, G, E	Data processing collection of programs
2	GSTATS (L)	H, G, E	Elementary descriptive statistics
2	PROFILE (M/B)	G	Displays slope profile and associated variables; scattergraphs drawn and correlation coefficients calculated.
2	DESCRIBE (NC)	H, G, E	Various statistical measures
2	SPATIAL (NC)	G	Calculates spatial statistics
3a	RUNNING THE BRITISH ECONOMY (L)	E	Effect of monetary and fiscal policies
3a	MAXPRO (L)	E	Theory of the firm
3a	DROPLET (GAPE)	G	Model of the hydrological cycle
3a	GRAVITY (L)	G	Predicting journey patterns
3a	WELF (L)	G	Social indices of deprivation
3b	PARAFFIN FILE (BP)	E	Case study of UK paraffin market
3b	RAIL (L)	H, G, E	Rival railway companies plan networks

Figure 19. Categories of CAL in History, Geography and Economics by program type (continued overleaf)

Category	Program name and source	Subject area	Topic
3b	DISRAELI (L)	H	Disraeli and Eastern question 1875–8
3b	CAMPAIGN (L)	H	Edward III's Normandy campaign
3b	FARM (L)	G, E	Making profits given weather variations
3b	ROUTE (L)	G	Motorway route planning
4	SLOPE MEASUREMENT (GAPE)	G	Slope angle estimation and forms of transport
4	INTRAD (L)	E	Gains from trade with Portugal in wine and cloth
4	CONTOURS (H)	G	Contour maps and sections of 54 geomorphological features
4	CLIMATE (H)	G	Recognition of climatic types

Key for sources of programs

AUCBE	Advisory Unit for Computer Based Education; Hatfield, Herts AL10 8AU
ILEA	Inner London Education Authority
L	Longman Micro Software
NC	Newman College, Bartley Green, Birmingham B32 3NT
GAPE	Geographical Association Package Evaluation, Department of Geography, University of Loughborough. Hutchinson
BP	British Petroleum Education Unit, PO Box 5, Wetherby, West Yorkshire LS23 7EH
H	Heinemann Computers in Education Limited, 22 Bedford Square, London WC1B 3HH
CICP	Computers in the Curriculum Project, Chelsea College
M/B	St. Martin/Brathay Project, MEP funded

Key for subject areas

H	History
G	Geography
E	Economics

Figure 19 (continued). Categories of CAL in History, Geography and Economics by program type

Other data collected, e.g. variations in depth, PH, and moisture content with distance downslope, can be displayed underneath the profile to give a visual impression. Hence, a result table can be entered simply and displayed. Scattergraphs can then be drawn and correlation coefficients calculated for the linear relationships between two variables. This program then is a combination of Categories 1 and 2 on Figure 19.

Simulations (Category 3) are now an accepted and successful teaching tool in history, geography and economics (Taylor and Walford 1978). Microcomputers can handle simulations of a model or system or a decision making exercise or game. The program RUNNING THE BRITISH ECONOMY (an example of Category 3a) offers the opportunity of emulating the Chancellor of the Exchequer! It allows the close appraisal of past actions and interrelationships and according to one teacher reporting to Longman, 'My students learn more from three hours . . . running their own economy than in a whole year of teaching macro economics. No other technique has the potential to teach interdependence and economic policy so efficiently'. Probably an exaggeration, but this is still a valuable program.

The DISRAELI program is a decision making game (an example of Category 3b) which pinpoints ten decision situations for British diplomacy between the outbreaks of revolts in Boznia and Herzegovina in the summer of 1875 and the attempts to revise the Treaty of San Stefano in the spring of 1878. Four alternative (mostly plausible) courses of action are provided for each of the ten situations. Students are invited to see events through Disraeli's eyes and to select the course of action which they believe he would have followed. A scoring system is devised whereby a cohesive policy, even if not technically 'correct', scores more highly than a series of decisions which oscillate markedly in terms of methods and aims.

Category 4 in Figure 19 can be exemplified by CLIMATE, a program which sets out to help 14–16 year old pupils in their study of world climatic regions through the recognition of climate type by data and/or graph analysis. For this program, an understanding of climatic types and data is essential. INTRAD gives a student the task of maximizing the welfare of England in its trade in wine and cloth with Portugal. There is control over the production possibilities, which goods to trade, and the output of the exported goods. Although, like CLIMATE, it can be used as an introduction to these ideas, it is best used for testing that students understand opportunity cost and the comparative advantage/cost model.

SLOPE MEASUREMENT also belongs in Category 4 but is very much a drill and practice program in that it reinforces the skill of slope estimation.

stly, a graphic representation of a slope is shown together with its easurement, in degrees, percentage, and as a ratio. Pupils can alter the slope raising or lowering it) and observe the changes in measurements. Secondly, the program will generate slopes at random, the pupils having to estimate their measurements. The program aims to relate visual impressions of slopes with their actual measurements.

Various other types of learning and related software are listed in Figure 19. CALUSG, published as *Data in Geography* (1979), produced a range of teaching materials using the computer as workhorse (5a in Figure 19). An example of the micro used as an electronic blackboard is provided by CIRCULAR FLOW OF INCOME (5b in Figure 19). Here a diagram is built up step by step under the teacher's control, just as it might be drawn on the blackboard. Obviously a micro needs to be connected to a large TV screen or monitor so that the tables and diagrams can be seen by the whole class.

Few departments have used micros to manage their resources (5c in Figure 19) but as Watson (1984a) suggests, 'From the micro in the classroom, they can explore the contents of the . . . department library, the central library, the list of slides or film strip sequences, the location of worksheets, and particularly if there is an appropriate piece of software which the pupil could use. In the future, the school's computing facilities will be able to down-load information which may be relevant from sources well outside their physical school base'.

Computer managed learning (CML) (Category 5d) offers four main facilities: the testing of a student's knowledge of a topic; records of past performance can be stored; further work can be set on the basis of the first two facilities as well as some decision rules by the teacher; reports can be produced for a topic, for a student, or on the progress of a particular teacher's students. The TIPS system (Kelley 1970) has been in use in the USA since 1967, while Broderick (1974) in Havering, has developed CML for science education. Finally, the integration of video and micro (Category 5e) offers enormous potential but remains underdeveloped at present.

At present most programs developed for history, geography and economics have a value for only one of those subject areas. However, the information handling and analysis programs have cross-subject applicability. There are also some examples of simulations which have wide applicability. RAIL for instance provides humanities courses with material of both geographical and historical interest. Groups of students play a competitive game planning railway routes as nineteenth-century company directors. Various other Computers in the Curriculum Project programs such as CANAL,

WINDMILL and COSBEN straddle subject boundaries. Indeed Killbery (1984) argues that CAL could help 'to overcome some of the real problems associated with cross-subject teaching. Properly designed units can ease the load of preparation by supplying much of the expertise required from other disciplines, and by structuring the approach to suit the differing slants required'. Watson (1984b) also argues that our discipline-based curriculum structure can be inhibiting to innovative thinking and points to 'broad sweeps of overlap, in the history/geography/economics area' which could be supported by appropriate CAL.

Cautionary notes

Before moving to the other sections of this unit it is important to sound a few notes of caution. The development of programs is a new element of the publishing industry and as yet some of the products are unsatisfactory — full of errors, user-unfriendly, poor in their use of graphics and so on. Any real impact of CAL across the curriculum will require the co-operation and understanding of the teaching force. Kelly (1984) speaks of the need to overcome computer-induced anxiety and Golby (1982) calls for a balance between 'The utopianism of those who may hope for and expect instant revolution and the luddite mentality of those who reject technological progress in any form'. Hoyle (1983) is over-pessimistic, in my view, as to how the innovation will take off, but on the other hand as Shepherd et al. (1980) rightly point out, 'the effectiveness of CAL . . . depends largely on the human element, particularly in the way in which teachers use the new resource'. Finally, the pace of change is so rapid that without care commercial considerations will outweigh considered educational viewpoints. As Walker (1981) rightly suggested, 'At the start of any new period of development, it is important to stand back and ask why we want it and what the pupils will gain from it, to think carefully about the purpose of . . . teaching and then to see how the computer can help serve that end'. Clearly there must be an important role here for educational research, including thorough software evaluations.

Description of CAL in different areas

Geography

Various general publications help the reader with particular interests in CAL and geography. These include Shepherd et al. (1980), Kent (1983), Watson (1984a) and Midgley with Walker (1985). The most comprehensive and up-to-date listing of programs has been compiled by Fox (1984). As argued above, geography showed early interest in CAL not least because the teaching of a modern geography course involves problem solving, decision making, model building, and handling and analysing data. CAL, because of its graphics potential, its data storage and processing capabilities, and its ability to recall and modify models and systems, is highly suited to the new content and pedagogy of the subject. A variety of programs have been published over the last few years. Some examples of these will now be considered.

GEOBASE is a spatial data base package at present undergoing evaluation. It is an interrogative system, displaying information in such a way that spatial trends and inter-variable relationships can be directly seen and analysed. In short it compiles maps and diagrams in response to questions posed by the user. At present a prototype program is available for teachers to build up their own databases and the interrogative program is on classroom trial.

Jane Richardson, formerly of the Brathay Centre for Field Studies, has developed a range of programs for number-crunching, data display, predictive modelling and calculating statistics using the micro in fieldwork.[2] HISTO is one example which displays and compares two histograms statistically. PUDDLE, on the other hand, shows what happens to rainwater. The program simulates the paths of water above and below the ground surface. The water is temporarily held in stores, before it eventually returns to the atmosphere or drains downslope. These movements are shown on the screen by an animated flow diagram. RICE is a decision-making simulation, which attempts to simulate the economic and environmental problems facing a 'typical' rice farmer in north-east India. The pupil is able to combat these problems by buying different types of rice, using fertilizer or pesticide, or by drilling a well.

A final example, this time with CAL as skills reinforcer, is provided by MAP SKILLS 1 and MAP SKILLS 2. Grid references, scale, the compass and its use, and a game called Yacht Race are the contents of these two packages. They are best used as a useful test and reinforcer of a pupil's understanding of some of the basic map skills.

History

The best guidance so far for history teachers interested in CAL is provided by Francis (1983) but earlier publications from the Historical Association (1979) and *Teaching History* (1982) are worth consulting. The Historical Association is at present trying to set up a catalogue of history programs and establish a standardized format for census and reference retrieval files.

The greatest enthusiasm has been shown for information handling programs which complement the 'New History'. This recent trend encourages pupils to consider historical methods and events through the examination of source materials and evidence. Allied to this is a move towards more recent economic and social history for which much data is available to be examined and quantified. Such work has been spearheaded by Peter Laslett at the Cambridge Centre for Population Studies and involves study of census returns, parish registers, wills, inventories, and records of many types. This data needs searching, quantifying and aggregating, and information handling CAL packages have great potential here. As Schurer (1984) argues, 'the increased interest in local studies has made the enumerators' returns the prime historical document to be "computerized" in schools'. Local instances of this abound, but an example known to this author is the ADEL parish register 1693–1702 (a Yorkshire parish) used by a west London school. Pupils are encouraged to interrogate this data base by asking questions such as: How many people came from Adel itself and how many from the surrounding villages? How many people died of fever? How many children died before they were five years old? Linked interpretative questions are asked, such as: Sometimes no cause of death is listed. Why do you think this is? Do you think the causes of death which are listed are likely to be true? However, different packages such as QUARRY BANK 1851 and CENSUS ANALYSIS handle the data differently. Entries are abbreviated to varying lengths and encoded according to various schemes, and information is variously added or suppressed. Thus no true exchange of data can take place outside of the circle of schools using the same package. This explains why at present a group of Cambridge historians[3] are trying to devise standards for census data transcription and analysis (Schurer 1984).

However, many history teachers regard CAL as no more than a gimmick and a passing fad, and are particularly scathing about CAL simulations. They see the danger of oversimplification to the point of distortion. They argue that such simulations suggest that certain events were inevitable (Blow 1982) and make the dangerous assumption that decisions were logical. Developments in artificial intelligence and in particular PROLOG[4] are described by Ennals (forthcoming) but are often regarded as either a pedagogical cul-de-sac, or as one Inspector put it, 'I take a sceptical but undismissive attitude'. Many teachers still share the view of Derek Turner (1982) who suggested that 'The long term importance of the computer in the history classroom is uncertain. It cannot become clear until more software programs are available and more schools have tried and shared their experience with others'.

Although history CAL has been relatively slow to take off, the signs are that interest in the last year alone (1984) has expanded massively. Not all history teachers will agree with Francis's (1983) view that the microcomputer presents the greatest opportunity since printing for a revolution in teaching and learning, but many are realizing the reasons why this was said.

Economics

The best review of the state of CAL in economics was Cotterell (1983) but this has now been superseded by another helpful booklet by Randall (1984). In that publication Randall argues strongly for the use of microcomputers in the teaching of economics and suggests six reasons. Firstly, micros allow students to explore the properties of models, which loom large in economic courses. Secondly, micros can simulate the dynamic form of many economics models, graphing their output. COBWEB, for instance, introduces the cobweb theories' fluctuations. The characteristics of the market can be changed by choosing different 'commodities' to produce, or by changing the slopes and lags explicitly. Thirdly, some programs allow students to explore the way in which certain processes approach a solution. The credit multiplier process (by which an increase in deposits in one of a system of banks enables the system as a whole to increase its lending by a multiplier of that deposit) is simulated by the program CREDIT, which allows students to see this process at work as one of its options. Fourthly, certain programs allow the simulation of experiments. So for instance MULTSC and UKMCRI can be used to determine the effect of the injections multiplier. Government expenditure can be changed and as a result national income changes and thereby the size of the multiplier can be calculated. Fifthly, economics CAL programs can genuinely simulate reality, often using real data and situations. For instance, AGCOM1 and AGCOM2 cover the present EEC system of price support and the former UK system. Each student has the role of the relevant commissioner/minister, and must decide on levels of support. A final reason given by Randall, in support of economics CAL, is that key statistics can be held in store, then presented in the most appropriate graphical fashion, and statistically analysed if necessary.

However, most economics programs seem to play a reinforcement role with respect to skills and/or knowledge. Some economics teachers are making a strong case for using computers to present simulations which make otherwise complex and seemingly abstract models reveal their important practical applications at a relatively early stage in an introductory course. Most software was until recently for the 16–19 age group, but the 14–16 Economics Project is now having an impact.

As yet, few economics teachers have ventured into CAL, a pattern equally true of history and geography teachers. Most economics software has been promised but little has materialized. In the related subject area of business studies there are some interesting developments in spreadsheets and statistical programs. Probably most used and best known, however, are the two business games of PARAFFIN FILE and SIXGAM. SIXGAM can be played by one to six firms for up to ten 'years', with the firms selling a single product in up to six countries. The results are stored for each year, which gives the option of discontinuous use and the possibility of displaying results as tables or simple barcharts. This is typical of the modern generation of CAL business games which are more friendly, flexible, less complex, and with simpler graphical output than the earlier games geared to mainframe computers.

Teaching process and content in the humanities

Geography

(a) Teaching process What CAL in geography has done since the late 1970s has been to complement geography's interest in games, models and decision making. Consequently, three commonly used programs are FARM (a simple weather-related crop choice game); DEMOG (a program which allows changes in birth and death rate and illustrates the effects on an age-sex pyramid model); and MILL (location of windmills, attempting to reduce costs) — in spite of their having been produced in the Paleotechnic era[5] of the 1970s.

The trend has been for geography teachers to use a CAL program first with a small group of sixth formers in the 'gatekeeper' mode (Shepherd et al. 1980) as an electronic blackboard. When expertise and confidence has been gained, more of a partnership mode has been used whereby computer, teacher and pupil interact in a three-cornered fashion. Wiegand (1984) has studied CAL in geography classrooms and has observed three ways of organizing lessons.

In *whole-class teaching* the teacher uses one micro in conjunction with one or more TV monitors, usually at the front of the class. Another style of micro use is *group work*, where for instance five micros are available and pupils sit around the keyboards and monitors. The final and at present most popular style is the *cafeteria style* of class management. Here the class is organized into groups who work mostly away from the micro and only occasionally have access to it. ROUTE, a motorway planning simulation, is often used in this way, with the micro evaluating the decisions taken in the groups.

(b) Content Most early programs in geography were based on enthusiasts' interests, rather than contemporary syllabuses. Nowadays the trend is to link with courses and textbooks such as HOLIDAY 1 and 2, and CITIES 1 and 2, which integrate well with two books produced by Nelson to support GYSL based courses. Curriculum development links have also been made, as is the case with four programs developed to complement the Geography 16–19 Project – PUDDLE, GROWTH, WELF and MINE.

History

(a) Teaching process Several history programs have reinforced the resource-based, enquiry approaches of the 'New History'. New programs are being developed in relation to the now highly successful 13–16 Project and SUFFRAGETTES is an example of this. Francis (1983) has identified four broad types of history CAL – simulations; data retrieval; reference retrieval; and assessment. Re-enactment simulations are of battles (CAMPAIGN – about the Hundred Years' War), voyages (DRAKE) and diplomatic crises (CHOICE). Replay simulations allow a different result the second time round (SUFFRAGETTES is an example). Model simulations deliberately simplify situations to emphasize particular historical ideas and influences (CASTLES and VILLAGE are example of these). Game simulations, through their stress on chance and competition/winning, are effective portrayals of some situations, SPANISH MAIN for example. The final type is simulated research, whereby historical research is re-enacted. SAQQARA and AMARNA, for instance, help a pupil to understand the problems of an archaeologist and can teach the need to search and excavate systematically and carefully. Data retrieval in history can be exemplified by CENSUS and QUARRY BANK, and reference retrieval, whereby the computer acts as a library catalogue, by JOEL and SIR. Finally, there is student assessment in history but as yet few examples exist.

Four classroom strategies in history CAL have been identified by Francis (1983). These are: *electronic blackboard* used by teacher for demonstration; *whole-class strategy* with pupils fully involved, though the teacher may well operate the keyboard; *group work* either of a competitive or cooperative nature; and the computer at the disposal of an *individual student*.

(b) Content In history, as in geography, many programs at first were peripheral to the main syllabi and reflected the personal interests of developers. Therefore the content of school history courses has not been affected, but this is quite possible with coursework elements of modern syllabi. A big question mark hangs over the likely influence of Ennals (forthcoming) who sees PROLOG having a much more radical influence on learning in history (and other) classrooms.

Economics

(a) Teaching process As yet, few economics teachers have made use of CAL in their classrooms. This is a direct comment on the limited range of software available until recently. As Cotterrell (1983) put it, 'There is a need for software which can be used for individualised learning: most of the software available at present is more suited to classroom work and requires detailed guidance by the teacher. There is an urgent need, particularly in applied microeconomics, and for courses which are less theoretical than GCE 'A' level, for well-written software presenting simulations and case studies with good screen layout, use of graphs and good documentation.'

(b) Content The early phase 1 Schools Council Programs published by Longman, which include ELAST, MAXPRO, FISCAL and MONPOL, are still the most used in schools even though they were published as early as 1978. Many more economics programs are now being published, not least through links between the Economics Education 14–16 Project (Manchester University), Computers in the Curriculum Project (Chelsea College), and a group of economics teachers at North Staffordshire Polytechnic.

Future possibilities

A critical yet constructive role must be played by teachers in developments at various levels. For instance, the Geographical Association through its journal *Teaching Geography* has a regular feature entitled the Computer Page. Also curriculum development projects, in the vanguard of innovation, must continue to link with software ventures. This has been true of the Economics 14–16, History 13–16 and Geography 16–19 Projects. Perhaps most helpful for teachers would be the creation of more local/regional groups of teachers evaluating and developing software. Existing curriculum subjects must take increasingly seriously their role in developing the computer awareness of pupils. Teachers will also have to bear in mind the increased sophistication of pupils, and make use of the vast number of micros in their homes — computer assisted homework is a real possibility!

Technological developments will include micro/videodisk developments, computer laboratories and networks in schools, and increasingly powerful micros. It is the duty of teachers to grasp the educational possibilities these technical developments offer, and not be taken over by commercial interests, without having a say. Software developments are bound to continue as reported in Kent (1984). But as Oakeshott (1982) suggested, 'a stabilized, tidy or predictable market seems a long way off'. What is likely is that television and radio will continue to show interest in educational computing. One recent innovation was the BBC's commissioning of four programs to run alongside an A-level school geography radiovision series for the summer term of 1984.

Most exciting, yet at the same time disturbing, is the likely future impact of micros on curricula and the role of teachers, as Papert (1980) and more recently Cartwright (1982) have suggested. Cartwright in his conclusion states, 'Whole areas of curriculum will have to be re-evaluated and perhaps even replaced. We will not change the way we teach, but what we teach as well. . . . The implications for classroom teachers are . . . vast. Their role will change significantly. They will become true managers of learners rather than information amplifiers'. In addition, Papert has argued that computers could become potent resources for deschooled communities as envisaged by Illich (1971). The enthusiasm of youngsters for home computers suggests that this prediction is already being proved correct. These points are discussed further in Part V.

Talking points

- *What are the CAL research directions that educational researchers should engage in?*
- *What is the role of CAL for less and more able youngsters?*
- *What will prove to be the most efficacious/liked classroom strategies?*
- *What are the likely roles of Logo, PROLOG and Artificial Intelligence in the humanities?*
- *Is there a role for teacher- and/or pupil-produced software?*[6]
- *Most fundamentally: Will the inertia of our educational system allow these exciting curriculum changes? What strategies could be adopted to enable the changes to take place?*

Notes

1. GAPE was the Geographical Association Package Exchange – now Geographical Association Package Evaluation.
2. Jane Richardson, Brathay and Bob Lewis, St. Martin's College, Lancaster developed these programs with MEP funding.
3. The ESRC Cambridge Group for the History of Population and Social Structure.
4. The Logic Programming group of the Department of Computing at Imperial College London have been investigating the teaching of logic as a computer language (PROLOG) for children.
5. A term used by Hall, D., Kent, W.A. and Wiegand, P. (1982) Geography teaching and computers. *Teaching Geography*, January. It refers to the mainframe era of CAL in the 1970s.
6. Midgley believes so, since his book (1985) includes modules around which teachers can build programs. In this book he explains how he has set about program development.

References and further reading

Blow, F. (1982) History and computers, the joint Schools Council 13–16 and Computers in the Curriculum Project. *Teaching History* **33**, June.

Broderick, W.R. and Lovatt, K.F. (1974) Havering computer managed learning system. *SSRC Newsletter* **25**.

Cartwright, G. (1982) *Educational Computing in the Distant Future* (Mimeo).

Cotterell, A. (1983) Computer programs for teaching economics, *Economics*, Spring.

Ennals, R. (Forthcoming) *History and Computing.* Ellis Horwood.

Fox, P. (1984) *List of Geography Microcomputer Software.* Geographical Association.

Francis, J. (1983) *Microcomputers and Teaching History.* Longman.

Golby, M. (1982) Microcomputers and the primary curriculum. In Garland, R. (ed.) *Microcomputers and children in the primary school.* The Falmer Press.

Gordon, P. (1984) *Purpose and Planning in the Humanities Curriculum.* An inaugural lecture. University of London Institute of Education.

Historical Association (1979) *Computers in Secondary School History Teaching* No. 40.

Hoyle, E. (1983) Computers and education. A solution in search of a problem. In Megarry, J. et al. (ed.) *The World Year Book of Education 1982/83 Computers and Education.*

Illich, I. (1971) *Deschooling Society.* Calder and Boyars.

Kelley, A.C. (1970) The economics of teaching — the role of TIPS. In Kelly, A.V. (ed.) (1984) *Microcomputers and the Curriculum.* Harper and Row.

Kemmis, S. (1976) *The Educational Potential of computer assisted learning: qualitative evidence about student learning.* UEA CARE.

Kent, W.A. (ed.) (1983) *Geography Teaching and the Micro.* Longman.

Kent, W.A. (ed.) (1984) The process of software development for geography in the UK. In Haubrich, H. (ed.) *Perception of People and Places Through Media* Vol 2. Geographical Education Commission, IGU.

Killbery, I. (1984) Not just geography. In Watson, D. (ed.) *Exploring Geography with Microcomputers.* CET.

Midgley, H. with Walker, D. (1985) *Microcomputers in Geography Teaching.* Hutchinson.

Oakeshott, P. (1982) *Microcomputers in Schools — A Market Overview.* Publishers Association.

Papert, S. (1980) *Mindstorms: Children, Computers and Powerful Ideas.* Harvester Press.

Randall, K. (1984) *Microcomputers and Teaching Economics.* Longman.
Schurer, K. (1984) Population history, microcomputers and education. *ESRC Newsletter* **52**, June.
Shepherd, I. et al. (1980) *Computer Assisted Learning in Geography.* CET with the GA.
Taylor, J.L. and Walford, R. (1978) *Learning and the Simulation Game.* Open University Press.
Teaching History (1982) June, No. 33.
Turner, D. (1982) Computer assisted learning in history, *Teaching History* June, No. 33.
Walker, D. (1981) Educational computing and geography. In Walford, R. (ed.) *Signposts for Geography Teaching.* Longman.
Watson, D. (ed.) (1984a) *Exploring Geography with Microcomputers.* CET.
Watson, D. (ed.) (1984b) Microcomputers in Secondary Education — a perspective with particular reference to the humanities. In Kelly, A.V. (ed.) *Microcomputers and the Curriculum.*
Wiegand, P. (1984) Listening at the classroom keyhole. In Watson, D. (ed.) *Exploring Geography with Microcomputers.* CET.

Program sources

History

Choice, Census Analysis, Campaign: Longman
Suffragettes, Village: Computers in the Curriculum Project
Castles, Spanish Main, Saqqara, Amarna: Ginn
Sir: British Library
Quarry Bank 1851: Heinemann
Drake, Joel: not published
Adel: school produced

Geography

Profile, Geobase, Histo: MEP funded
Puddle, Rice, Farm, Route, Growth, Welf, Mine: Longman
Climate: Heinemann
Slope Measurement: Hutchinson
Holiday 1 and 2, Cities 1 and 2: Nelson
Map Skills 1 and 2: Cambridge

Economics
Intrad, Circular, Flow of Income, Cobweb, Credit, Multsc, Agcom 1 and 2, Slant, Maxpro, Fiscal, Monpol: Longman
Running the British Economy, UKMCR1: Heriot-Watt

Business Studies
Paraffin File: BP Educational Service
Sixgam: Pitman

Interdisciplinary
Rail, Demog, Canal, Mill, Cosben: Longman
Query, Quest: Chiltern Advisory Unit

Ashley Kent is a lecturer at the University of London Institute of Education. He has taught in various schools and now has a keen professional interest in computer assisted learning.

UNIT 16

SCIENCE EDUCATION

Clive Opie

This unit discusses:

- *reasons for using microcomputers in science education*
- *sources of software*
- *using the microcomputer in the classroom*
- *using a microcomputer for the purpose of simulation*
- *using a microcomputer as a monitoring/control unit*
- *the future — microcomputer or microprocessor?*

Reasons for using microcomputers

Although details of the potential uses of microcomputers have been given, it is worth noting some of them again with reference to their use in science teaching. They can:

(a) perform complex calculations extremely quickly;
(b) provide a means of displaying experimental data in a number of formats, a graphic display being probably the most interesting of these;
(c) provide interactive simulations of experiments either impossible (e.g. manufacture of ammonia) or normally difficult (e.g. Young's experiment) in the classroom;

(d) monitor a variety of parameters, e.g. voltage, current, pH, temperature, light, time intervals, radioactive decay and pressure, from a range of science experiments, and also act as a storage unit for any relevant data from such experiments;
(e) be used to control external equipment.

Talking point

- *Consider the points above and try to formulate at least four examples in science for each, where you feel a microcomputer could play an important role. It is likely that your examples will overlap in some areas.*

Sources of software

A couple of years ago anyone wishing to use microcomputers in their science teaching would have been hard pressed to name more than a dozen sources of what might be reasonably described as usable software. Today the array of software provides the newcomer with such a vast range of material to investigate that it is extremely difficult to know where to start looking. However, if you are to exploit the microcomputer in your science teaching, then this mass of software and its literature must be sifted through.

There is no easy way out of the problem but the following guidelines might help:

1. Be clear in your own mind that the use of a microcomputer will help your teaching of a particular science topic. Be certain you are using the microcomputer because it is providing something that other media cannot. It is amazing what overhead projectors, videos etc. can achieve. (Examples of some of the software that I have either used or seen used to great effect in science teaching are outlined later.)
2. Check with your own establishment if software suitable to your needs already exists. This can save you an immense amount of time looking through software catalogues. You should also find out if funds are available to buy any software should you find some.

3. To find your software look at the main distributors of science software, which are Longmans, Heinemann, and Edward Arnold. The December 1983 issue of the *School Science Review*, the quarterly publication of the ASE, started providing software reviews. This is now a common feature and one which a science teacher would be advised to browse through. Several other software houses also produce materials for science.
4. Once you have found a piece of software that will suit your needs, check that it is available for the microcomputer that you have to work with. Until the advent of the BBC Microcomputer most software in Britain was written either for the RML 380Z, Commodore Pet or Apple microcomputers. Most of this latter software is being, or has been, rewritten for the BBC machine. Where you find statements such as 'not yet published' or 'coming soon' you would do well, if things are urgent or important, to contact the company concerned. Such is the speed of development in this field that catalogues can be out of date by the time they are published.
5. If at all possible, and it usually is, preview the software before you purchase it. This will give you the chance to check if the program will meet your needs. It is possible to preview all published material, from the main suppliers of software, at any of the Microelectronics Education Programme (MEP) Regional Centres. Your local Teachers' Centre is also likely to have some software which you can look at. Do not be surprised if the software does not ideally fit your requirements: you will be very lucky if it does. Previewing software is undoubtedly the most time-consuming suggestion I have to offer. However, your time will be wisely spent, as only then can you be reasonably confident that the software is a worthwhile investment.

A checklist to help in choosing software has been produced (Wellington 1984). This has some extremely useful suggestions.

Using the microcomputer in the science classroom

Spending time on choosing your software is important. But as much consideration and attention must be given to the use of the software in the classroom. The questions you need to ask yourself are:

1. Do I need the use of several micrcomputers or will a single one be sufficient? If I need a number of microcomputers will I be able to get the use of them? Are there enough power points in the room?

2. If I have to use a single microcomputer, do all the pupils need to be able to see the screen at the same time? If the answer is yes, then will they be able to?
3. Is the software really suitable for the class that I am teaching? If you are using a piece of software available in your establishment, and you teach more than one class in any one year, it could be that what works for one class will have disastrous consequences in another.
4. Do I need any additional material, e.g. work cards? This could be necessary either to use the software effectively or to keep those not using the microcomputer actively engaged in some worthwhile exercise, probably related to the software.
5. Do my pupils need training in the use of the microcomputer? If the answer is yes, then what training do I need to provide? You will probably best find the answers to these questions by talking to the teaching staff in your establishment. Do not rely wholly on the views of your class — they will often claim to be able to cope with far more than they actually can.

Talking point

- *Plan and execute a lesson where you are going to use a piece of commercial software.*
- *Having completed the lesson ask yourself what might have helped to improve the lesson. Then, if possible, try to implement any changes you decide upon and see if the lesson is improved.*

Having considered how you obtain and implement the use of your software let me give a short review of two packages that I have used. Both have been used as revision pieces and I will reserve discussion of other areas of software that I have outlined in my preview until later.

Program name: ELEMNT
Suppliers: Longman Micro Software

This is a competitive game intended to review the properties of some elements and their compounds. You are provided with a rough description of a mystery element and a points total of 200. To ascertain its identity you can ask for various pieces of information on it or its compounds. Asking each question subtracts from your points total and the amount subtracted is dependent on the question and the usefulness of its answer. The aim is to guess the identity of your element with the minimum loss of points.

I have used this software with immense success with A-level students, and with less success with a good O-level set. The reason for this is simply that a number of the elements in the software package had not been covered in the O-level syllabus.

Program name: Titrations
Suppliers: System Software

The software provides revision material for the calculations resulting from acid/base and acid/carbonate titrations. Such calculations can be computer generated or stem from pupils' own titration results. It has very useful prompts for incorrect answers which give progressively more help.

I have only seen this software in use with a fifth year CSE/O-level group. The general feeling from the pupils was that the program was very useful.

Simulations and the use of microcomputers

Within science teaching there are many occasions where a microcomputer can be used to extremely good effect; for instance where an experiment is very difficult or impossible to carry out in a school environment for practical reasons. Examples of such occasions across the science curriculum are: in chemistry, rates of fast reactions and industrial manufacture, e.g. sulphuric acid; in biology, enzyme kinetics and pollution experiments, e.g. pond ecology; and in physics, mass spectrometry, and Young's experiment.

In such cases microcomputer simulations can be valuable. They eliminate the inherent difficulties of the experimental set-up while still being able to extract all the valuable educational points from it. Here is a software example for each of the areas indicated above:

Rates of reactions
Program name: DECOMP
Suppliers: Longman Micro software

This program studies the rate of decomposition of hydrogen peroxide. You can vary the concentration and volume of hydrogen peroxide, the temperature at which the reaction takes place and the catalyst used for the reaction. The last variant allows a comparison between organic and inorganic catalysts, with astounding results. Good graphical displays of rates of reaction are given, allowing visual interpretation of what is going on. Some of the reactions can take less than a pico-second so, clearly, trying to monitor them in the school laboratory would be impossible.

Manufacture of sulphuric acid

Program name: CONTCT
Suppliers: Longman Micro Software

This program invites you to produce sulphuric acid at the lowest possible cost. This game-type software is generally more stimulating to the pupil and generates interest — something we, as teachers, might like to think we can do, but seldom achieve. Being able to vary the conditions for the manufacturing process of temperature, pressure and molar ratio of oxygen to sulphur dioxide allows admirable demonstration of all of Le Chatelier's principles. At the same time the inclusion of a costing exercise and a pollution control check based on conditions used provides the game element of the package. Do not be surprised if industrial espionage becomes rife in the class that you use it with. I have found using this with O- and A-level students very worthwhile, with the game situation being achieved best if they work in groups of four.

Enzyme kinetics

Program name: ENZKIN
Suppliers: Edward Arnold

Practical facilities and laboratory time available to A-level students mean that only a few of the factors that affect the catalytic action of enzymes can be thoroughly investigated. This program allows the student to vary the enzyme, make changes to pH, temperature, enzyme and substrate volumes and incubation time. The speed of the presentation of the results of employing certain conditions is the obvious advantage of using this computer package. The student's notes provide clearly explained information, thought-provoking questions and carefully selected schedules for practical work. These all help to provide the student with the confidence to use the simulations and to derive the maximum benefit from them.

Pollution pond ecology

Program name: POND
Suppliers: Longman Micro Software

Demonstrating the effect of adding pollutant to a pond would be easy if it were not morally and socially unacceptable. So here is another way in which a computer simulation can be used, i.e. to display the effects of pollution without physical damage to any natural pond. The program allows you to vary the quantity of pollution that you add to your pond, and predicts the effects of that addition over several years in terms of the numerical content of the plankton, herbivores and fish. Excellent graphics displays are used. Overfishing can also be studied. The problem admirably highlights the delicate balance that exists in the ecosystem.

Mass spectrometry

Program name: MASPEC
Suppliers: Longman Micro Software

Mass spectrometry is an extremely important tool in analysis work. The cost of a mass spectrometer obviously prohibits its use in schools, who will visit higher educational establishments if they wish to see one in operation. However, the educational value of such equipment is in its data output not its operation. MASPEC provides mass spectral data on a range of samples useful to students at school. It allows them to investigate and eventually identify ions of an unknown sample. It also allows the addition of further samples to the simulation. This program also has uses in chemistry.

Young's experiment

Program name: Young's Slits
Suppliers: Heinemann Computers in Education

This program is produced by Five Ways Software. It provides a dynamic model of Young's experiment, which is an important part of many physics courses and extremely difficult to demonstrate using conventional apparatus. The amplitude and wavelength of the source waves, the separation of the slits and the position of convergence can all be varied and the results discussed.

Talking point

- *Examine the software of at least two pieces of science simulation material. Try to get some new material if possible but if not then use those given above. Write down your views on the software you study in terms of:*
  (a) Its overall presentation, including teacher/student notes and work sheets if provided.
  (b) Whether you feel it would be useful in the classroom, and if so how you would use it, i.e. with the whole class as a demo, or small groups or individually.
  (c) The classes that you feel it would be most suited to.

Monitoring control with a microcomputer

One of the more interesting and useful attributes of a microcomputer in science teaching is its ability to monitor conditions of experiments and to control external equipment. Such facilities, although always available with microcomputers, have only really become apparent since the arrival of the BBC Microcomputer. This is because all the necessary interfaces to do such work are standard features of the BBC machine. Removing the need to purchase or build anything except the circuitry to interface your experiment has stimulated development in this area. Unfortunately the software and interfacing, which is still required, has still to be done by the practising teacher unless relatively costly interfaces are bought. However, the relevant information to produce the necessary home-made hardware is now more readily available and the software is also often provided.

This is one area where *knowing a little programming could be useful.* Commercial software is copyright and often uses machine code, so that it is difficult to alter to your exact needs. However, home-made software is likely to be in BASIC and therefore easily altered to your own requirements if you know how. This means that not only can you interface your equipment, but you can manipulate the display of the data you are handling so that it appears as you want it to.

Using the BBC or any other microcomputer, it is possible to:

(1) Monitor pH, light intensity, temperature and pressure. All these can be measured as varying voltages. Such measurements require the use of an analogue to digital converter (A to D). The BBC Model B has four A to D connections built in as standard, and so is capable of monitoring four voltages at a time. The BBC machine can read the voltage at each A to D every 10 ms. Figure 20 outlines the work carried out by the author (Opie et al. 1984).
(2) Monitor pulses of voltage. For instance, in radioactive decay experiments a disintegration can be used to produce a logic (5V) signal, or pulse. This in turn can be fed into the BBC Microcomputer User Port where it can be detected (Opie et al. 1984) Figure 21 shows the arrangement.
(3) Control equipment, e.g. heaters, lights, pneumatic or hydraulic valves, motors. The User Port of the BBC Microcomputer can send as well as receive logic signals. If these signals are in turn used to switch on a relay through a transistor circuit then the equipment can be controlled. Figure 22 shows the idea.

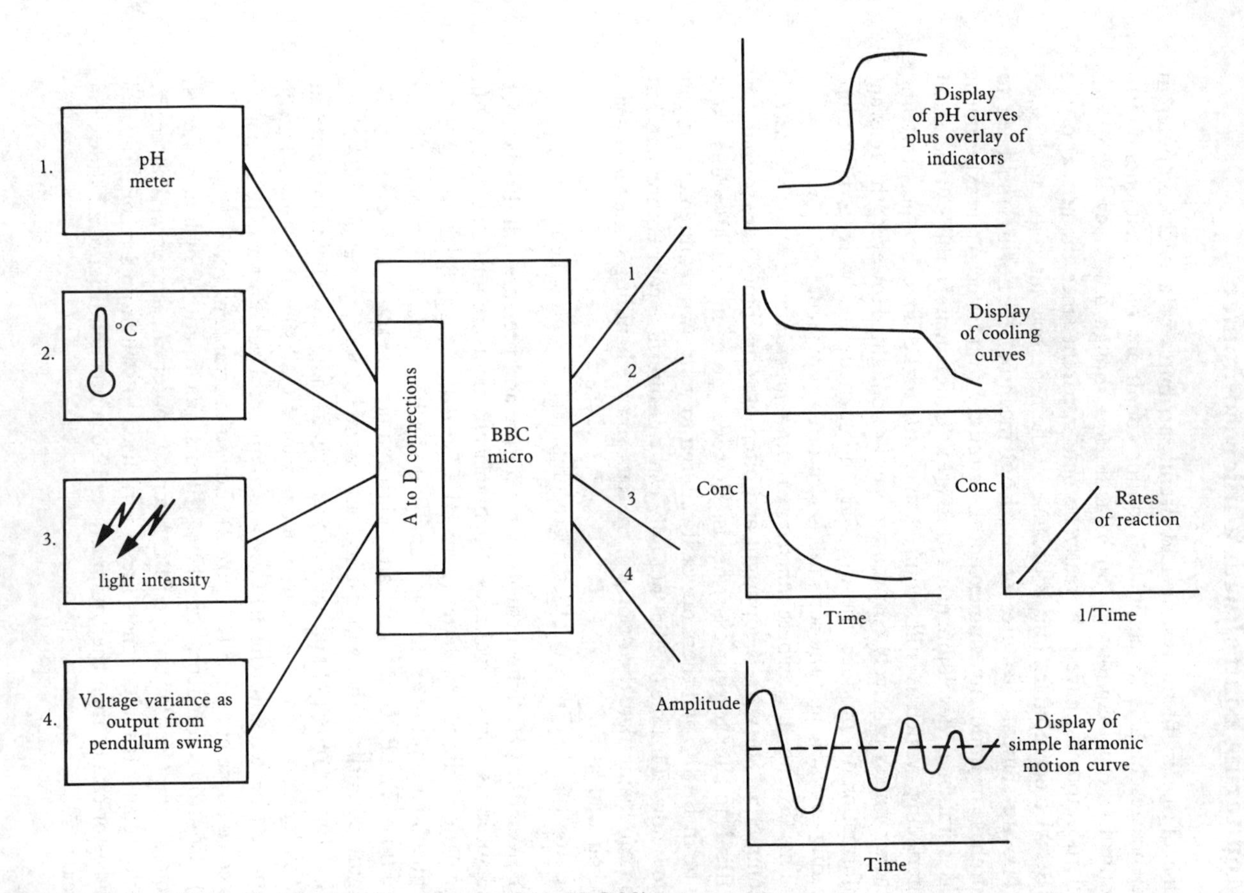

Figure 20. Possible uses of the A to D converter of the BBC Micro

It is impossible to indicate all the sources of information in this area but the following list will provide you with enough material to get started. You will inevitably find references to other sources of relevant information through reading these.

1. MEP publications MEP has sponsored the preparation of a number of articles all related to computers and control. Many of these are the result of Curriculum Development Projects and Opie et al. (1984) have produced a very useful introduction to this field. Their report covers everything the beginner needs to know to start monitoring/control work with the BBC, Commodore Pet, Sinclair or Apple microcomputers. It also provides all the relevant details to allow experimentation with all of the ideas expressed above. However, this is not the only work on control and various other articles are available from MEP. MEP centres also hold the main hardware/software examples presently available for control. (A new BBC Control BASIC should be available by the time this is published, which will make using the BBC Microcomputer for this work even easier.)

2. Electronic System News This is a half-yearly journal published by the Institution of Electrical Engineers. It is free to educational establishments and provides a range of information for those interested in electronics and computing. Some of this information is ideally suited to science teachers wishing to exploit their computer facilities for control work. It also gives details of current technology/electronic materials and courses.

3. Acorn User Finding a commercial publication that provides information on control is not easy. However, this (and the next) publication have produced details on interface circuits and programs to use with your hardware. A most interesting article in the March 1983 issue is 'Making and using a light pen for the BBC'. The publication is biased towards the BBC Microcomputer, but as this is likely to be the standard machine in British schools for several years and as the ideas can generally be re-orientated for use with other microcomputers, this is not really a disadvantage.

4. Educational Computing This monthly publication reviews and presents articles on all aspects of computers in education. The February 1983 to November 1983 issues provide a month-by-month build up of knowledge on computers and control. Although a little technical at times, this is worth looking at. Other articles have appeared which describe circuits of use to the beginner. It's worth subscribing to.

5. Association for Science Education (ASE) The *School Science Review*, the quarterly journal of the ASE, often has details of computer software or hardware related to science teaching.

6. MUSE The initials stand for Microcomputers Users in Secondary Education but its title belies its operations, as it caters for microcomputer users in all areas of school education. It publishes a quarterly journal, *Computers in Schools*, which at times (e.g. October 1982 and April 1983) contains information related to the area of control/monitoring. It also publishes a yearly report – *MUSE Report*. The October 1982 issue entitled 'School microcomputers: Interfacing to the real world', is worth looking at.

7. Books There are many books in this area. To help you on your way I have found the following sources of literature useful: Sparkes (1982); a BP Educations Service/MEP joint publication (1982); Bettridge (1984); Johnson et al. (1984).

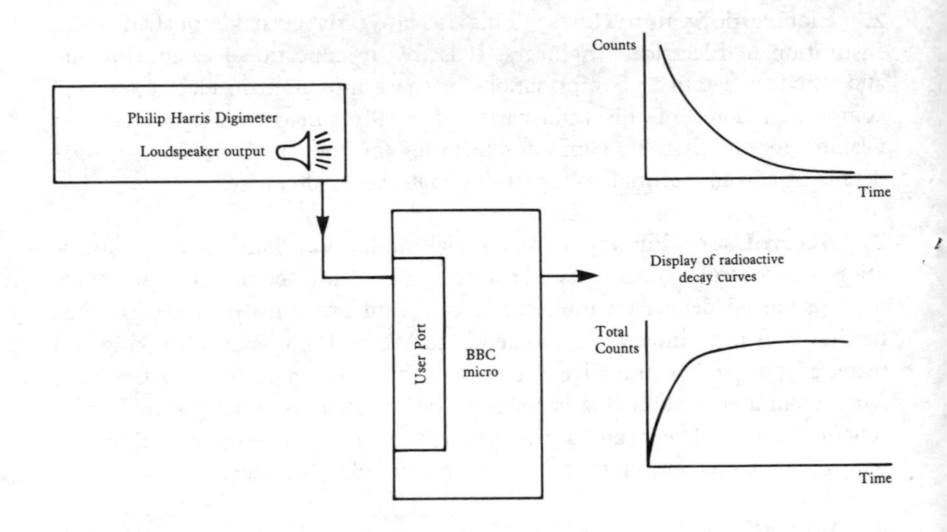

Figure 21. Using the User Port on the BBC Micro to monitor radioactive decay

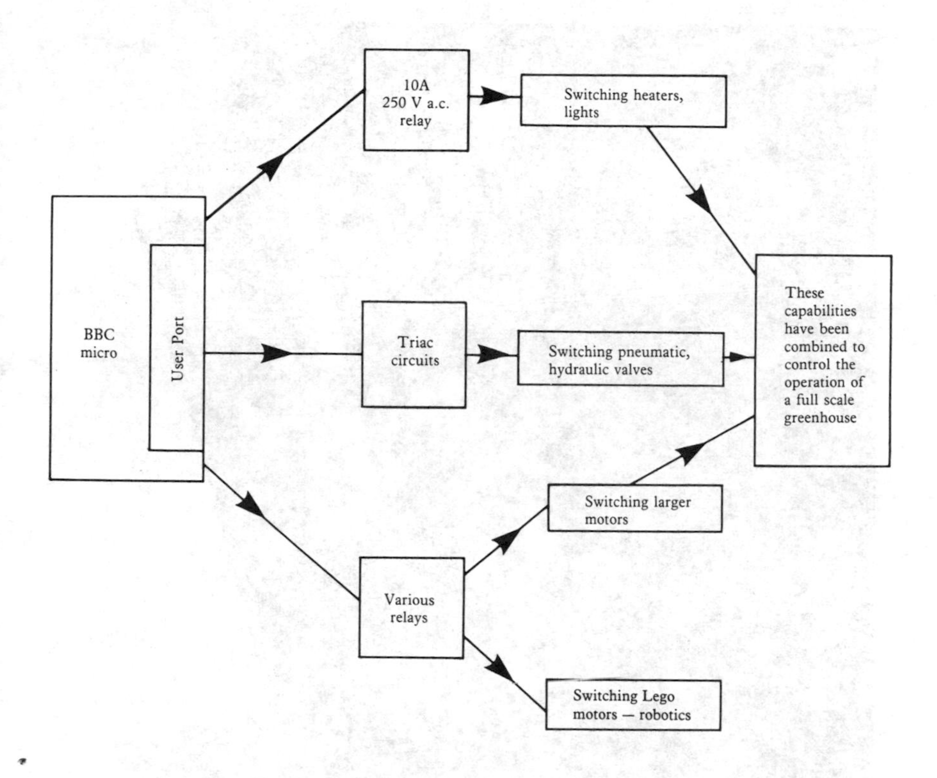

Figure 22. Capabilities of the BBC machine's User Port

The future — microcomputer or microprocessor?

Since about the beginning of 1983 there has been considerable interest in the development of microprocessor-based units which interface to a microcomputer. The reason for this is that it gives teachers the facility to link scientific experiments to their computer without the need to build anything. With teachers' workloads, this is an obvious advantage to those who would like to explore more deeply into control or monitoring techniques, but do not have the time or know-how.

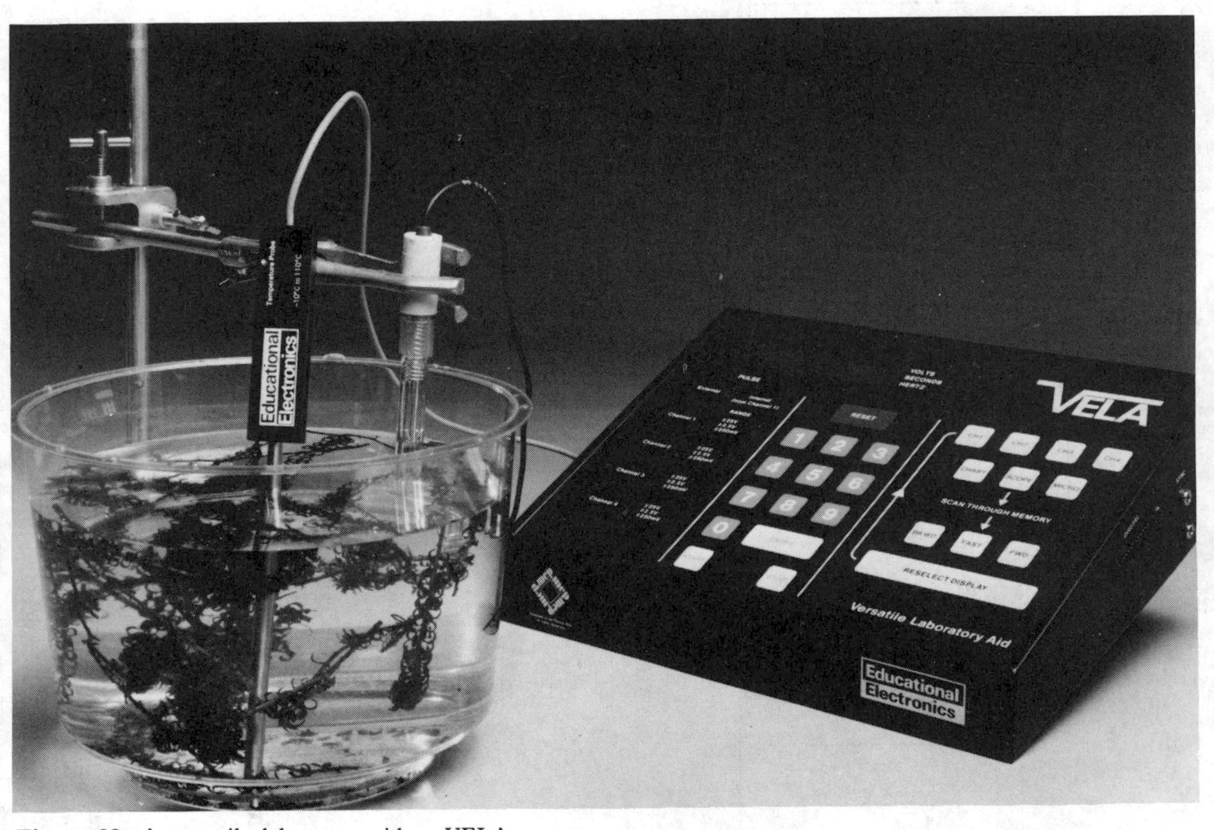

Figure 23. A versatile laboratory aid — VELA

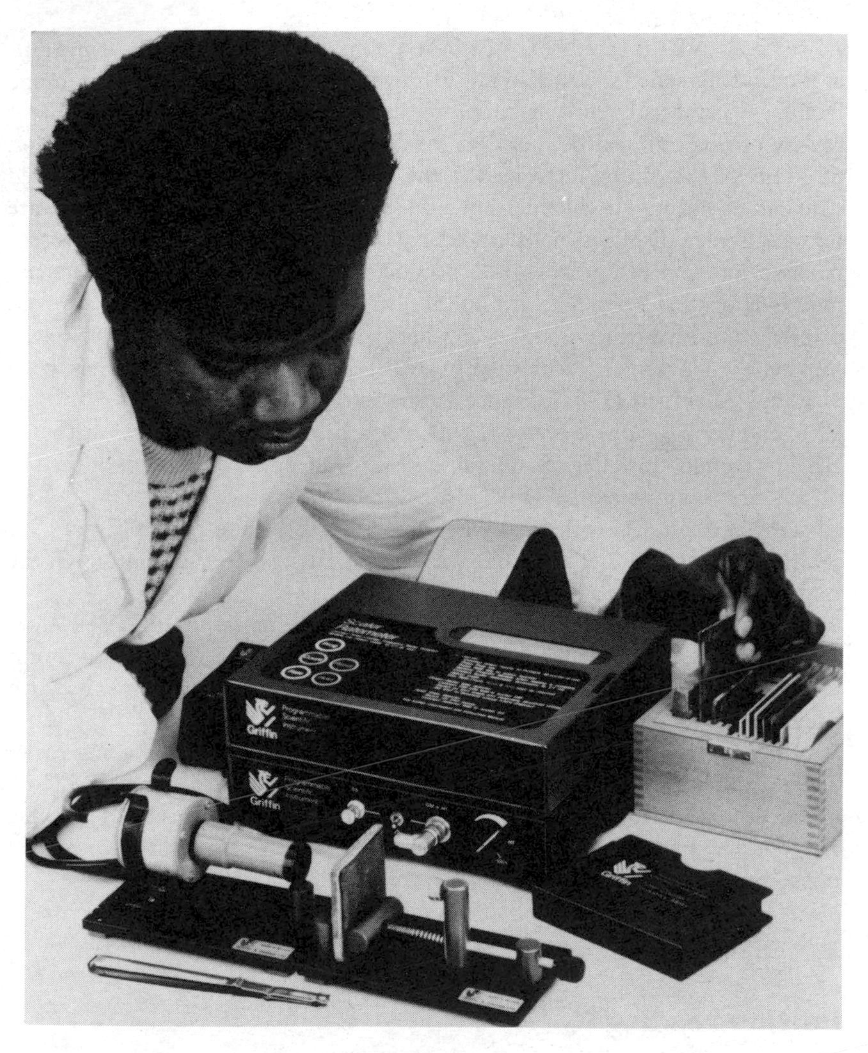

Figure 24. Another versatile laboratory aid – GIPSI

Examples of such units are:

1. VELA VELA stands for VErsatile Laboratory Aid. It is in its own right a monitoring/control unit having its own built-in programs and storage facility. It is robustly built making it useful for work in the field. An excellent review of this unit can be found in the *School Science Review*, No. 230, Vol. 65. The VELA can be interfaced to the BBC Microcomputer so that stored data can be output via the micro to a screen. Unfortunately, present software for such screen display is not particularly exciting and in my opinion this area needs a lot of development. The producers of the VELA consider its use mainly as a stand-alone machine and in this capacity it is excellent. However, pupils are motivated by pictures and hence my feeling is that there is a need for some good screen display software. A review of the VELA has been written by Lambert (1983). Figure 23 shows the unit in use.
2. Cambion Interface System This interface unit makes control with the BBC or Commodore Pet considerably easier. A detailed discussion of the use of this unit is provided by Opie et al. (1984).
3. Griffin Gipsi As with the VELA, this is a stand-alone system (Figure 24) which will interface with the BBC Microcomputer. I feel that although the unit is reasonably priced, its add-ons are expensive.
4. Unilab microcomputer interface This unit is similar to the VELA in terms of its functions. However, the significant difference is that it is a unit made to be interfaced with the BBC whereas VELA contains its own programs in its own ROM memory.
5. Interspec and Interbeeb These are two interfaces aimed at making easier electrical monitoring and control with the Spectrum or Sinclair ZX-81 microcomputers (Interspec) and BBC Microcomputer (Interbeeb). Both these are good value for money. Further details on the use of this unit are provided in the report by Opie et al. (1984)

Further reading

Ball, D. (ed.), Tallon, B. and Tomley, D. (1983) Microcomputers and biology teaching, *School Science Review* **65**, 231, p.255.
Gill, R.A. (1984) Microcomputer simulation of enzyme kinetic behaviour, *School Science Review* **65**, 233, p.670.

Harris, F.O. (1983) Computer programs in chemistry — the present and the future, *School Science Review* **65**, 231, p.318.
Margham, J.P. and Hale, W.G. (1983) *BASIC Biology: An introduction to biological computing*. London: Collins.
Moore, J.L. and Thomas, F.H. (1983) Computer simulation of experiments, *School Science Review* **64**, 229, p.641.
Sparkes, R.A. (1984) *The BBC Microcomputer in Science Teaching*. Colchester: Hutchinson Educational.
Wellington, J. (1984) Aid to intuition, *Times Educational Supplement* 25 May, p.42.
Johnson, R., Procter, C. and Reglinski, A. (1984) *Interfacing and Control on the BBC Micro*. London: National Extension College.
Opie, C.T. (ed.), Boden, B., Harris, K., Horsley, M., Porter, P., Thorpe, G. and Walton, J. (1984) *Computers and Control.* MEP Curriculum Development Project.
Lambert, A. (1983) VELA — a microprocessor based laboratory instrument, *School Science Review* **65**, 230, p.38.

Clive Opie is Head of Computer Education at King Ecgbert Comprehensive School in Sheffield. In recent years he has been heavily involved in initial and in-service education for teachers, and in developing curriculum material for computer studies and awareness courses.

PART FIVE

INFORMATION TECHNOLOGY AND THE CURRICULUM

UNIT 17

WHAT IS INFORMATION TECHNOLOGY?

The words 'information technology' are being used more and more by writers, journalists, educationalists and television presenters. This unit sets out to explain these words, and offer possible definitions. It then goes on to describe some of the present and future manifestations of the new technology in people's everyday lives.

Later units discuss the uses and possible effects of information technology in both education and society. Finally, speculations about its effect on schooling and the curriculum are offered in Unit 20.

Attempting to define IT

The umbrella definition of information technology generally offered is usually something like: the application of new technology to the creation, storage, processing and communication of information. This is unlikely to carry much meaning for the uninitiated. What is 'new technology'? What does the 'processing of information' involve? Haven't people been creating and communicating information for centuries? The last question is probably the best starting point. People *have* been creating, storing and distributing information for centuries. The use of stone tablets, papyrus scrolls, smoke signals, the printing press, morse code, semaphore, and the telephone, are all examples of information technology. They have been followed, and added to, in this century by the use of satellites, cables, fibre-optics, and computers.

The main difference between new information technology and the old is the *speed* at which information can now be collected, transformed, distributed and retrieved. This in turn has catalysed the almost exponential increase in the *amount* of information now 'held' – in journals, papers, books, and magnetic media such as tapes and disks.

These developments are due almost exclusively to the growth of one technology: microelectronics.

Converging technologies

Within the last forty years, the handling of information has gradually moved away from the use of *mechanical* means towards the use of electronic devices. Handwritten and hand-delivered letters, paper in filing cabinets, mechanical sorting devices, mechanical adding machines, cash, questionnaires with boxes to tick for collecting information: all these mechanical media for collecting, sorting and distributing information are still with us. But they are now accompanied, and sometimes replaced, by electronic media and systems. Electronic mail, electronic transfer of funds (instead of cash), calculators and computers, videotex, word-processing, and magnetic databases now exist side by side with more traditional information technology.

All these devices involve *electronics*. There are three main electronic devices: transistors, capacitors and resistors. All have been used for the last thirty years. Until quite recently (about 1964) each of these devices was made separately and then wired together to make an electronic circuit. This can still be done. But nowadays electronic circuits are commercially produced by making and connecting all the devices on a tiny wafer of silicon in *one continuous process*. These tiny integrated circuits on thin silicon wafers are called 'chips'. The science of designing, making and using these chips is called *microelectronics*. There are two main types of chip: processing chips and memory chips. Chips used for processing data are called microprocessors. They can be designed to carry out arithmetic and logic processes, or to *control* the flow of data. Microprocessors are used in microcomputers – but they are also used in washing machines, calculators, robots, cameras, watches, sewing machines, and so on. The list is constantly growing. Memory chips are designed to store data, including computer programs.

Microelectronics can be viewed as a sort of 'umbrella' technology covering and influencing two other technologies: *computing* and *communications*. Computing involves microelectronics as one of its parts or foundations – but the computing industry involves an awful lot more. The technology of computing involves: designing and analysing systems; producing software; collecting and coding data; producing clear and readable information; developing new hardware; and so on. Computing is a slightly older technology than microelectronics. Today's computers of all sizes contain one or more microprocessors, e.g. the BBC Micro has a processing chip called the Motorola 6502, and ROM and RAM chips. But computing existed well before the first chip was ever made.

The oldest aspect of IT is *communications*. Modern forms of communication are often called *telecommunications*. This is likely to involve at least three parts: telephones, television and radio waves, and fibre-optics:

1. *Telephones*: One French expert estimated that in 1970 there were about 200 million telephones in the world. By the year 2000 there may be 2 billion — by 2020 A.D. he forecast a total of 10 billion telephones worldwide — more 'phones than people. If the telephone network does spread this widely, computer terminals will be linked by telephone throughout the world to form global computer networks. The number of computer terminals may one day equal the number of telephones.
2. *Radio waves*: Radio waves travel through air, or empty space, at the speed of light ('television waves' are simply shorter wavelength radio waves). They are ideal for sending messages, including messages from one computer to another. Satellites are now used to help the passage of radio waves from one part of the globe to another.
3. *Fibre optics*: The latest development in communications is the *optical fibre*. This is a strand of glass only as wide as a human hair, but often several kilometres long. Light or laser messages can be transmitted along these fibres. The message is first *coded* into binary form. A pulse of light represents ONE; no pulse represents ZERO. At the receiving end the pulses are decoded. Optical fibres can carry over 40 million bits of data every second — at the speed of light. The fibres are collected together (perhaps 24 in all) into a narrow cable.

Telephones, radio waves and satellites, and fibre-optic cables will form the communications systems of the future. The three industries of microelectronics, computing and communications will form a tripod for the 'Information Technology' age. The convergence of these three technologies will vastly improve the *storage*, *processing* and *communication* of information. But what about information itself? Why should information be so important?

Information

This section discusses perhaps the two most important aspects of information: the huge growth in the amount of information, commonly termed the 'information explosion'; and the predicted importance of information as a key resource in the economies of the future, the so-called 'information society'. Both points will be discussed briefly here, with suggestions for almost endless further reading at the end of the unit. But first, a few comments on the nature of 'information' itself are necessary.

The nature of information

The study of information, and information theory, has become almost a discipline in itself, starting perhaps with Shannon and Weaver (1949). Some of the main points about information which might be useful to people involved in education can only be sketched here. Firstly, the distinction between information and data is worth making. Data provide the raw material, the basic building bricks, for information. The word 'data' is the plural form of *datum*, the Latin word for 'fact'. Datum is defined as that which is given or granted, i.e. 'something known or assumed as fact, and made the basis of reasoning or calculation' (Oxford English Dictionary). In other words, data on their own carry no *meaning* — they may be a collection of measurements, a string of symbols, or a table of facts and figures. Data only provide *information* after some *meaning* or interpretation has been attached to them, i.e. information can be seen as data in a meaningful and useful form. A debate exists as to whether information exists as an entity in itself (for example, people talk about the 'information content' of the universe) or whether information can only exist inside the human brain, as Illich (1975) suggests. The debate is perhaps an important one for education since it partly determines one's view of the learning process and of education itself. Is information actively created by each individual or is it a ready-made entity to be passively absorbed and acquired? The problem of defining information, and the philosophical issues surrounding it, must be ignored here although suggestions for further study are given at the end of the unit. One important point *will* be followed up in a later unit. This is the idea that there is some kind of hierarchy in the structure of knowledge, with data and information at the bottom, and knowledge and something called *wisdom* at the top.

The information 'explosion'

This is another label which has become rather hackneyed, so its meaning is worth spelling out in factual terms. The 'flow' of information across the Atlantic Ocean is said to double every four and a half years. This flow began with the telegraph and the telephone and expanded with the growth of satellite communications. Indeed the flow of information is now an industry in itself. The information explosion is usually quantified in terms of the number of articles published in journals and periodicals each year. These show that the exponential growth in information is not new. Between 1920 and 1960, for example, the number of articles on Economics in periodicals increased eight-fold from 5000 to 40,000 each year. The periodical literature in Psychology increased from 30,000 to 90,000 articles per annum. In other words, by 1960, if a person wished to keep abreast of Psychology by being aware of all the published articles, he would need to peruse more than 200 articles *each day*. Clearly this is a ridiculous aim, but it raises the question of what it means to keep 'abreast of one's subject'. Does it mean that 'one's subject' necessarily becomes increasingly narrow? The growth of published literature since 1960 is even more daunting. In medicine, for example, 390,000 articles were published in 1970, i.e. rather more than 1000 each day. This inevitably leads to increasingly narrow specialization. Table 8 shows the growth in published articles in the sixties in a variety of disciplines. You can see that the total number of articles virtually doubled in that decade. This growth is almost certain to continue.

Such a vast expansion in information is bound to raise doubts about our current notion of *subject specialists* in secondary schools. No teacher, or lecturer, can be expected ever to become a subject specialist, let alone remain one for twenty years. To keep abreast of a whole subject or discipline (such as mathematics, physics or biology) is as impossible a task for a school teacher as for a university lecturer. Perhaps teachers should stop pretending (as a small minority do) that they are an *authority* in their discipline and are capable of answering any question posed to them. The vast increase in the amount of information published in any one discipline could foreseeably have two effects on the secondary curriculum. At one extreme it could lead to increasingly narrow subject specialism in the hope that a given teaching specialist could cope with that area. This is undesirable, in my view, as well as highly unlikely in the light of falling roles and reduced resources. On the other hand it may lead to a welcome erosion of the teacher as a subject authority figure: infallible, expert, and all-knowing. Teachers need no longer adopt this role in

the eyes of pupils. No teacher can be expected to know the whole of physics and chemistry in the sense of knowing its *information content*. Teaching strategies may therefore evolve in two ways:
(a) by increasing the emphasis on the skills and concepts of a discipline, whilst de-emphasizing information content and factual recall as primary aims;
(b) by adapting the teacher-pupil relationship in the classroom to make it clear that no one individual can be aware of the whole of the information content of a subject and is therefore *not* to be seen as an infallible authority figure – the school 'Mastermind' in that specialism.

The effect of exponential information growth on learning and teaching, and the curriculum, is discussed more fully in Unit 20.

Table 8

Number of articles published in periodicals during 1960 and 1970

Subject	1960	1970
Mathematics	15,000	30,000
Physics	75,000	155,000
Civil engineering	15,000	15,000
Mechanical engineering	10,000	20,000
Electrical and electronic engineering	80,000	150,000
Aerospace engineering	35,000	75,000
Industrial engineering	15,000	15,000
Chemistry	150,000	260,000
Metallurgy	35,000	50,000
Biology	150,000	290,000
Geosciences	91,000	158,000
Agriculture	150,000	260,000
Medicine	220,000	390,000
Psychology	15,000	30,000
Other subjects	929,000	1,882,000
Totals	1,985,000	3,780,000

Source: Heaps, H.S. (1978) *Information Retrieval – computational and theoretical aspects.* Academic Press, New York, p.3.

Information as a resource

Although the information explosion is not new, its scale and importance have rapidly increased because of the growth and convergence of both computing and communications. On the one hand, widely available computing power, i.e. information processing, enables far more information to be *produced* from its raw material, data. On the other hand, modern electronic communications allow the rapid flow of information and data from one person or institution to another. It has also made information more rapidly and readily *accessible*, for good and for evil (see Lindop 1978)

The growing importance of high-quality, up-to-date information in a modern economy has led to the assertion that information is the fourth major *resource* in any society, along with land, labour and capital (see, for example, Bell 1973). This has led to the notion of an information society or post-industrial era with high-quality information as a dominant commodity. This notion is discussed fully in the next unit, since any such major change in society is bound to influence the education and curriculum within it.

Information technology in action

The use of computers is just one small aspect of information technology. In the same way, the use of computer assisted learning (CAL) is just one example of the potential use of information technology in education. Information technology may involve, and be involved in, any of the following:

videodisks	fibre optics	radio and television
video cameras	robotics	control technology
computer networks	satellite communications	telephones
videotex	weapons and warfare	the electronic office

The list is almost endless. It would be impossible to discuss all the instances and applications of information technology here, and further reading is suggested at the end of the unit. For the purposes of this unit four examples are discussed briefly here, all of which may have an increasing influence on education. They are *videotex, computer networks, fibre-optics* and *videodisks.*

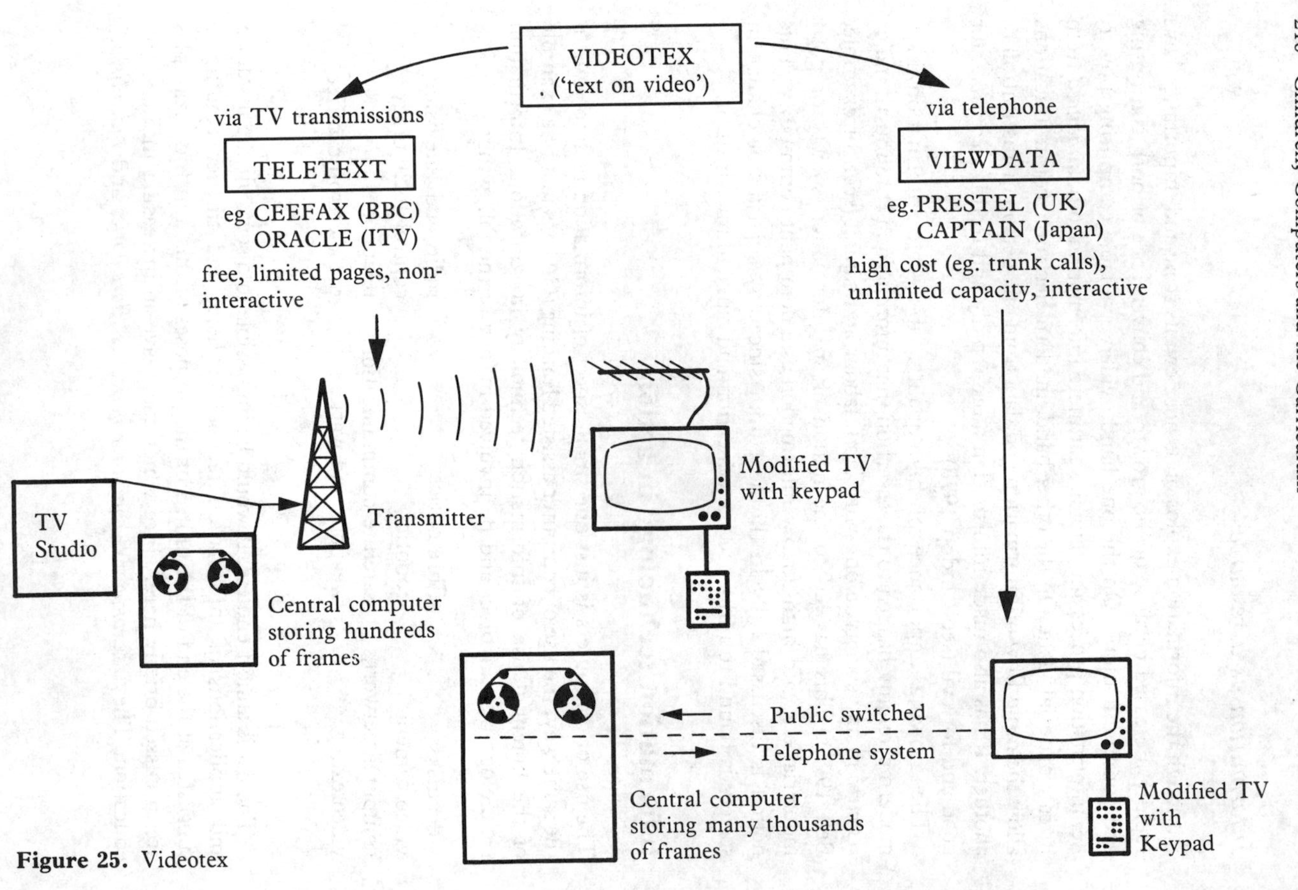

Figure 25. Videotex

Videotex

The general name usually given to information which can be displayed on a television screen is videotex (i.e. text on video). There are two different types: (Figure 25)

Viewdata With this system information can be called up from a large computer by telephone, and displayed on a television screen. The best example is Prestel, British Telecom's version, which is explained fully later. Viewdata is a two-way *interactive* system. All the information is stored in the central computer in a *database*. A viewdata user can interrogate this database to get to, or *access* the exact information she wants.

Teletex This is the name given to information which is sent from a TV transmitter, received by your television aerial, and displayed on your television screen. Two examples are CEEFAX ('see facts') on BBC, and ORACLE on ITV. These are both one-way or non-interactive types of videotex. You can receive information, but you cannot send it back. You can call for a particular 'page' of information using a keypad.

The main advantage of teletext is that it is free — once you have a proper keypad and television. On the other hand, Prestel can be quite expensive to use. Prestel was invented and developed in Britain, through the British Post Office (now British Telecom). It is simply a *computer-based information service*. To use it you need three things: a special Prestel television set, or an adaptor on your present television; a telephone, and a jack-plug to connect it to the television; and a keypad, which looks a bit like a pocket calculator.

Prestel can also be used by 'connecting' a telephone to a microcomputer, e.g. the BBC Micro, with a special device called an *acoustic coupler* (Figure 26). By pressing the right buttons on the keypad or keyboard you get in touch with the central Prestel computer via the telephone line. Pressing another key will give you an index of all the information available. Hundreds of thousands of pages of information are stored on Prestel. To help find the page you want a free directory is supplied to users. A user can then access any Prestel page by keying-in the full number, or can browse through various pages, pressing a single key each time. Every Prestel user has to pay a rental charge *and* the cost of the telephone calls. This means that many users make a note of the page numbers they use most, just to save time and their phone bill! Some pages actually cost extra money if you use them (they have a 'frame charge'). Information is supplied to Prestel by *Information Providers*. These people rent pages from British Telecom and display their information on those pages. Information is provided on travel, farming, imports and exports, hotels, the law, houses, business news, the world's economies, theatres, cinemas, currency exchange rates, share prices, even the weather. The use of Prestel as a source of information in education is therefore almost unlimited. Its educational use, as an example of a database, is discussed in Unit 19. It is worth noting, finally, that computer programs can be disseminated using Prestel. They can be received and recorded on either tape or disk — this is often referred to as *telesoftware.*

Figure 26. Prestel in use. (Photograph reproduced by courtesy of Prestel British Telecommunications plc)

Computer networks Computers and other devices which use computer-coded data, can be connected together to form *networks*. Using a network, coded data can be sent from one device to another. The signals are digital signals, or on/off pulses. These signals can be sent along wires, telephone lines, via television transmitters, or along optical fibres. A network of microcomputers can be formed in a room or a house just by linking them with wires or cables. A local area network (e.g. in a large school, factory or university) can be made in a similar way. A wider network can be called a district network; for example a village, town or city linked by telephone lines and possibly cables. Wider still is the national network, and then the international or global network. On these networks data will be sent by telephone line, land or submarine cable, radio waves and satellites. How are these networks used? Here are just two examples:

(a) *The electronic office.* In a large office or company all the electronic devices used can be linked together to form a local data network. Microcomputers, word processors, high-speed printers, mass storage tapes and disks, can all be joined together. Another device in the network will be used to send and receive communications to and from other local, national and international networks.

(b) *Electronic mail.* Using a data network, messages can be sent from one computer terminal to another. The message to be sent is converted to an electronic digital signal, transmitted via a cable, telephone or satellite, and then converted back again at the receiving end. It may be displayed on a television screen for the receiver to read, and then perhaps stored on file or disk. No paper is necessary. This system for sending messages is one type of electronic mail.

The possibilities for computer networks in education, and the education *system*, are huge in number. Administration could be helped by linking schools to LEA offices, and to each other. This could totally change, for example, the dissemination of information and the contact between schools, e.g. by the use of electronic mail. Networks within, and between, schools could also have *direct* educational value. These possibilities are again taken up in Unit 19.

Fibre-optics Optical fibres are very thin strands of glass which are used to carry messages in the form of light pulses, often laser pulses. Glass fibres can be tightly packed together into cables which can carry many messages separately (Figure 27). Glass is cheap, plentiful and light, and this means that cables of optical fibres will be the message-carriers of the future. They are likely to be used in:

- *banking*: sending messages from one bank to another;
- *publishing:* electronic magazines and newspapers, newsletters and advertising could be sent via cable;
- *information services, similar to Prestel:* information could be requested and received from a database using optical cable instead of a telephone line;
- *electronic shopping*: goods could be advertised using a cable network, and the chosen article could be ordered via optical cable.

These are just a few uses for cable networks. They already bring cable television to millions of viewers in the United States who have twenty or thirty channels to choose from. But their main use will be in *two-way* communications – between people, groups, offices, companies, and from a viewer *back* to the television centre! Their potential use in education is almost totally untapped. Larger, possibly national, cable networks could be widely used for 'distance learning' along the lines of the Open University. More local networks could be used for communicating ideas, or swapping information.

Figure 27. Producing an optical fibre thinner than a human hair. (Photograph reproduced by courtesy of Prestel British Telecommunications plc)

Videodisks and lasers Laser beams are now being used to send, receive, store and process information. They have become an essential part of information technology. As well as sending information, lasers can be used to *record* information by writing it onto special disks. A high-power laser burns tiny holes onto the surface of the disk and the information is read from the disk by scanning it with a low-power laser beam.

The picture and sound of a television video can be stored on laser video disk. Inside a videodisk player a laser reads the information. This is converted into a television signal and carried into the aerial socket of a television set.

Laser disks have three big advantages: there is no contact between the playing head and the disk – this means that they should never wear out; they can store huge amounts of information – figures such as '30 encyclopaedias on a single disk' have been quoted; and they can be easily and precisely *controlled*. This latter point is perhaps the most important. Disks that can be controlled and manipulated by the user are called *interactive videodisks*. Video is truly interactive when it offers questions or alternatives, and invites the viewer to choose, ask their own questions or provide answers. The viewer's response determines what follows. This interaction between viewer and video is usually controlled by some sort of computer system, with a computer program offering various branches and routes. Interactive video is still in its infancy — but its use, and influence on patterns, in education is likely to be radical. Existing uses and likely developments of interactive video in education are discussed in Unit 19.

Summary

This unit has attempted to provide a sketch, or rather a Cook's tour, of information technology. It is intended to provide a useful introduction to its meaning and use for people primarily concerned with education.

For those who wish to delve deeper, some readable commentaries are suggested under Further reading — these books in turn will suggest numerous further references on the topic. Indeed, the subject of IT is itself subject to the 'law of exponentially increasing information'.

The applications and manifestations of information technology are almost certain totally to pervade people's lives in the next decade, and will therefore influence education via society. This is the subject of the next unit.

Further reading

1. Two readable introductions to information technology are: *Information Unlimited* by Ian Sommerville (Addison-Wesley, 1983); and *Information Technology* by P. Zorkoczy (Pitman, 1982).
2. Material which can be used in schools, or for other introductory courses, is contained in the last two parts of *Computers and Communication* by Steele, R. and Wellington. J.J. (Blackie, 1985).
3. Those who require more detailed accounts of the 'new information era' might try *The Wealth of Information* by Tom Stonier (Thames Methuen, 1983); and *The coming of post-industrial society: a venture in social forecasting* by David Bell (New York: Basic Books, 1973).
4. People who wish to delve into the rigours of information theory in its original form should read *The mathematical theory of communication* by Shannon, C. and Weaver, W. (Chicago: University of Illinois Press, 1949).

Talking points

- *The views of Ivan Illich on the nature of information are summed up in the following paragraph:*

'The world does not contain any information. It is as it is. Information about it is created in the organism through its interaction with the world. To speak about storage of information outside the human body is to fall into a semantic trap. Books or computers are part of the world. They can yield information when they are looked upon. We move the problem of learning and of cognition nicely into the blind spot of our intellectual vision if we confuse vehicles for potential information with information itself. We do the same when we confuse data for potential decisions with decision itself.'

(*From* Tools for Conviviality, *page 86 (London: Calder and Boyars, 1973))*

- *Do you agree with Illich's view? What implications does such a view have for education? Does the way we conceive 'information' have an effect on the way we view education?*
- ***Here are some definitions of information technology. Which of them carries the most meaning for you?***

- *'... the creation, storage, selection, transformation, and distribution of information'*
- *'... the science of information handling'*
- *'... the coming together of three technologies: microelectronics, computing and communications'*
- *'... the scientific, technological and engineering disciplines and the management techniques used in information handling and processing; their applications; computers and their interaction with men and machines; and associated social, economic and cultural matters.' (UNESCO)*
- *'Information Technology is concerned with systems for the creation, acquisition, processing, storage, retrieval, selection, transformation, dissemination and use of vocal, pictorial, textural and numerical information. Current systems typically utilize a microelectronics based combination of computing and telecommunications which may, in turn, act in conjunction with other technologies to multiply their effects.' (CGLI National Advisory Committee for IT. June 1983)*
- *Ergonomics Unit, University College, London: Information Technology is 'The production, transformation, storage and transmission by electronic means of information in the form of representations.' (Information Technology: a 'core' for YTS, Report to MSC, April 1983)*

UNIT 18

INFORMATION TECHNOLOGY IN SOCIETY

This unit introduces some of the present and future effects of information technology upon society by raising some of the important issues involved. Much of the discussion is speculative and necessarily superficial — further reading and sources of more detailed information are suggested at the end of the unit.

Why consider society?

It is a statement of the obvious that any society influences the education and the educational system within it. Therefore any changes in society will, hopefully, lead to changes in education. In previous decades changes in society have been relatively slow. This is no longer the case. In *The Two Cultures and the scientific revolution* (Cambridge University Press, 1959) C.P. Snow remarked that during all of human history until the present century the rate of social change has been sufficiently slow as to pass unnoticed in one person's lifetime (p. 45). This so-called 'rate of social change' has accelerated in the last two decades, largely due to the growth of microelectronics. The notion of social change and the problems it may bring (sometimes described as 'future shock' or culture shock) are discussed at the end of this unit. The important point to note here is that the pace of social change is now so rapid that any speculative discussion of education necessarily involves a consideration of society and its development. Any such discussion is bound to be laden with value judgements, i.e. speculations on what the future *ought* to be like, as well as predictions of what it *will* be like. This unit attempts to consider both.

There is one other related reason for considering the effects of information technology upon society in a book on education. The impact of information technology and microelectronics upon education will arguably be far greater as a result of its influence on society than through its *direct* influence on the education system (see Figure 28). In other words the *indirect* influence of information technology on education through its pervasion of society is likely to be far more fundamental than its direct influence on teaching, learning and schooling. Indeed, as has been stated earlier, the use of computers in education might be in some danger of proving a passing fad or fashion (like the teaching machines of the 1960s) if their use and influence were only a direct one. But the presence of computers and information technology in society is already so ubiquitous that their indirect influence on education cannot possibly fade — although the novelty, mystique, mystery and status attached to their use in education probably will.

Figure 28. Solving the unemployment problem?

Changing patterns of employment

Quantity

In Britain in the 18th century almost everyone who did work, worked on the land — about 92 people in every 100 were working to feed themselves and the eight others. By 1980 only 2 per cent of all workers were employed in agriculture. These two in every 100 worked to feed the other 98. The figures are even more extreme in North America. One American farmer now feeds about 60 people — indeed farming in the USA has been cynically described as the process of converting oil into food. This trend is still continuing, as the figures show. The percentage of the civilian labour force employed in non-agricultural industries has decreased since 1979. This, presumably, is due to the increase in the percentage who are unemployed. In the USA in June 1982 9.5 per cent of the labour force was unemployed — this compares with a figure of 1.9 per cent employed in agriculture. In other words the number of people unemployed in the USA in 1982 was exactly *five times greater* than the number employed in feeding the whole of the population (source: *Statistical Abstract of the U.S.,* tables 624 and 625, page 375).

It is interesting to break these statistics down further by considering the different sectors of employment under the heading 'non-agricultural'. In the USA these are classed as *Information, Service* and *Industry.* The statistics shown in Figure 29 indicate a decrease of employment in Industry with a sharp increase in numbers employed in both Information and Service. The graph shown is misleading however since it only shows figures for those *in employment.* At first glance the graph may imply that the sharp decline in numbers employed in both industry and agriculture since 1960 has been compensated for by growth in the Information and Service sectors. This conclusion is, however, false. Total unemployment in the USA has risen from roughly 3.8 million (5.5 per cent) in 1960 to roughly 10.4 million (9.4 per cent) in 1982. In other words, it appears that the number of jobs *created* by the growth in the so-called information and service industries had fallen short of those displaced by the decline in manufacturing industry by a figure of several million in the early 1980s. Whether or not this trend wil continue is a matter for debate, and depends upon both political and technological factors. Growth in the industries connected with information technology (both hardware and software) will undoubtedly produce new jobs. But the capital-intensive nature of the work involved is unlikely to reduce unemployment greatly. The other hope for full (or fuller) employment — the service industries — depends

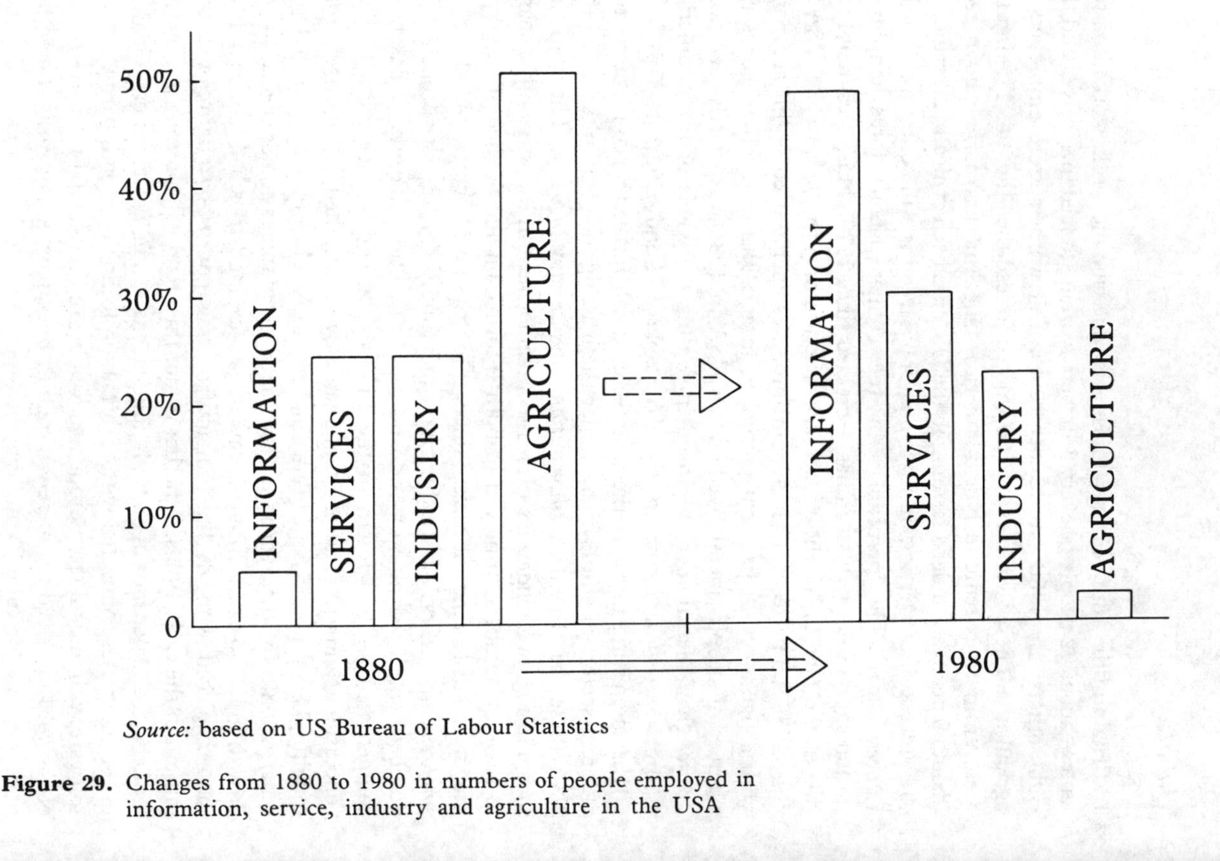

Source: based on US Bureau of Labour Statistics

Figure 29. Changes from 1880 to 1980 in numbers of people employed in information, service, industry and agriculture in the USA

almost totally on political decisions. It is worth noting that between 1979 and 1981 almost half a million jobs were lost in the service sector of Britain. Jobs in service industries are necessarily labour-intensive and (in a strict sense) inefficient and non-profit making. It may be argued that they can only be supported and expanded if they are 'paid-for' by the wealth-earning industries, particularly those involving new technology.

The full intricacies of the employment debate are well beyond the scope of this book. But certain tentative conclusions can be drawn which are likely to have a direct bearing on education:

- there will be a decline in the numbers employed by the manufacturing industries;
- there may be an increase in the numbers employed in the information and possibly the service sectors, though the latter depends largely on political decisions;
- in the short term the number of jobs created will almost certainly be less than the number displaced.

Quality of employment

The other important discussion in considering changing patterns of employment is the notion of *quality*. One optimistic view is that the majority of dull, boring, repetitive jobs now done by human beings will eventually be done by machines — the replacement of car workers by robots on an assembly line is just one existing example. This use of machines would free human beings to carry out more flexible, creative and rewarding tasks. The pessimistic view is that the use of machines for boring, repetitive work will simply increase unemployment.

The nature and quality of employment in the information sector is also likely to change. Hundreds of workers in large, commercial city centres are involved in *handling information.* They may be office workers, secretaries, bank clerks, insurance workers, or simply messengers carrying information from one place to another. Computers are excellent for handling and storing information, and new communications will be excellent for sending it from one place to another. So the new technologies of computers and communications will alter or even end the jobs of thousands of white collar workers — the so-called 'pen pushers' and 'paper-handlers', administrators and clerks, messengers and telephonists, newspaper workers and printers. If you live in London you may not yet have noticed unemployment as much as a person who lives in a manufacturing city like Coventry, Bradford or Sheffield. This may not be true for much longer. Most of Britain's information handlers travel into, and out of, London every day. The London rush hour could become a thing of the past. In other words, the complete introduction of new technology into information handling will totally change the nature of the 'information handler's' job, and the skills required. These qualitative and quantitative changes will apply equally to clerks, secretaries, bank employees, administrators and newspaper workers.

One final point worth noting on quality of employment is that future technological changes will almost certainly result in a *polarization of skills.* An increasing number of skilled and semi-skilled jobs will become 'de-skilled' by the use of new technology. This will result either in the replacement of a semi-skilled worker by an unskilled worker, or in the loss of a job. At the other extreme there is likely to be an increasing demand for highly skilled, often technical labour in a high technology society. Yet some computer scientists believe that even highly skilled 'experts' could be affected by new technology. Computer scientists are working to make systems which can make decisions and give advice just like an expert doctor, lawyer or accountant for example. These are called expert systems or intelligent knowledge-based systems. A system has already been tried which can diagnose certain illnesses by asking the right questions. Leading doctors need to be involved in producing it, of course, and giving it the right data. But some expert systems are quicker and more reliable than even people who helped to develop them.

The brief discussions above simply serve to show that no one can predict with any certainty the nature and number of skills that will be required in the future. Prediction is equally uncertain for both low- and high-level skills. This uncertainty is particularly important for education. Much current educational discussion involves talk of 'relevant skills for the future', 'pre-vocational training and education', and 'skills for the information era'. Yet no one can point with any certainty to the skills that are likely to be most relevant, or the vocations most calling, in a future society.

Education for leisure

Although future development skills cannot be predicted with any certainty, it is a fairly safe prediction that the *leisure* time available to people will increase steadily. This may be caused by any, or all, of four reasons: increased unemployment; a shorter working week; work-sharing and the end of overtime; and earlier retirement. The only factor of uncertainty is whether leisure time, and work time, will be spread out and shared equally between all members of society, i.e. by job and work-sharing; or whether higher unemployment will lead to total 'leisure time' for millions and no increase for those in paid employment. Indeed, the latter outcome may arise from the polarization and narrowing of skills mentioned earlier. There may be increasing demands for the highly skilled, highly technical person whose leisure time may actually decrease.

However leisure is shared in the future the *total* time available for it is bound to increase. This will make demands on education in three important ways. Firstly, more time must be devoted in schools, in the school curriculum, to the *enrichment* of leisure, i.e. education in the ability to make full and rewarding use of it. This, in turn, will involve education in *attitudes* towards work and leisure. The traditional boundary between work and leisure will, and should, become blurred. The traditional identification and categorization of a person (usually male) in terms of job-description must somehow be educated away. This is coupled with the Protestant ethic in most western societies that 'hard work' is the only really serious and worthwhile activity. In addition, work is implicitly defined as paid work, so that voluntary work, work done in leisure time or *unpaid* work (such as bringing up children) is afforded a lower status and lesser esteem. Education has a responsibility to undermine these attitudes. The third demand on education is that *it should not be seen as the province or responsibility of the school.* Education must be seen as a life-long activity which begins before the age of five, does not end at sixteen or eighteen, and is not confined to the school hours of each day. The equation of education with schooling must be questioned (this point is developed further in Units 19 and 20).

To sum up: education in a society dominated by information technology has a responsibility to devote more time to enriching 'leisure', to change people's attitudes to work and employment, and to provide life-long education rather than a narrow concentration on school hours and school years.

The notions of 'change' and 'appropriate technology'

This last section of the unit discusses two notions which are increasingly important in modern society, and both have implications for those involved in education.

Technological change is often described as exponential, i.e. the rate at which change takes place is itself steadily accelerating. In other words in a given time interval, say 1985 to 1990, the magnitude of change will be bigger than in the previous time interval, i.e. 1980 to 1985. This increasing rate of change seems likely to continue. 'Change' applies not only to technology, its machines and devices, but also to values, norms, attitudes, communities and institutions. This, in the words of Stonier (1983), leads to 'cultural disorientation':

> The accelerating pace of technological development brings with it not only rapid changes in the economy but, as a consequence, in society as a whole. It leads to a form of cultural disorientation [which] may prove to be the most dangerous and unpredictable of the problems emerging in the closing decades of the 20th century.
>
> (Stonier, T. *The wealth of information.* Methuen, 1983, p. 24)

The term 'cultural disorientation' coined by Stonier conveys a similar idea to the notions of culture shock and 'future shock' proposed by Alvin Toffler (see Toffler 1970 and 1980 in Further reading). Toffler suggests that education must now prepare school-children to cope with rapid change. This differs from the notion of 'education for change' proposed by radical teachers' groups and others in recent years. Toffler is suggesting that education should *prepare* young people for change so that they can both anticipate it and adapt to it, in their workplace and their everyday lives. Amidst rapid change, existing skills and knowledge can become redundant virtually overnight. Both education *and* training must therefore be flexible and 'future-oriented' (to use Toffler's term). The notions of a career, and careers education, may well become too rigid. In future it may become the norm for a person to train, retrain, and change 'careers' two or three times during their so-called working life. The traditional idea of a career as a linear progression or course through life is perhaps no longer useful.

One thing perhaps not emphasized enough by Toffler is the positive view that education can itself help to *influence* and *determine* future change as well as preparing people to cope with it. It is the responsibility of people themselves to ensure that new technology is used in appropriate and convivial ways. People are determinants of change as well as victims of it.

The notions of appropriateness and conviviality can only be touched upon here and references are given later for further reading (see Burns (1981) and Illich (1973)). Burns lists eleven requirements that any technology should satisfy in order for it to be deemed appropriate:

1. The technology must be intelligible to the community as a whole.
2. It must be readily available at a price within the range of most individuals.
3. It must fulfil a socially useful purpose.
4. The tools and processes utilised must be under the maintenance and operational control of the local workforce.
5. It should use indigenous resources and skills.
6. It should create employment.
7. The production and use of the technology should present no health hazards to the personnel concerned.
8. It should be non-pollutant, ecologically sound and where applicable it should recycle materials.
9. It must prevent external cultural domination.
10. It should where possible allow fulfilling, flexible, creative and innovatory use.
11. It should fit into the existing social infrastructure.

In short, an appropriate technology is one that is understood by the bulk of the population, uses skills which are readily available, does not adversely affect the environment or community, and which achieves a social objective. Technologies in our society which may be termed appropriate are: The telephone network (if it were somewhat cheaper), local bus and train services (if more accessible), domestic water supply (if environmental disturbances due to reservoirs could be minimised), and a number of energy sources, such as hydroelectric, geothermal, solar and wind.

A technology, according to Burns, is appropriate when it is socially beneficial and socially oriented.

Talking points

- *Does new information technology satisfy all, or even any of the eleven requirements listed above?*
- *Can new information technology be described as an appropriate technology?*
- *How can education for the future help to satisfy any of the above requirements?*

The questions of how far new information technology is appropriate and how education can make it more appropriate, are left to the reader to consider. I will simply conclude this unit by stating rather crudely some of the ideas (or ideals) for the future which have been put forward by 'The Pessimists' and 'The Optimists'. Firstly the views of 'The Pessimists' can be sketched as follows: the growth and application of new technology will lead to:

- massive unemployment: millions of people condemned to a 'life of leisure' — too much leisure time, not knowing how to use it, no money to spend on it.
- upheaval of people and communities: more people will be forced to leave their towns and communities to seek work.
- more isolation of human beings; there could be less social contact between people as communities are uprooted and more communications are made via computers.
- lucky people in the new jobs will earn higher wages, *but* they may have to work longer hours, e.g. shift work to make full use of computer time.
- 'more work for some, less for others' could widen the gap between the haves and the have-nots — people on high wages in new industries, and people on the dole.

At the other extreme, 'The Optimists' believe that new technology could actually improve the *quality* of people's lives:

- There could be a shorter working week for those who have a job. Fewer people would need to work overtime, on night shifts, or unsociable hours to produce the goods we need. People could retire at an earlier age if they wish to.
- Many of the boring, repetitive jobs in unpleasant conditions would disappear — they could be done by machines. There might be less drudgery and boredom in the work place.
- If efficient farms and factories, helped by microelectronics and computers, produce the goods we need more people could be employed in the *service industries.* These people could do socially useful jobs, e.g. nursing; caring for elderly people; helping the handicapped; protecting and conserving our surroundings; teaching; and so on.
- There are hundreds of jobs that cannot be done by machines. These are jobs of the craftsmen — wood carving, sculpture, painting, stone masonry, and so on. The age of microelectronics could allow the return of the craftsman.
- More leisure time will be available for those who want it.

Few people would be either pessimistic or idealistic enough to believe that either of these extremes will become reality in the near future. But the two extremes do provide a useful starting point for debate. Most of all, the latter provides a valuable goal for those involved in education who should surely be concerned that new technology be used *appropriately,* i.e. to serve people, not to master them.

Talking points

- *Consider the following passage from Tom Stonier:*
  'The automation of production systems will mean that some time early in the next century it will take no more than 10% of the labour force to provide us with all the food we eat, all the clothing we wear, all the furniture, all the textiles, all our housing, all our appliances, all our cars . . . what will the other 90% be doing?' (From 'Looking to the future', page 35, Book L of the *Science in Society* project, Heinemann 1981).
  Do you consider this a realistic forecast? What implications would it have for education? What will *the other 90 per cent be doing?*
- *Do you agree with the main suggestion of this unit that the influence of information technology on education will be more* indirect *than* direct?
- *How important do you consider the notions of 'cultural disorientation' and 'future shock' suggested by Stonier and Toffler respectively? What effect should they have on education? Are you a victim of future shock yourself?*

Further reading

1. The ideas of 'appropriateness' and 'conviviality' are discussed fully and readably in: Burns, A. (1981) *The Microchip: Appropriate or Inappropriate Technology?* Ellis Horwood, Chichester; and Illich, I. (1973) *Tools for Conviviality.* Fontana.
2. Alvin Toffler's notions of future shock and the third wave (a post-industrial revolution) can be found in: Toffler, A. (1970) *Future Shock.* Pan; and (1980) *The Third Wave.* Pan.
3. Two texts that provide an introduction to information technology and its effects on society which can be used in schools are: Ruthven, K. (1983) *Society and the New Technology.* Cambridge University Press; and the second half of Steele, R. and Wellington, J.J. (1985) *Computers and Communication.* Blackie.
4. Two rather more substantial tomes which contain a wide range and large number of varying contributions are: Forrester, Tom (ed.) (1980); *The Microelectronics Revolution.* Oxford: Blackwell; and Friedrichs and Schaff (eds.) (1982) *Microelectronics and Society: for Better or for Worse.* Pergamon. The latter work, particularly, elaborates some of the points introduced in this unit.
5. One of the classic, and often-quoted, books on the future of work and employment is written by two trade unionists: Jenkins, C. and Sherman (1979) *The Collapse of Work.* Eyre/Methuen.

Page			
		21173030	Home Economics
		21173031	Humanities
21173000	Archaeology	21173032	Information Technology
21173001	Arithmetic	21173033	Languages
21173003	Astronomy	21173034	Law
21173004	Biology	21173035	Literature
21173005	Building	21173036	Local History
21173006	Business	21173037	Mathematics
21173007	Careers	21173038	Medicine
21173008	Chemistry	21173039	Metalwork
21173044	Child Development (was Nutrition)	21173040	Microcomputing
21173009	Classics	21173041	Music
21173010	Commerce	21173043	Nursing
21173011	Computers	21173045	Photography
21173013	Crafts	21173046	Physical Education
21173014	Design Technology	21173047	Physics
21173015	Drama	21173048	Politics
21173016	Economics	21173049	Pollution
21173017	Electronics	21173050	Public Admin
21173018	Energy	21173051	Religious Studies
21173019	Engineering	21173052	Science
21173020	English Lanaguage	21173053	Sea
21173021	English Literature	21173054	Social/Community Education
21173022	Environmental Studies	21173055	Social Studies
21173023	Farming	21173056	Sport
21173042	Fashion & Textiles (Needlecraft)	21173057	Statistics
21173012	Food & Nutrition (Cookery)	21173058	Study Skills
21173024	Geography	21173059	Surveying
21173025	Geology	21173060	Technical Studies
21173026	Government	21173061	Technology
21173027	Health	21173066	Travel
21173028	History	21173063	Weather
21173029	Hobbies	21173064	Woodwork
21173065	Home & Community	21173062	World Studies

Figure 30. Directory of subjects related to the school curriculum available on Prestel (as at April 1984)

O'Shea and Self suggest that the most likely use of videodisks will be for direct *industrial training*, e.g. for familiarizing sales staff with their product. They take a similarly cautious line on the use of videotex in education: '. . . viewdata systems are beginning to expand in the business world, but there is still little sign that educationalists yet see viewdata as a solution to any of their problems' (p. 257). One new technology which they do enthuse about is the extension of the use of the *optical disk* to replace magnetic disk and tape as a means of storing data, i.e. secondary storage. With such an optical disk, data are written on and read from the disk using a laser beam. O'Shea and Self estimate that one side of such a disk can now hold 'about five times the textual information in the *Encyclopaedia Britannica*'.

It is clear that views on the potential of IT in education do vary, and that most forecasts should be treated with caution. However, it is surely true that the potential for learning with *new* technology of all kinds, from videotex and videodisk to cable and computer, is enormous. It is impossible to publish a printed book which can give an up-to-date account of new developments, trials and evaluations (such is the time lag between manuscript and final product). The only possibility for keeping abreast of developments in learning with new technology is by reading weekly or monthly publications. A similar problem exists in learning *about* new technology, and maintaining an awareness of wider uses of information technology. The nature and content of technology awareness courses is the subject of the next section.

IT awareness and computer literacy

The growth of computer awareness courses, running sometimes in parallel and sometimes in conflict with computer studies courses, has already been mentioned. The actual content of computer awareness courses is however a matter of some debate. What are pupils or recipients to be made aware of: uses, effects, or inner workings? Should pupils learn programming — if so, in which language? The lack of agreement over the content of computer awareness courses is limited to (perhaps caused by) confusion over the notion of 'computer literacy'. It is popularly suggested, by the media for example, that lack of computer literacy will be as serious a social handicap in the future as illiteracy and innumeracy are now. But the last two are easily defined and identified, usually in terms of the three R's. Is computer literacy to be seen as the fourth 'R'? If so, exactly what does it entail?

One publication which has had the courage to state, in fairly concrete and comprehensible terms, the essential elements of computer literacy is the Further Education Unit handbook *Computer Literacy – a Teacher's Guide* (FEU 1983). Its definition is summarized as follows:

'A computer literate student should:
(i) Understand what computer systems are
(ii) Use computer vocabulary
(iii) Operate a microcomputer in a work related situation
(iv) Appreciate what a program is and why it works
(v) Be aware of applications of computing in commerce, industry and other settings
(vi) Be aware of current trends in Information Technology and its social implications' (p. 5).

This statement may not receive universal agreement, but has value in providing a useful working definition and a starting point for discussion (see Talking points). Some may feel that certain criteria are too demanding if interpreted strictly; 'awareness of current trends' in IT, for example, requires a tremendous amount of reading. On the other hand, it could be argued that for a person to be computer literate (s)he should acquire the art of programming, and learn a high-level language. This point will be discussed later, but my own observations suggest that only a minority of school computer awareness courses delve into either programming or the learning of a computer language in any depth. This view is supported by Walton (in Galton and Moon 1983)* who suggests the following content for a computer awareness course in the second or third year of secondary school:

'1. Two or three "hands on" sessions for every pupil, each lasting about thirty minutes, and illustrating the various facets of the machine. Given a limited number of microcomputers, this would be spread throughout the course, probably outside the lesson time itself.
2. Information retrieval – including a demonstration of a general-purpose information retrieval package and of PRESTEL.
3. Social implications – including data bases, issues of privacy, etc., implications for jobs for the future; the benefits for the handicapped.
4. Historical perspective – the rate of development of hardware over the last four decades.

* Galton, M. and Moon, B. (eds) (1983): *Changing Schools: Changing Curriculum.* Harper and Row.

5. A *brief* demonstration of the elements of programming, using graphical work as a vehicle, rather than arithmetic. A heavy emphasis on programming is likely to be counter-productive for the majority of children.
6. Word processing and the electronic office — including a demonstration of a word-processing package.
7. Applications — a look at the range of applications in the world today, from robots to making cars, to computers in banking, to farm management with a microcomputer.
8. Control technology — a demonstration of simple control: using the microcomputer to control motors and mechanisms, and reading data from light cells, thermometers, etc.
9. Terms — an explanation of some of the simple terms in computing: hardware, software, input, output, processor, memory, backing store (including disks and cassettes), microcomputer etc.' (Galton and Moon 1983, p. 125).

This should form a timetabled course in the *short term* only, as Walton partly implies. Gradually some of the elements will be integrated into *all* subjects (points 1, 2 and 6 for example). Other aspects could be integrated into specific subject studies such as science (point 8) and history (point 4).

Debate on the content and timetabling of computer awareness courses is certain to continue at least as long as the demand for them continues. A sub-discussion within that debate, yet one raising wider issues, is the topic of the next section.

Who should learn to program?

The issue of *who* should learn to program computers, *when*, and in *what language* has been widely debated by people concerned with primary education up to higher education and teacher training. The debate is far too complex and many-sided to examine closely here, so the main points are summarized below with several suggestions for further reading at the end of the unit:

1. One of the arguments *against* teaching computer programming in schools comes from those involved in higher education, particularly teachers in Computer Studies and Computer Science departments. They argue that teaching programming to children, usually through the BASIC language, encourages and inculcates bad programming habits which need to be undone by higher education. This view is reflected by the lack of demand by undergraduate Computing departments for O- or A-level Computer Studies

as an entrance requirement. Indeed, some departments appear positively to discourage the school study of these subjects. This attitude is seen by some school teachers as sheer academic snobbery, or perhaps an attempt to protect and preserve territory. More generously, it can be seen as one aspect of the structured versus unstructured programming debate which has been going on for some years now, and is likely to continue (see Further reading). My own view is that it is both unwise and unfair for specialized departments in higher education, who are involved with a tiny minority of able students, to dictate a policy for all pupils in schools. There may be good educational reasons for not teaching BASIC, but this is a separate issue (see point 4).

2. It can be argued that to teach computer programming in schools is both unwise and misleading. It is *unwise* because only a small minority of school leavers will ever be employed as computer programmers. Indeed, some computer scientists believe that the demand for programmers will actually decrease in the future, It is therfore *misleading* to teach computer programming to the majority of pupils under the pretence that it is either a 'relevant skill', 'a skill for the future' or, worse still, vocational preparation. As a preparation for life after school the most effective argument for teaching computer programming is that it could provide an interesting and rewarding *leisure activity.* To suggest, or even tacitly pretend to pupils that the ability to program a computer is essential pre-vocational education is downright dishonest. It may provide a valuable leisure pursuit, but it is far from a passport to a job.

3. Perhaps the most persuasive argument for teaching and learning programming (although there is little research evidence to back it up) is the view that it is educationally valuable and desirable in itself. In other words, to learn the art (or science) of programming a computer is *intrinsically* worth while, e.g. it provides valuable mental exercise, develops good mental discipline, and enhances the ability to solve problems. Seen in this light, it has been described as 'the Latin of the 80s'.

This description prompts the slightly facetious question: what happened to the curriculum between the decline of Latin in state schools and the growth of programming? Were those educated in this interim period (myself included) disadvantaged at school in terms of mental discipline and skills in problem solving? Perhaps a more serious question is the problem of *transfer* of learning from one sphere to another. Will the development of mental discipline and problem solving, inculcated by the correct approach to programming, transfer to other school subjects, or even other aspects of everyday life? To prove, or even disprove, such a hypothesis would be a virtually impossible research ask. However, it is taken almost as a basic assumption by some who advocate programming as an essential part of computer education.

4. A more recent aspect of the programming debate centres on the distinction between learning to program and learning a computer language:

> Many primary schools are now giving priority to just three areas: information handling, word-processing, and programming. It is this last area, that of programming that, until now, has caused particular problems in UK schools. For in order to teach children to program, it is necessary to provide them with a suitable programming language. BASIC is not a suitable programming language. At present the only contender at primary level is LOGO. (From 'Powerful Packages' by R. Noss in *Times Educational Supplement,* 25 May 1984, p. 45).

It is argued that programming is a valuable educational activity if the right language is used (in partial agreement therefore with the higher education view, point 1). A full discussion of Logo, and the educational ideas of its main founder Seymour Papert, requires a book in itself (see Further reading). More recently other contenders such as PROLOG and SMALLTALK have been suggested by Ennals (1984) and others.

Arguments over which language, at what age, and for what purpose, will continue in the debate on the value of programming in education. Hopefully this section has made you aware of some of the main questions without pretending to answer them. It is certainly one of the larger and more important issues in deciding the place of information technology in education. Finally, it is worth noting that the use of programming in computer education cuts across the earlier distinction between learning *with* new technology and learning *about* new technology. A correct approach to programming surely enables both, as does the development of information skills. The latter is the topic of the next section.

Information skills and information education

The plea for the introduction of information skills into the school curriculum is not new. It has simply become more pressing with the growing use of information technology in schools, coupled with talk of the information era or the post-industrial age as the next phase in modern society. A useful starting point for discussion occurred in 1981 with the publication of the Schools Council Curriculum Bulletin *Information Skills in the Secondary Curriculum* (ed. M. Marland). The booklet is important for suggesting in fairly concrete and explicit terms the *content* of a school's information skills curriculum. A detailed breakdown of the steps involved in 'any finding-out activity' is put forward for both teachers and pupils to follow. The nine stages or 'question steps' are as follows:

What do I need to do?
(formulate and analyse need)

Where could I go?
(identify and appraise likely sources)

How do I get to the information?
(trace and locate individual resources)

Which resources shall I use?
(examine, select and reject individual resources)

How shall I use the resources?
(interrogate resources)

What should I make a record of?
(record and store information)

Have I got the information I need?
(interpret, analyse, synthesize, evaluate)

How should I present it?
(present, communicate)

What have I achieved?
(evaluate)

With the availability of computerized databases such as Prestel and the use of other databases on micros these nine question steps are particularly relevant today.

My own view is that 'information education' should now be broadened to include not only information skills but *wider* considerations of the nature, use and implications of the information explosion. I have suggested below four topics which could be considered in a broader information education. They have been presented as questions, followed by a very brief outline of some answers which could be given to school pupils:

1. *What is a database? What's the use of databases?*
Prestel is often called a national database. A database is any collection of facts, items of information or data which are related in some way. A telephone directory is a database, so is an address book. Some other examples could be:

a collection of recipes	a library of books
a filing cabinet	a folder full of schoolwork
the Oxford English Dictionary	a textbook

Every database should contain data which is *organized* in a sensible and systematic way, for example by placing names in alphabetical order. This should allow anyone using a database to put in, or get out, the information they want as easily and quickly as possible. The main advantages of computerized databases are: (i) unlike printed guides or books they can easily and quickly be kept up to date; (ii) the information they store can be accessed easily, quickly and directly — and often from hundreds of miles away.

2. *What is 'good' information? What is meant by the quality of information?*
Suppose you telephone your local railway station to inquire about trains to London. Your reply comes back: 'A train will probably be leaving some time today'. This is poor quality information — it is vague, uncertain, and inexact. A more helpful reply would be something like: 'A non-stop train is leaving at 10.12 a.m. from Platform 2, reaching London-King's Cross at 12.24 p.m.' The table below summarizes the differences between high and low quality information:

High quality	*Low quality*
reliable	misleading
accurate	inaccurate
up to date	out of date
complete	incomplete
precise	vague/imprecise
clear	unclear
well presented	poorly presented

In other words, the greater the uncertainty the worse the information. As information technology spreads, the *quality* of information will become more and more important. High quality information about banks and money supply, current prices, world markets and trends, crops and agriculture, the weather, in fact almost anything, will become a valuable commodity. It will be the key *resource* in the society of the future — a resource which can be bought and sold, imported and exported.

3. *What are the dangers for individual people in society as the information stored on them grows and becomes more readily available?*
No brief answers for pupils to this question will be suggested here! A huge number of issues are involved: which companies or institutions hold information about people — the Police, the NHS, credit companies? How do they hold this information? Who has access to it? Could *all* the information on an individual held by various sources be pooled into one central database? How could information held about individuals be misused? By whom? What information held on individuals are people most *sensitive* about — their weight, age, bank balance, sexual activities, political beliefs? All these questions could be raised and discussed with pupils as part of their 'information education'. An ideal and original source for teachers is the 1978 Lindop Report on Data Protection (see Further reading).

4. *What is the difference between information and data? What is the connection between information, knowledge and wisdom?*
These points are somewhat subtle and debatable and will therefore need a fairly cautious approach. The distinction between data and information has already been made (page 26); this could be discussed, using examples, with all pupils; e.g. how does a string of symbols such as XKW141T acquire any meaning? Only when given a *context* (i.e. it is my car number) can such data be interpreted and used, e.g. to calculate the age of my car. Similar examples could be created and discussed.

The important distinctions between merely acquiring information, possessing worthwhile knowledge, and more elusively developing *wisdom* should also be drawn (Figure 31). The mere ability to acquire, record and store information and to use modern information retrieval systems should be afforded no higher status than the *possession* of information and the

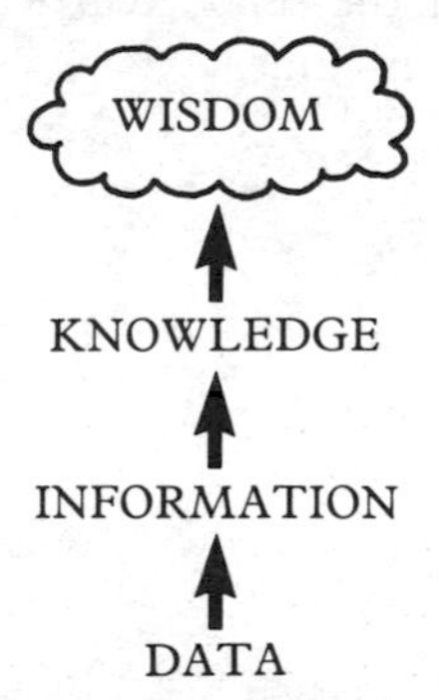

Figure 31. Data, information, knowledge and wisdom: an imaginary hierarchy

acquisition of facts. The important elements in information education involve using and interpreting information, questioning and examining its sources, and finally in deciding why and whether that information is relevant and valuable (see Further reading for a fuller discussion of these points).

Education for an information society

The view of this unit has revolved through 180 degrees. It has moved from a consideration of the role of information technology in education to a discussion of the education needed for a so-called information society. It is perhaps inevitable that an information society should have far more influence on the schooling and education within it than an industrial society. It therefore follows that the links between education and society will become closer, and their mutual influence become inseparable. Some of the ideas to be introduced into a broad information education were suggested in the previous section. A full general education should encompass not only those issues but also a discussion of a future society dominated by information technology. This would involve a broad treatment, across the curriculum, of (for example) the following topics: the rapid changes in society; the implications of an information explosion; the effect on work, leisure, and the quality of life of newer technology; the place of the individual in a society dominated by information; and finally the place of machine or artificial intelligence in a human society. Will computers of the future make man's *mind* as obsolete as the machines of the industrial revolution made his *muscle*? This rather glib suggestion forms an ideal starting point for a debate on new technology which could be carried right across the school curriculum.

The influence of IT upon the school curriculum and on education in general is the subject of the next unit.

Further reading

1. One of the most useful and detailed sources of information connected with Unit 19 is *New Information Technology in Education* by David Hawkridge (London: Croom Helm, 1983).
2. References on the structured versus the unstructured programming debate are too varied and numerous to list here. I suggest that readers watch out for articles and viewpoints in *Educational Computing, Computer Education* and the *Times Educational Supplement.* An important reference to the issue was made in the Alvey Report, *Advanced Information Technology* (HMSO 1982): '...it is no good just providing your BASIC programmers. Universities in fact are having to give remedial education to entrants with A-level computer science. Teachers must be properly trained, and the language taught chosen with an eye to the future'.
3. References on learning through programming and the choice of programming language are again numerous but the following are perhaps the basics:
(i) Logo: *Mindstorms: Children, Computers and Powerful Ideas* by Seymour Papert (Harvester Press, 1980); and *Learning and Teaching with computers* by Tim O'Shea and John Self (Harvester Press, 1983), which also discusses Smalltalk (pp. 200–214).
(ii) Prolog: *Beginning Micro-Prolog* by Richard Ennals (Ellis Horwood and Heinemann, 1984).
(iii) A collection of views can be found in *New Horizons in Educational Computing* by M. Yazdani (Ellis Horwood, 1984).
4. (i) A full discussion of information skills can be found in the Schools Council Curriculum booklet (No. 9) *Information Skills in the Secondary curriculum,* edited by Michael Marland (Methuen, 1981).
(ii) The notion of a broader information education is raised in Wellington, J.J. 'The knowledge we have lost in information', *Times Educational Supplement* 31 August, 1984.
5. An excellent and surprisingly readable source book on information education is the 1978 Lindop Report on data privacy *Report of the Committee on Data Protection* (London: HMSO, 1978).
6. 'Interactive Videodiscs in primary schools: an evaluation study' by Colin Mably is available free from its author at North East London Polytechnic, Londbridge Rd., Dagenham, Essex.
7. The use of Prestel in schools is discussed in *Prestel and Education: a report of a one-year trial* by Vincent Thompson (London: Council for Educational Technology, 1981).

8. A brief but vivid account of information skills in the primary school is given by Alistair Ross, 'Information handling Skills' in *Micros in the Primary Classroom,* ed. R. Jones (London: Edward Arnold, 1984).
9. A sobering view of the short history of Prestel, which describes it as 'a dismal and expensive flop', was provided by Jack Schofield in *The Guardian* (13 September 1984), 'How the Post Office Failed to Deliver'.

Talking points

- *Study again the definition of computer literacy offered by the Further Education Unit. Do you agree with all the suggested objectives? Do you feel that you are 'computer literate' yourself, according to these criteria? Are these criteria too demanding, (v) and (vi) for example, to be workable?*
- *Who* should *learn to program computers? Should you? If so, why? What are your reactions to computer programming: fear, excitement, boredom . . .? Have you observed children's reactions or attitudes to programming?*
- *Do you consider that a distinction can be made between learning* with *new technology and learning* about *new technology? Or are the two inseparable in practice? Is the distinction a useful one anyway?*
- *How much do you know about the information held on you? E.g. do you know* which *bodies hold the information,* what *this information is, and* who *has access to it?*

UNIT 20

EDUCATION AND THE CURRICULUM IN AN INFORMATION SOCIETY

It has already been suggested that information technology will affect education and the curriculum both directly, and indirectly through the changes it brings in society. This unit speculates upon the future of education, curriculum and the learning process in a society increasingly dominated by information technology.

Changing views of the curriculum: horizontal and vertical

Traditionally, the secondary school curriculum has been viewed through the spectacles of the subject specialisms. The curriculum, and therefore the school timetable and school day, have been divided into 'school subjects' usually based on well-founded, historically based disciplines. Many a secondary pupil can look forward to a daily diet of, say, mathematics followed by English, French, with physics and geography in the afternoon. This approach, which I will call the *vertical* approach to the curriculum as in Figure 32, has been supported by the 'forms of knowledge' thesis. A full account of this thesis can be found in the references under Further reading. For my purposes here the approach can be crudely summarized as follows. There are a number of clearly distinguishable *forms of knowledge* which are necessary for making sense of reality i.e. in becoming educated. Unless a

SKILLS/ ISSUES ↓ / SUBJECTS →	MATHS	ENGLISH	SCIENCE (Physics, Chemistry, Biology)	HUMANITIES (Geography History)	MODERN LANGUAGES (French, German)	CRAFT, DESIGN & TECHNOLOGY	PHYSICAL EDUCATION	COMPUTER STUDIES	COMPUTER AWARENESS	R.E., MUSIC etc. etc.
Language skills										
Problem-solving skills										
Life & social skills										
Information skills										
Communication skills										
Information technology awareness										
Multi-cultural education										
Peace and conflict education										

Figure 32. Two ways of viewing the curriculum

person has acquired, been initiated into, these forms they cannot be said to be educated. Education, and therefore the curriculum, should be defined and structured according to these forms.

This vertical approach, along the lines of the above caricature, seems to have dominated both philosophical thinking and school practice for the last twenty years. The secondary curriculum is still almost exclusively structured by translating 'forms of knowledge' into separate subject specialisms. The opposite view prevails almost totally in primary education. The curriculum is seen and structured in terms of skills, themes, issues and abilities. The dominant secondary theme of 'initiation into existing forms of knowledge' is, perhaps thankfully, ignored. My analogy of horizontal and vertical views of the curriculum is visualized in Figure 32.

The influence of information technology, along with other developments in education, will almost certainly promote a more horizontal approach to the curriculum. Indeed, education in and awareness of information technology itself will increasingly become cross-curricular as opposed to a vertical slot on the curriculum and the timetable. *Skills* which run horizontally in Figure 32 will play a more dominant part in the curriculum. The development of information skills (discussed in Unit 19) are a key example. Language and communication skills, to be developed in *every* subject specialism, will also become increasingly important in a society based on information. (This suggestion in fact goes back to the 1975 Bullock Report: *A Language for life.*) *Issues*, as much as skills, will be increasingly treated in a cross-curricular or horizontal way. This must be reflected as much in a teacher's approach to education (and therefore in teacher-training) as in the content of a pupil's curriculum. Issues such as multi-cultural education, sex-stereotyping, the Third World, and education for international co-operation (my non-emotive term for the much maligned 'peace studies') must all be treated across the curriculum by every teacher in every subject specialism.

To cut a long discussion short: the development of skills and concepts, the discussion of key topical issues, and the development of abilities for coping with rapid change will surely be the guidelines for a future curriculum, rather than the dominance of traditional subject specialisms. In the post-industrial era a crude 'forms of knowledge' thesis, in which pupils are initiated into traditional disciplines (rather like sheep-dipping), cannot survive.

On the other hand a totally horizontal approach to the curriculum based purely on skills and concepts is both practically and philosophically impossible. Quite simply, how can skills and concepts be acquired without the subject-matter, facts, content to pin them onto? This is based on an important warning from the 19th century philosopher Immanuel Kant. He suggested that knowledge is only possible when we have both a perception and a concept working together: 'Thoughts without content are empty. Perceptions without concepts are blind'.*

This has direct bearing on the way we should view the curriculum. The curriculum cannot be viewed *either* vertically *or* horizontally. It must be seen in some way as a two-dimensional matrix. The two extremes must be married in a future curriculum if schools hope to survive. This two-dimensional approach can be summarized by caricaturing Kant: 'Skills without content are empty. Facts without concepts are blind'.

The curriculum and educational software: mutual influences

The primary approach to the currriculum is perhaps one of the reasons why imaginative and innovative educational software is most likely to be seen in the early years of education. In secondary and tertiary education so much of the software has been asked for, and been written, by subject specialists. As yet, few exciting examples of CAL programs which deliberately cut across subject boundaries can be seen in secondary schools. Perhaps teachers simply wouldn't, or don't, buy them — the curriculum and educational software are mutual influences upon each other.

In accordance with the model of the curriculum put forward in the previous section there are two ways of developing software for the curriculum: vertically and horizontally. The first approach involves producing software *within* the traditional disciplines or forms of knowledge, i.e. to slot into existing timetabled subjects such as mathematics, physics, English, geography, French and so on. This approach has the advantage of developing both content and concepts within existing subject specialisms, hopefully enhancing and improving teaching and learning in traditional disciplines. It is therefore likely to be favoured by secondary teachers who see themselves as subject specialists and (to put it crudely) as 'teachers of their subject' rather than 'teachers of children'. This approach to software development is likely to have least effect on existing curriculum patterns. The micro serves the curriculum (see Watson 1984, under Further reading).

A horizontal approach to software development involves producing software to develop *skills* and concepts, or to raise and stimulate *issues*, which cut across traditional disciplines and subject boundaries. Such software will

* Kant, I. (1968) *Critique of Pure Reason* (trans. by Kemp Smith). Macmillan, p. 93.

reflect broader aims in teaching and learning, cross-curricular skills, and often (as Watson 1984 points out) be 'firmly aligned with innovative movements' in education. Clearly, software of this kind will, if accepted by teachers, have far more influence in changing the curriculum. The curriculum will need to *adapt* to the software. One worrying aspect of this approach, particularly for commercial publishers, is that teachers may simply not buy it. Constrained by the examination system and the consequent strait-jacket of the secondary curriculum, teachers may plump only for the safe approach to software, i.e. to enhance existing subject teaching. A similar situation exists in book publishing. How many commercial publishers produce books which are cross-curricular and not geared to a particular examination? Book publishing is surely notorious for *serving* the existing curriculum rather than trying to adapt it — will software publishing for the secondary range follow the same path?

Teaching and learning processes

So far only the curriculum has been discussed in relation to the growth of information technology. This section speculates on some of the changes that might occur in the actual processes of *learning* and *teaching*. In my view, the distinction between teaching and learning is often difficult to perceive let alone maintain. Therefore all the points on teaching and learning processes are mixed in together in this section. I present them as a series of separate points which the reader is invited to ponder and discuss. Some of the changes listed as possibles below are more probable than others:

1. The traditional role of the teacher as a giver or purveyor of knowledge and information will gradually fade. The teacher will increasingly become a counsellor, a guide and a motivator in the learning process. The view of the teacher as a subject-based authority will also diminish.
2. As a result, the widely held bucket or hydraulic theory of learning will die. This is the view that knowledge is a liquid with unique properties that resides in teachers and must be poured into pupils. Its properties are unique in that, despite transfer from one vessel to another, the reservoir level is unchanged. This *tabula rasa* or empty vessel view of the learning process, and of the *job* of a teacher, is still remarkably prevalent in pupils and parents. Many pupils still feel that a teacher is failing them in some way, and breaking a kind of unwritten contract, if he doesn't actually *teach them something.* Encouraging class discussion, facilitating learning, developing the right

attitudes, or improving learning skills are all seen as lesser aspects of the teacher's role. His main job is seen as *imparting information*, i.e. to pour liquid simultaneously into several small empty vessels, preferably into as many and as quickly as possible.

This view of the learner/teacher situation will surely fade, but don't underestimate the time it takes. Leading government figures have, within the last five years, spoken of 'teachers' *productivity*' and of increasing class sizes having no adverse effect on children's learning. Both smack of the hydraulic theory.

3. The importance of *home* learning is almost certain to increase with the spread of items of information technology like videodisks, viewdata, and microcomputers into homes. In 1983 there were less than 1 million micros in UK homes, by 1984 there were over 2 million, at the end of 1985 an estimated 5 million. Educational use of home micros will enhance existing school learning in traditional subjects, e.g. in revising for public examinations. It will also affect the way pupils perceive school learning and home/school connections. The homework/school work distinction will become blurred. Closer links between home, school and hopefully the wider community could be encouraged. Eventually the distinction between informal and formal learning, never a particularly useful one, will no longer be tenable.

4. It follows that pupils will be far more in *control* of their own learning than they are at present. A pupil's learning will no longer be teacher controlled, monitored, or dominated. Who knows what a pupil will be learning outside school, given access to the right technology? Indeed this is already a worry to many parents with the huge growth of video hardware and software.

5. This leads to another problem for teachers. An expansion in so-called informal learning will lead to even greater ranges in ability and experience in the classroom. Teachers will be confronted with wider mixtures of ability and experience then ever before, making the bucket theory of learning increasingly less tenable. Indeed, many teachers will know far less about certain subjects than the pupils in front of them. This will be particularly true at the end of a long 'finding-out' project for example.

Computer studies teachers are already finding that one or two of their teenage pupils have far more ability and experience in programming than they do. This situation will gradually be duplicated right across the school curriculum, from history to mathematics. Pupils, teachers and parents must learn to accept this. The unwritten contracts and expectations of school life must adapt.

6. It follows, finally, that the present norm of teachers teaching and learners learning will often be inverted, particularly as their technological expertise diverges. Pupils are already more adept, at home with, and less 'hung up about' new technology than many teachers. Attitudes among teachers to computers, for example, seem to vary from outright fear to total obsession. Pupils' attitudes are far more healthy — they rarely deify it or become obsessed with it, nor are they afraid of it.

Teachers have a lot to learn from pupils.

The future of schooling: speculations

Compulsory schooling has been in existence for over 100 years. One view of its future holds that compulsory schooling as we know it may not last until the next century, let alone for another hundred years. Such views are discussed at the end of this section. A less extreme, and therefore more widely held view, is based on the following tenet: schools must adapt and change in order to survive in a changing society. The view is widely held but few people have suggested in other than vague terms exactly how schools and their curricula might grow, evolve and develop. One exception is an excellent booklet produced by the MEP entitled *All Change* (see Further reading). The authors of the book put forward seven propositions which offer definite guidelines for a future curriculum:

- Proposition 1: Every school should analyse its activities in terms of the skills each fosters. The curriculum should develop skills and attitudes which will help young people to thrive in tomorrow's world at least as much as it promotes the acquisition of knowledge.

- Proposition 2: Key skills in the information/automation era will be:
  - life and social skills;
  - problem-solving skills;
  - communication skills;
  - information skills.

- Proposition 3: Leisure education should become a major concern of every school.

- Proposition 4: All students need to be technologically literate and to have an understanding of the concept of 'information'.

- Proposition 5: Schools should seek opportunities to give pupils more experience of regulating their use of time.

- Proposition 6: The content of 'lessons', and teaching and learning styles, must encourage students to want to be in school. Any amount of theorising about what students 'ought' to be doing will be pointless if the young people are motivated neither by the prospect of a job at the end nor by the current activity itself.
- Proposition 7: Schools should increasingly place the emphasis on 'learning' rather than 'teaching'. Teachers should help students to learn 'how to learn' and help them to manage their learning.

Some of the points contained in these propositions have already been discussed — the nature of teaching and learning processes for example. Others are perhaps more problematic, especially when based on the authors' predictions of future society. Proposition 3 for example is based on the view that 'work' and 'leisure' are, and will continue to be, distinct activities. However, for many analysts of society the notion of leisure has ideological overtones. Proposition 2 is hard to disagree with but the task of translating these 'key skills' into concrete objectives is the difficult step. The notion of 'problem-solving skills' is particularly hard to define. What is problem solving? Is there a common 'problem-solving ability' which cuts across different domains and disciplines, e.g. mathematics, craft, programming, everyday life? Is there any evidence to suggest that skill in problem solving in one area can transfer across to another? Are skilled computer programmers particularly adept at solving 'life's little problems'? (This whole notion of key skills for the information era is discussed in the final section.)

Despite the problematic nature of some of these seven propositions they form an excellent starting point for a discussion of future curricula. Perhaps Proposition 6 is the most important of all: how can students be encouraged to 'want to be in school'? Such doubts have prompted a return in the minds of some authors to the de-schooling days of the early 1970s. The radical ideas of Reimer, Illich and Goodman have been revived in several circles (see Further reading). Seymour Papert, for example, believes that the educational revolution made possible by computers (with of course the use of Logo) will not take place within the social context of conventional schools:

> The model of successful learning is the way a child learns to talk, a process that takes place without deliberate and organised teaching . . . I see the classroom as an artificial and inefficient learning environment that society has been forced to invent because its informal environments fail in certain essential learning domains, such as writing or grammar or school math. I believe that the computer presence will enable us to so modify the learning environment outside the classroom that much if not all the knowledge schools presently try to teach with so much pain and expense and such limited success will be learned, as the child learns to talk, painlessly, successfully, and without organised instruction. This obviously implies that schools as we know them today will have no place in the future.
> (Papert, S. (1980) *Mindstorms.* Harvester Press, pp. 8–9)

Papert admits the influence of the ideas of Ivan Illich. Illich suggests that learning must be an *active* process, in which pupils take the initiative (see Proposition 5 above). He suggested establishing *informal networks* to enable individuals to contact each other to learn new skills, share experiences and co-operate in activities. Such networks, enhanced by new information technology, would allow skill and interest matching and motivate true learning. Compulsory education by schooling would be abolished.

The ideas of Papert, Illich, Reimer and others are well worth reading with new information technology in mind. Unfortunately there is no room to discuss them fully here. Another, much-quoted, writer who casts doubts on our present educational system is the American paperback prophet, Alvin Toffler. Toffler argues persuasively that compulsory schooling is a second-wave institution. Toffler (1980) describes three waves or eras in western society over the last few centuries: the agricultural era (heralded by the agricultural revolution), the industrial era (caused by the industrial revolution) and now the third wave leading to a post-industrial society. In Toffler's scheme, schools are a phenomenon of the second wave, the industrial era. Existing schools face backwards, in his view, towards a disappearing era rather than forwards to a newly emerging and rapidly changing society.

I cannot hope to do justice to the debate on the future of schooling here. At least some of the issues have been raised. Perhaps the only point that can be made with certainty is that *the equation of education with schooling will become increasingly less tenable.* This mental equation still prevails in the minds of many people, most seriously in the views of parents and teachers. The equation is made in two important respects: *time* and *responsibility.* The first view holds that a child's or a student's education takes place in *school time*, i.e. education time is equated with school time. Education, therefore, takes place from school-starting age to school-leaving age and ends there, usually at the age of 16. During that period education takes place largely between 9.00 a.m. and 3.30 p.m. Few people would openly subscribe to such a view, but its influence lingers on in many minds. The second part of the equation concerns responsibility. The responsibility for educating a child is abdicated to the school from 5 to 16. It is seen as the 'school's job' to 'take care of education' for once and for all, almost to the point of believing that pre- and post-school education are rendered unnecessary.

The conflation of education with schooling has direct parallels with the equation of health with the health service, which is dominant in so many minds. The very presence of an elaborate health service may encourage people to abdicate responsibility for their own health. Illich (1973) labels institutions such as schooling and the health service *manipulative*. Their presence, however well-intentioned, often manipulates a person's outlook on, for example, both health and education. This is perhaps the most optimistic hope for the future with new information technology: that schools should become less manipulative and more 'convivial' (Illich), and thereby education may become less equated with schooling.

Skills for the future?

Perhaps the key question in any debate on the future of education and the curriculum is: What skills will be needed for the information era? The question is a huge one since it involves both assumptions and predictions of a largely political nature. Any answer will therefore be based on an *ideology* of the future: a vision of future employment, political structures, social networks, and so on.

Proposition 2 in *All Change* (page 18) suggested that 'key skills in the information/automation era will be: life and social skills; problem-solving skills; communication skills and information skills'. These are excellent as overall aims but they are often very difficult to break down into specific objectives, let alone classroom practice. One useful analysis of 'lifeskills' was given by Hopson and Scally and is shown in Figure 33. They provide a valuable and largely neutral starting point for schools but even so some of the objectives could be seen as ideologically based. 'How to be a skilled consumer', for example, begs the question of whether or not society should be based on consumption — similarly with the suggested skill of 'how to use my leisure to increase my income'.

LIFESKILLS: TAKING CHARGE OF YOURSELF AND YOUR LIFE

ME

Skills I need to manage and grow

- how to read and write
- how to achieve basic numeracy
- how to use computers
- how to find information and resources
- how to think and solve problems constructively
- how to identify my creative potential and develop it

- how to manage time effectively
- how to make the most of the present

- how to discover my interests
- how to discover my values and beliefs
- how to set and achieve goals
- how to take stock of my life
- how to discover what makes me do the things I do
- how to be positive about myself

- how to cope with and gain from life transitions
- how to make effective decisions
- how to be proactive
- how to manage negative emotions
- how to cope with stress
- how to achieve and maintain physical well-being
- how to manage my sexuality
- how to learn from experience

ME AND SPECIFIC SITUATIONS

Skills I need for my education

- how to discover the education options open to me
- how to choose a course
- how to study

Skills I need at work

- how to discover the job options open to me
- how to find a job
- how to keep a job
- how to change jobs
- how to cope with unemployment
- how to achieve a balance between my job and the rest of my life
- how to retire and enjoy it

Skills I need at home

- how to choose a style of living
- how to maintain a home
- how to live with other people

Skills I need at leisure

- how to choose between leisure options
- how to maximise my leisure opportunities
- how to use my leisure to increase my income

Skills I need in the community

- how to be a skilled consumer
- how to develop and use my political awareness
- how to use public facilities

Figure 33. An analysis of life skills

Source: Hopson and Scally, *Lifeskills: Taking Charge of Yourself and Your Life*, Lifeskills Associates, Leeds.

It is easy to nit pick and make pedantic criticisms of any suggested list of objectives, however. What is more important is to examine the various centres, programmes and initiatives which have been established by central government. Such schemes, often directed by civil servants, offer direct central control of the school curriculum – previously the restricted and autonomous territory of the teaching profession (even if this autonomy was often more imaginary than real).

Information technology education centres (ITECs), the Technical and Vocational Education Initiative (TVEI), the Youth Training Scheme (YTS) and the Certificate for Pre-Vocational Education (CPVE) all seem to be expected to provide skills for the future or *relevant* skills. The following questions should all be asked of any scheme, centre or school which purports to offer relevant or pre-vocational skills:

- What skills are relevant? What are they relevant *to* — a future society or to an individual? Is there still meaning in the notion of 'relevance'?
- Which skills are currently being offered by various programmes and government initiatives? Is there a discernible group of skills (problem solving, social, information skills etc.) which is common to them all?
- Is there a common rationale underlying various schemes, e.g. a vision of the future, a notion of 'future literacy'? Is there any rationale underlying them?
- What is meant by a 'skill' – as opposed to, say, an understanding, a competence or an awareness? Is there more to education than merely the development of skills?
- Does the notion of 'pre-vocational education' make any sense?

I would not even dare an attempt at answering these questions here. They are posed simply for the reader to ask, and ponder on, in considering the curriculum of the future.

Talking points

- *The short passage below describes a view of how the role of the teacher is likely to change:*

  All this implies a certain stance in teachers — the teacher becomes a different professional from the time-honoured one. His tradition has been the purveyor of information and knowledge and for years he has struggled to change his role in the light of changed circumstances. One hundred and fifty years ago the teacher worked in an environment where there was little information, the possession of which was the legitimate key to power. Information has a fairly long lasting usefulness. There was no television; film was primitive; radio and other printed materials were non-existent. There was no free library system. Now not only is the life outside school transformed for all youngsters and their families but also the microcomputer, computing and microprocessing developments have transformed the means of retrieving knowledge. The teacher knows too that the parent and wider community possess information, knowledge and skill which can enable him to do his job better. For what is the teacher's new role today? It is threefold. Firstly, he needs to be a facilitator — a person who can diagnose and make connections between the learner and the resources so that the learner may develop his potential. Secondly, he needs to be a mediator between the learner and his resources with the skilled eye of a diagnostician of learning difficulties. Finally, and perhaps most importantly, he needs to be an animator who by his inspiration, love of learning and above all his infectious enthusiasm provides the spark from which motivation grows.

  (From 'A Glimpse of the Future' by Tim Brighouse in *Changing Schools . . Changing Curriculum)*

- *Do you agree with the threefold suggestion for the teacher's new role, i.e. facilitator, mediator, and animator? Which of these three aspects do you consider most important?*

- *Do you see a total end to the teacher's function as a 'purveyor of knowledge'? Can this function be defended in the light of Ryle's distinction between 'knowledge that' and 'knowledge how'?*

- *Isaac Asimov is quoted as saying: 'A person should be ashamed of doing what a machine can do better'. Do you agree with this view? What effects might this have on employment, and people's life-styles, if taken to an extreme? Where, how, and by whom should the line be drawn between 'jobs done better by machine' and 'jobs done better by humans'?*

Talking points

- *Try reading the following anecdote:*
  'Two men were watching a mechanical excavator on a building site. "If it wasn't for that machine," said one, "twelve men with shovels could be doing that job." "Yes," replied the other, "and if it wasn't for your twelve shovels, two hundred men with teaspoons could be doing that job." ' (IBM advertisement)
- *One of the themes of Ivan Illich's writing is that insularity and competition in education should be replaced by collaboration and co-operation. Is this view realistic in your opinion? Certainly, the importance of collaboration and group-work is likely to grow in the future — for example in the so-called space race. But will this lead to the end of* competition, *e.g. between groups?*
- *Is there any place for a 'forms of knowledge' approach to the curriculum in a rapidly changing society based on the growth and availability of* information *as its key resource?*

Further reading

1. Full accounts of the 'forms of knowledge' thesis can be found in: *Ethics and Education* by R.S. Peters, especially Chapter 5 (George Allen & Unwin, 1966); and 'Liberal education and the nature of knowledge' by P.H. Hirst, in Archambault, R.D. (ed.) (1965) *Philosophical Analysis and education.* Routledge & Kegan Paul. Numerous discussions and attacks on these views have appeared in print. One attack, on philosophical grounds, is Wellington, J.J. (1981) Determining a core curriculum, *Journal of Curriculum Studies* **13**, No.1, pp. 17–24.
2. An excellent introduction to the study of the curriculum is *The Curriculum: Theory and Practice* by A.V. Kelly. (Harper and Row, 1982, second edition).

3. The 1970s debate on de-schooling (before the influence of IT) can be *found in Reimer, E. (1971) School is Dead,* Penguin; Illich, I. (1973) *De-schooling society,* Penguin; and Goodman, P. (1971) *Compulsory Mis-education,* Penguin. A critique of these and similar approaches occurs in Barrow, R. (1978) *Radical Education.* London: Martin Robertson.
4. A clear and critical account of the place of microcomputers in the secondary curriculum is 'Microcomputers in Secondary Education', by Deryn Watson. It occurs in *Microcomputers and the Curriculum*, ed. A.V. Kelly (Harper & Row, 1984), a book which contains several other useful articles.
5. A provocative booklet for discussion is: *All Change* by Brenda Prestt, Peter Dutton and Peter Nicholls (MEP and National Extension College, 1984).
6. One book which provides several fresh approaches and viewpoints on educational computing is *Young Learners and the Microcomputer* by Daniel Chandler (Open University Press, 1984). Its first sentence sets the tone for the rest of the book: 'The microcomputer is a tool of awesome potency which is making it possible for educational practice to take a giant step backwards into the nineteenth century.'
7. An excellent article speculating on the new roles of home and school in future education is: 'How will the new technology change the curriculum?' by R. Meighan and W.A. Reid in *Journal of Curriculum Studies*, 1982, vol. 14, no.4, pp. 353–8.
8. Two useful books relating to the whole of Part V have been written by John Maddison: *Information Technology and Education: an annotated guide to resources* (Milton Keynes: Open University Press, 1982); and *Education in the Microelectronics era* (Milton Keynes: Open University Press, 1983).
9. There is a valuable collection of articles on new technology, computer literacy and the curriculum in the June 1984 issue of *British Journal of Educational Studies.*

Postcript

At the risk of appearing pretentious, I would like to put forward three personal hopes for information technology in education for the future.

Firstly, that *technological* expertise should not dominate the use of IT in education, as it often has done in educational computing. 'Technology push' has so far outweighed 'market pull'. This is likely to continue, but perhaps educational expertise will eventually match technological skill in using and applying IT. Education buffs are far less dangerous, and less boring, than computer buffs. May the micromafia, who talk of ROMs, RAMs, Peeks and Pokes at parties, become a dying breed.

Secondly, that the use of information technology in education should follow the guidelines for an *appropriate* technology listed earlier. This should follow from my first hope above. In particular, 'the technology must be intelligible to the community as a whole'. This must be education's primary aim — to remove fear, anxiety, and (most dangerous of all) *awe*.

Thirdly, I would suggest that no one should take forecasts of the future too seriously. Here are some forecasts that have supposedly been made:

- IBM made less than 20 of its first model of computer. They thought that the world could not possibly cope with, or need, more.
- As telephones began to spread in 1920 it was predicted that by 1970 all women would be employed as telephone operators.
- In 1978 the British Post Office (now British Telecom) forecast that by 1982 there would be one million viewdata receivers. In June 1982 there were only 16,350.
- In the late 1940s British computer experts predicted that five of their new-fangled, giant machines would suffice for Britain's computing needs. By 1980, equally powerful computers could be carried in a plastic bag. Computing had moved from high centres and institutions to people's front rooms. The technological reformation had taken place.

These forecasts, yesterday's tomorrows, are all worth remembering when you read today's predictions.

Another view from MIT

Joseph Weizenbaum, Ph.D., a Professor of computer science at the Massachusetts Institute of Technology, made the following comments in a telephone interview conducted by Donna Osgood, a BYTE associate editor, on the effectiveness of computers as learning tools.

We in the United States are in the grip of a mass delusion with respect to the education of kids with computers. The belief that it is very urgent that we put computers in primary and secondary schools is based on a number of premises, of which only one is true. The true premise is that the whole world is becoming increasingly pervaded by computers. But then people infer that in a world pervaded by computers, everybody must be "computer literate" in order to be able to cope with the world at all. A second inference is that a high degree of computer literacy assures one a good job, while computer illiteracy condemns one to life on the margin of the coming information society.

I think most people imagine computer literacy to consist largely of the ability to communicate with computers, to operate them and to be able to correctly interpret their output. Hence, computer literacy is generally interpreted to mean knowing a computer language or two, and probably involves facility with the computer's keyboard.

Another illusion is that computer-language learning is like other kinds of learning. That, of course, is best done very early in life, indeed, the earlier the better. This provides a lot of fuel for the pressure on the schools to begin computer training very early and to make it part of the school curriculum from kindergarten to grade 12.

Again, all of this is based upon the true assumption that the computer is beginning to pervade and will continue to pervade our society. I would like to draw an analogy to something else that is ubiquitous in our society — the electric motor. There are undoubtedly many more electric motors in the United States than there are people, and almost everybody owns a lot of electric motors without thinking about it. They are everywhere, in automobiles, food mixers, vacuum cleaners, even watches and pencil sharpeners. Yet, it doesn't require any sort of electric-motor literacy to get on with the world, or, importantly, to be able to use these gadgets.

Another important point about electric motors is that they're invisible. If you question someone using a vacuum cleaner, of course they know that there is an electric motor inside. But nobody says "Well, I think I'll use an electric motor programmed to be a vacuum cleaner to vacuum the floor".

The computer will also become largely invisible, as it already is to a large extent in the consumer market. I believe that the more pervasive the computer becomes, the more invisible it will become. We talk about it a lot now because it is new, but as we get used to the computer, it will retreat into the background. How much hands-on computer experience will students need? The answer, of course, is not very much. The student and the practicing professional will operate special-purpose instruments that happen to have computers as components.

The emphasis on learning computer languages early is misplaced. It is clear to me that computer languages are not like natural languages. I think they are more like mathematical languages or physics. They require a certain intellectual maturity, and when you have that intellectual or mathematical maturity, you can learn them relatively quickly. It isn't worth spending a lot of time on at an early age.

The counterargument that we should begin with baby steps early, like teaching BASIC to eight-year-olds, is going in exactly the wrong directions. BASIC is, from a pedagogic point of view, an intellectual monstrosity that we should start to eradicate and not attempt to use as a basis for anything.

I'm trying to argue that the introduction of computers into primary and secondary schools is basically a mistake based on very false assumptions. Our schools are already in desperate trouble, and the introduction of the computer at this time is, at very best, a diversion — possibly a dangerous diversion.

Too often, the computer is used in schools, as it is used in other social establishments, as a quick technological fix. It is used to paper over fundamental problems to create the illusion that they are being attacked.

If Johnny can't read and somebody writes computer software that will improve Johnny's reading score a little bit for the present, then the easiest thing to do is to bring in the computer and sit Johnny down at it. This makes it unnecessary to ask why Johnny can't read. In other words, it makes it unnecessary to reform the school system, or for that matter the society that tolerates the breakdown of its schools.

INDEX OF NAMES

INDEX OF SUBJECTS

MICROCOMPUTERS AND THE CURRICULUM

edited by A. V. Kelly, Goldsmiths' College, University of London

A collection of case studies which explore sound practice in the use of microcomputers in education, not only in areas of secondary education such as mathematics, science and technology, but also in primary education, special education and the humanities. The major advantage of the microcomputer is not that it can think for one but that it can make one think, so that it has enormous potential for promoting the development of childrens' thought processes. The contributions to this book investigate this kind of use of microcomputers, rather than the more widespread use of the new technology as a sophisticated teaching aid, or as a device to keep children quiet and occupied.

Features

- Looks at actual practice of microcomputer use in schools
- Deals with primary and secondary areas and special education

Contents

ISBN 0 06 318273 4/Paper

208pp/1984

Harper Education Series